A DICTIONARY OF ACRONYMS & ABBREVIATIONS

EPALA   **ERIC PUGH**
Associate of the Library Association

ADOAAA   # A DICTIONARY
OF ACRONYMS &
ABBREVIATIONS

SAMTIS   *Some abbreviations in management, technology and information science*

CBL   **CLIVE BINGLEY** *b* LONDON

The compilation of this work, which contains more than 5,000 entries, was commenced early in 1965 and little retrospection from that date has been attempted, though some organisations no longer in existence have been included because reference is still made to their publications. In the case of United Kingdom organisations the nationality has been excluded from the definition.

It is hoped that yet another guide to the literature of science and technology, both in book and report form, will be of value to the librarian and information officer newly entering this field and also to the general reference librarian. There would also appear to be some justification for the belief that this book can be of assistance to members of other professions.

No abbreviations which cover only the titles of businesses or trade unions located either in the United Kingdom or the United States are included. In the case of acronyms, however, the name of the company or other body is included where it forms an integral part of the definition. Some abbreviations covering the full names of commercial concerns in other parts of the world are included. It must be stressed that certain of the acronyms listed are registered trade names and care must be exercised, therefore, in their use.

I would like to acknowledge the forbearance of my wife during the period I have been compiling this work, the assistance given by my son, and the efficient typing of Miss Angela Belcher who helped me to prepare the final draft. Acknowledgment is also made to Mr S G Berriman FLA, Mr D W King OBE FLA, and Dr A J Walford MA PhD FLA, for their kindly interest, though I must emphasise that the errors, which perhaps are inevitable in a work of this type, are entirely mine.

Teddington, Middlesex   ERIC PUGH
August 1967

CONTENTS

A A	Aluminum Association (USA) Australian Academy of Science (Australia) Automobile Association
A A A	Army Audit Agency (US Army)
A A A I P	Advanced Army Aircraft Instrumentation Program (US Army)
A A A S	American Association for the Advancement of Science (USA)
A A C C	American Association for Contamination Control (USA)
A A C E	American Association of Cost Engineers (USA)
A A C O B S	Australian Advisory Council on Bibliographical Services (Australia)
A A C S	Airborne Astrographic Camera System
A A E C	Australian Atomic Energy Commission (Australia)
A A E E	Aeroplane and Armament Experimental Establishment (MINTECH)
A A F S S	Advanced Aerial Fire Support System
A A I N	American Association of Industrial Nurses (USA)
A A L	Arctic Aeromedical Laboratory (USAF)
A A M	Air-to-Air Missile
A A M V A	American Association of Motor Vehicle Administrators (USA)
A A N	American Association of Neuropathologists (USA)
A A O	Abastumanskaya Astrofizicheskaya Observatoriya (USSR) (Abastumani Astrophysical Observatory)
A A P	*Apollo* Applications Programme
A A P G	American Association of Petroleum Geologists (USA)
A A P S	American Association of Plastic Surgeons (USA)
A A R	Association of American Railroads (USA) Average Annual Rainfall
A A S	Advanced Antenna System American Astronautical Society (USA)
A A S H O	American Association of State Highway Officials (USA)
A A S U	Department of Aeronautics and Astronautics, University of Southampton
A A T C C	American Association of Textile Chemists and Colorists (USA)

A B A	American Bankers Association (USA)
A B A C	A Basic Coursewriter
A B A C U S	Air Battle Analysis Center Utility System
A B B F	Association of Bronze and Brass Founders
A B B M M	Association of British Brush Machinery Manufacturers
A B C	Abridged Building Classification for Architects, Builders and Civil Engineers
	Approach by Concept
A B C A	United States-United Kingdom-Canada-Australia
A B C M	Association of British Chemical Manufacturers (now Chemical Industries Association)
A B D	Association Belge de Documentation (Belgium) (Belgian Documentation Association)
A B E M	Association Belge pour l'Etude, l'Essais et l'Emploi des Materiaux (Belgium) (Belgian Association for the Study, Testing and Use of Materials)
A B L	Automated Biological Laboratory
A B L E	Activity Balance Line Evaluation
	Agricultural-Biological Literature Evaluation
A B M	Anti-Ballistic Missile
A B M A	American Boiler Manufacturers Association (USA)
A B M A C	Association of British Manufacturers of Agricultural Chemicals
A B N T	Associaco Brasiliera de Normas Tecnicas (Brazil) (Brazilian Technical Standards Association)
A B P I	Association of the British Pharmaceutical Industry
A B R E S	Advanced Ballistic Re-Entry System
A B R O	Animal Breeding Research Organisation (of Agricultural Research Council)
A B S	Acrylonitrile Butadiene Styrene
A B S W	Association of British Science Writers
A B T I C S	Abstract and Book Title Index Card Service (of the Iron and Steel Institute)
A C A D I	Association des Cadres Dirigeants de l'Industrie (France) (Association of Industrial Executives)
A C C A	Associated Colleges of the Chicago Area (USA)
A C C E L	Automated Circuit Card Etching Layout
A C D	Acid-Citrate-Dextrose
A C D B	Association du Catalogue Documentaire du Batiment (France) (Building Catalogue Association)

8

A C E	Air Cushion Equipment
	American Council on Education (USA)
	Automated Cost Estimates
	Automated Computing Engine
A C E - S/C	Acceptance Checkout Equipment-Spacecraft
A C E A A	Advisory Committee on Electrical Appliances and Accessories
A C E C	Ateliers Constructions Electriques de Charleroi (Belgium)
A C G I H	American Conference of Government Industrial Hygienists (USA)
A C I	American Concrete Institute (USA)
	Automatic Car Identification ('Car' here is US word for Railway Carriage/Wagon)
A C I C	Aeronautical Chart and Information Center (USAF)
A C I M	Axis-Crossing Interval Meter
A C L	Allowable Cabin Load
A C L S	All-weather Carrier Landing System
	American Council of Learned Societies (USA)
A C M	Associated Colleges of the Midwest (USA)
	Association for Computing Machinery (USA)
	Association of Crane Makers
A C M R R	Advisory Committee on Marine Resources Research (of FAO)
A C M S	Advance Configuration Management System
A C O	Admiralty Compass Observatory
A C O R N	Associative Content Retrieval Network
A C P M	American Congress of Physical Medicine and Rehabilitation (USA)
A C R	Antenna Coupling Regulator
	Automatic Compression Regulator
A C R L	Association of College and Research Libraries (USA)
A C R S	Advisory Committee on Reactor Safeguards (USA)
A C S	American Ceramic Society (USA)
	American Chemical Society (USA)
	Attitude Command System
	Attitude Control System
A C S I L	Admiralty Centre for Scientific Information and Liaison (now NSTIC)
A C S M	American Congress on Survey and Mapping (USA)

A C S P	Advisory Council on Scientific Policy
A C T	Adrenocorticotrophin
	Advisory Council on Technology
A C T O	Automatic Computing Transfer Oscillator
A C T O L	Air Cushion Take-Off and Landing
A C T S	Acoustic Control and Telemetry System
A C U	Address Control Unit
A C V	Air Cushion Vehicle
A D	Air Dried
	prefix to numbered series of reports issued through Defense Documentation Center (USDOD) and usually sold by CFSTI
A D A	Action Data Automation
	Air Defense Agency (USA)
	Aluminium Development Association (now part of the Aluminium Federation)
	American Dental Association (USA)
	Automatic Data Acquisition
A D A C	Automated Direct Analogue Computer
A D A M	Advanced Data Management
	Advanced Direct-landing *Apollo* Mission
	Air Deflection And Modulation
	Automatic Distance and Angle Measurement
A D A P S O	Association of Data Processing Organisations (USA)
A D A P T	Adaption of Automatically Programmed Tools
A D A P T I C O M	Adaptive Communication
A D A R	Advanced Design Array Radar
A D C	Analogue-to-Digital Converter
A D C I	American Die Casting Institute (USA)
A D D D S	Automatic Direct Distance Dialling System
A D E	Automated Draughting Equipment
A D E P T	A Distinctly Empirical Prover of Theorems
A D E T I M	Association pour le Developpment des Techniques des Industries Mecaniques (France) (Association for the Improvement of Mechanical Engineering Techniques)
A D F	Automatic Direction Finder
A D G E	Air Defence Ground Environment
A D H	Antidiuretic Hormone
A D I	Alternating Direction Implicit
	American Documentation Institute (USA)
	Attitude Director Indicator

A D I S	A Data Interchange System
	Automatic Data Interchange System
A D L S	Automatic Drag-Limiting System
A D M	Activity Data Method
A D M I R E	Automatic Diagnostic Maintenance Information Retrieval
A D M S C	Automatic Digital Message Switching Centers (of DOD)
A D P	Adenosine Diphosphate
	Automatic Data Processing
A D P L A N	Advancement Planning
A D P S	Automatic Data Processing System
A D R S	Analogue-to-Digital Data Recording System
A D S	Accessory Drive System
	Activity Data Sheet
	Air Development Services (of FAA)
A D S A	American Dairy Science Association (USA)
A D S A F	Automated Data Systems with the Army in the Field (US Army)
A D S A S	Air-Derived Separation Assurance System
A D S S	Australian Defence Scientific Service
A D X	Automatic Data Exchange
A E	Aero-Electronic
	Aktiebolaget Atomenergi (Sweden) (Atomic Energy Authority)
A e	prefix to numbered series of publications issued by the Aerodynamics Division of NPL
A E A	Agricultural Engineers Association
	Atomic Energy Authority
A E C	Atomic Energy Commission
A E C B	Atomic Energy Control Board (Canada)
A E C C	Associacion Espanola par el Control de la Calida (Spain) (Spanish Association for Quality Control)
A E C D	Arnold Engineering Development Center (USAF)
A E C L	Atomic Energy of Canada Ltd (Canada)
A E D	ALGOL Extended for Design
	Automated Engineering Design
A E E	Airborne Evaluation Equipment
	Atomic Energy Establishment
A E E T	Atomic Energy Establishment, Trombay (India)
A E G	Allgemeine Elektricitats-Gesellschaft (Germany)
A E I	American Enterprise Institute for Public Policy Research (USA)

A E P	Averaged Evoked Potential
A E P B	Association pour l'Emploi des Plastiques dans le Batiment (France) (Association for the Use of Plastics in Building)
A E R A	Association pour l'Etude et la Recherche Astronautique et cosmique (France) (Association for Astronautics and Cosmic Study and Research)
A E R D L	Army Electronics Research and Development Laboratory (US Army)
A E R E	Atomic Energy Research Establishment
A E S	American Electroplaters Society (USA)
	Apollo Extension System
A E S O P	An Experimental Structure for On-line Planning
A E W & C	Airborne Early Warning and Control
A E W E S	Army Engineer Waterways Experiment Station (US Army)
A F	Audio Frequency
A F A	Air Force Association (USA)
A F A C	American Fisheries Advisory Committee (USA)
A F A L	Air Force Avionics Laboratory (USAF)
A F A P	Association Francaise pour l'Accroissement de la Productivitie (France) (French Association for Increased Productivity)
A F A P L	Air Force Aero Propulsion Laboratory (USAF)
A F A S E	Association For Applied Solar Energy (USA)
A F B	Air Force Base
A F C	Automatic Frequency Control
	Atomic Fuel Corporation (Japan)
A F - C C B	Air Force Configuration Control Board (USAF)
A F C E A	Armed Forces Communications and Electronics Association (USA)
A F C I Q	Association Francaise pour le Controle Industriel de Qualite (France) (French Association for Industrial Quality Control)
A F C R L	Air Force Cambridge Research Laboratories (USAF)
A F C S	Adaptive Flight Control System
	Automatic Flight Control System
A F D	Accelerated Freeze Drying
	Appointed Factory Doctor
A F E L I S	Air Force Engineering and Logistics Information System (USAF)
A F F D L	Air Force Flight Dynamics Laboratory (USAF)
A F F T C	Air Force Flight Test Center (USAF)

A F I - R A N	Africa, India Ocean Region Air Navigation
A F I C C S	Air Force Interim Command and Control System (USAF)
A F I N E	Association Francaise pour l'Industrie Nucleaire d'Equipment (France)
A F I P	Armed Forces Institute of Pathology (USDOD)
A F I P S	American Federation of Information Processing Societies (USA)
A F I T	Air Force Institute of Technology (USAF)
A F I T A E	Association Francaise d'Ingenieurs et Techniciens de l'Aeronautique et de l'Espace (France) (French Association of Aeronautical and Space Engineers and Technicians)
A F L - C I O	American Federation of Labor-Congress of Industrial Organizations (USA)
A F L C	Air Force Logistics Command (USAF)
A F L C O N	AFLC Operations Network
A F M	Air Force Manual (numbered series issued by USAF)
A F M R	Antiferromagnetic Resonance
A F M T C	Air Force Missile Test Center (USAF)
A F N O R	Association Francaise de Normalisation (France) (French Standards Association)
A F O S R	Air Force Office of Scientific Research (USAF)
A F P	Air Force Pamphlet (numbered series issued by USAF)
A F P A	Australian Fire Protection Association (Australia) Automatic Flow Process Analysis
A F P T R C	Air Force Personnel and Training Research Center (USAF)
A F R A S E C	Afro-Asian Organisation for Economic Co-operation
A F R P L	Air Force Rocket Propulsion Laboratory (USAF)
A F R R I	Armed Forces Radiobiology Research Institute (USDOD)
A F S	American Fisheries Society (USA) American Foundrymens Society (USA)
A F S A B	Air Force Science Advisory Board (USAF)
A F S C	Air Force Systems Command (USAF)
A F S C M	Air Force Systems Command Manual (series issued by USAF)
A F Q T	Armed Forces Qualification Test (USDOD)
A F T A C	Air Force Technical Applications Center (USAF)
A F T N	Aeronautical Fixed Telecommunications Network

A F T P	Association Francaise des Techniciens du Petrole (France) (French Association of Petroleum Technicians)
A F V	Armoured Fighting Vehicle
A F V G	Anglo-French Variable Geometry
A G A	Aerodrome, Air Routes and Ground Aids (a division of ICAO)
	American Gas Association (USA)
A G A C S	Automatic Ground-to-Air Communications Systems
A G A R D	Advisory Group for Aeronautical Research and Development (of NATO)
A G E D	Advisory Group on Electron Devices (USDOD)
A G E T	Advisory Group on Electron Tubes (USDOD)
A G F	Arbeitsgemeinschaft Getreideforschung (Germany) (Grain Research Association)
A G I	American Geological Institute (USA)
A G I F O R S	Airlines Group of International Federation of Operations Research Societies
A G I L E	*Autonetics* General Information Learning Equipment
A G M	Auxiliary General Missile
A G M A	American Gear Manufacturers Association (USA)
A G O R	Auxiliary General Oceanographic Research
A G R	Advanced Gas-cooled Reactor
A G R E E	Advisory Group for Reliability of Electronic Equipment (USDOD and US Industry)
A G R R	Association Generale de Retraite par Repartition (France)
A G U	American Geophysical Union (USA)
A H A M	Association of Home Appliance Manufacturers (USA)
A H E M	Association of Hydraulic Equipment Manufacturers
A H F	Antihaemophilic Factor
A H M I	Appalachian Hardwood Manufacturers, Inc (USA)
A H R	Acceptable Hazard Rate
A H S	American Helicopter Society (USA)
A H S B	Authority Health and Safety Branch (UKAEA)
A H S E	Assembly, Handling and Shipping Equipment
A I A	American Institute of Architects (USA)
	American Inventors Association (USA)
A I A A	American Institute of Aeronautics and Astronautics (USA)

14

A I A G	Aluminium Industrie AG (Switzerland)
A I B	Association des Industries de Belgique (Belgium)
A I B S	American Institute of Biological Sciences (USA)
A I C	Agricultural Institute of Canada (Canada)
A I C A	Association Internationale pour le Calcul Analogique (International Association for Analogue Computing)
A I C B M	Anti-Intercontinental Ballistic Missile
A I C E	American Institute of Consulting Engineers (USA)
A I Che E	American Institute of Chemical Engineers (USA)
A I C M A	Association Internationale des Constructeurs de Material Aerospatial (International Association of Aerospace Material Designers)
A I C M R	Association Internationale des Constructeurs de Material Roulant (International Association of Rolling Stock Manufacturers)
A I C P A	American Institute of Certified Public Accountants (USA)
A I C Q	Associazione Italiana per il Controllo della Qualita (Italy) (Italian Association for Quality Control)
A I D	Agency for International Development (USA) Automated Industrial Drilling
A I D S	Aircraft Integrated Data System
A I D S C O M	Army Information Data Systems Command (US Army)
A I E A	Agence Internationale de l'Energie Atomique (International Atomic Energy Agency)
A I E E	American Institute of Electrical Engineers (now IEEE) (USA)
A I E N D F	Atomics International Evaluation Nuclear Data File
A I E S E C	Association Internationale des Etudiants en Sciences Economiques et Commerciales (International Association of Students of Economic and Commercial Sciences)
A I F	Arbeitsgemeinschaft Industrieller Forschungsvereinigungen (Germany) (Association of Industrial Organisations)
A I G A	American Association of Graphic Arts (USA)
A I H A	American Industrial Hygiene Association (USA)
A I H C	American Industrial Health Conference (USA)

A I I S U P	Association Internationale d'Information Universitaire et Professionnelle (International Association for Educational and Vocational Information)
A I L	American Institute of Laundering (USA)
A I M	Aerotriangulation by observation of Independent Models
	Air Intercept Missile
	Australian Institute of Management (Australia)
A I M A	All-India Management Association (India)
A I M E	American Institute of Mining, Metallurgical and Petroleum Engineers (USA)
A I M I L O	Army/Industrial Material Information Liaison Offices (USA)
A I M P	Anchored Interplanetary Monitoring Platform
A I M S	Air traffic control/Identity friend or foe/Mark II Military classified Systems
	Auerbach Information Management System
A I N A	Arctic Institute of North America (USA)
A I P	American Institute of Physics (USA)
A I P C	Association Internationale des Ponts et Charpentes (International Association for Bridge and Structural Engineering)
A I R	Aerospace Information Report (series issued by SAE)
	American Institute for Research in the Behavioral Sciences (USA)
	Air Intercept Rocket
A I R S	Automatic Image Retrieval System
A I S	American Interplanetary Society (USA) (later American Rocket Society)
A I S C	American Institute of Steel Construction (USA)
A I S E	Association of Iron and Steel Engineers (USA)
A I S I	American Iron and Steel Institute (USA)
A I T	Auto-Ignition Temperature
A I T C	American Institute of Timber Construction (USA)
A I U	Advanced Instrumentation Unit (of NPL)
A I W	Auroral Intrasonic Wave
A K E W	Arbeitsgemeinschaft Kernkraftwerk der Elektrizitatswirtschaft (Austria)
A L A L C	Asociacion Latinoamericana de Libre Echange (Latin-American Free Trade Association)
A L A R M	Automatic Light Aircraft Readiness Monitor
A L B M	Air-Launched Ballistic Missile

16

A L C A	American Leather Chemists Association (USA)
A L C H	Approach-Light Contact Height
A L D E P	Automated Layout Design Programme
A L D P	Automatic Language Data Processing
A L F	Automatic Letter Facer
A L G O L	Algorithmic Language
A L M C	Army Logistic Management Center (US Army)
A L M S	Analytic Language Manipulation System
A L O R	Advanced Lunar Orbital Rendezvous
A L O T S	Airborne Lightweight Optical Tracking System
A L P	*Autocode* List Processing
A L P H A	Automatic Literature Processing, Handling and Analysis
A L P S	Advanced Liquid Propulsion System
A L R I	Airborne Long Range Input
A L S	Approach-Light System
	Associative List Searcher
A L S E P	*Apollo* Lunar Surface Experiment Package
A L T A I R	ARPA Long-range Tracking and Instrumentation Radar
A M	Amplitude Modulation
	prefix to series issued by Office of Aviation Medicine (FAA)
A M A	Adhesives Manufacturers Association of America (USA)
	Air Materiel Area (USAF)
	American Management Association (USA)
	American Medical Association (USA)
	Automatic Message Accounting
A M B I T	Algebraic Manipulation By Identity Translation
A M C	Air Materiel Command (USAF)
	American Mining Congress (USA)
	Army Materiel Command (US Army)
A M C S	Airborne Missile Control System
A M D	Aerospace Medical Division (USAF)
	Aerospace Material Document — numbered/ lettered series of Specifications issued by SAE
A M E D S	Army Medical Service (US Army)
A M E T A	Army Management Engineering Training Agency (US Army)
A M E T S	Artillery Meteorological System
A M F I S	Automatic Microfilm Information System
A M I C	Aerospace Materials Information Center (USA)
A M I C O M	Army Missile Command (US Army)

A M I S	Automated Management Information System
A M L	Admiralty Materials Laboratory
	Aeronautical Materials Laboratory
A M N I P	Adaptive Man-machine Non-arithmetical Information Processing
A M O	Alternant Molecular Orbit
A M O S	Acoustic Meteorological Oceanographic Survey
	Automatic Meteorological Observing System
A M P	Adenosine Monophosphate
A M R A	Army Materials Research Agency (US Army)
A M R L	Aerospace Medical Research Laboratory (USAF)
A M S	Administrative Management Society (USA)
	Aeronautical Material Specification (series issued by SAE)
	Agricultural Marketing Service (USA)
	American Mathematical Society (USA)
	American Meteorological Society (USA)
A M S A	Advanced Manned Strategic Aircraft
A M S C	Army Mathematics Steering Committee (US Army)
A MS I C	Army Missile Command (US Army)
A M S O C	American Miscellaneous Society (USA)
A M T C L	Association for Machine Translation and Computational Linguistics (USA)
A M T R A N	Automatic Mathematical Translator
A M U	Associated Midwestern Universities (USA)
	Astronaut Manoeuvring Unit
A M V E R	Atlantic Merchant Vessel Report
A N A A S	Australian and New Zealand Association for the Advancement of Science
A N A R E	Australian National Antarctic Research Expedition
A N C A R	Australian National Committee for Antarctic Research (of Australian Academy of Sciences)
A N C S	American Numerical Control Society (USA)
A N E D A	Association Nationale d'Etudes pour la Documentation Automatique (France) (National Association of Automatic Documentation Studies)
A N F	Anti-nuclear Factor
	Atlantic Nuclear Force
A N F O	Ammonium Nitrate and Fuel Oil
A N I	Automatic Number Identification
A N I P	Army-Navy Instrumentation Program (USDOD)
A N K O R	*Autonetics Kalman* Optimum Reset

A N L	Argonne National Laboratory (of USAEC)
A N O V A	Analysis of Variance
A N P	Aircraft Nuclear Propulsion
A N P P	Army Nuclear Power Program (US Army)
A N R T	Association Nationale de la Recherche Technique (France) (National Association of Technical Research)
A N S	American Nuclear Society (USA)
A N V A R	Agence Nationale pour la Valorization de la Recherche (France) (National Agency for the Evaluation of Research)
A O A	American Ordnance Association (USA)
A O A C	Association of Official Agricultural Chemists of North America
A O C	Air Operation Centrals
A O C S	American Oil Chemists Association (USA)
A O I N S T	numbered series issued by Administrative Office, Department of the Navy (USN)
A O I P	Association Ouvriers Instruments Precision (France) (Association of Precision Instrument Operatives)
A O Q L	Average Outgoing Quality Limit
A O R B	Aviation Operational Research Branch
A O R E	Army Operational Research Establishment (now DOAE)
A O R G	Army Operational Research Group (now DOAE)
A O S	Amphibious Objective Studies
A O S O	Advanced Orbiting Solar Observatory
A O S P	Automatic Operating and Scheduling Programme
A O U	Apparent Oxygen Utilisation
A P	Air Pollution (numbered series by US Public Health Service)
	Air Publication (numbered series issued by Ministry of Defence (Air Force Department))
	Applied Physics (numbered series issued by Applied Physics Division, National Physical Laboratory)
A P A	American Plywood Association (USA)
A P A C H E	*Aldermaston* Project for the Application of Computers to Engineering
	Analogue Programming And Checking
A P C	Automatic Phase Control
	Auto-Plot Controller
A P C A	Air Pollution Control Association (USA)

A P E X	Assembler and Process Executive
A P F	Atomic Packing Factor
A P F C	Asia-Pacific Forestry Commission
A P G	Aberdeen Proving Ground (USDOD)
A P G C	Air Proving Ground Center (USAF)
A P H A	American Public Health Association (USA)
A P H I	Association of Public Health Inspectors
A P I	American Petroleum Institute (USA)
A P I C	*Apollo* Parts Information Centre (NASA)
A P I C S	American Production and Inventory Control Society (USA)
A P L	Applied Physics Laboratory
	Association of Programmed Learning
A P L E	Association of Public Lighting Engineers
A P M I	Area Precipitation Measurement Indicator
A P O	Asian Productivity Organization (Headquarters are in Japan)
A P O E	Aerial Port of Embarkation
A P P	Advance Procurement Plan
A P P C	Advance Procurement Planning Council (USDOD)
A P P I	Advanced Planning Procurement Information
A P R	Airborne Profile Recorder
A P R C	Army Personnel Research Committee (of Medical Research Council)
A P R E	Army Personnel Research Establishment (MOD)
A P R O	Army Personnel Research Office (now BESRL) (US Army)
A P R O B A	Association Professionelle pour l'Accroissement de la Productivite dans l'Industrie du Batiment (France) (Association for Increasing Productivity in the Building Industry)
A P R S	Automatic Position Reference System
A P S	Alphanumeric Photocomposer System
	American Physical Society (USA)
	American Physiological Society (USA)
	Assembly Programming System
	Automatic Patching System
	Auxiliary Power System
A P T	Automatic Picture Transmission
	Automatically Programmed Tools
A P W	Augmented Plane Wave
A Q L	Acceptable Quality Level
A R A	Amateur Rocket Association (USA)
	Area Redevelopment Administration (USA)

A R A D C O M	United States Army Defense Command
A R A L	Automatic Record Analysis Language
A R B	Air Registration Board
A R C	Aeronautical Research Council (MINTECH)
	Agricultural Research Council
A R C R L	Agricultural Research Council Radiobiological Laboratory
A R D	Arbeitsgemeinschaft der Oeffentlich Rechlichen Rundfunkanstalten der Bundesrepublik Deutschland (Germany)
A R D C	Air Research and Development Command (USAF)
A R D E	Armament Research and Development Establishment (now RARDE)
A R D I S	Army Research and Development Information System (US Army)
A R E A	American Railway Engineering Association (USA)
A R I	Air-conditioning and Refrigeration Institute (USA)
A R I A	*Apollo* Range Instrumented Aircraft
A R I E M	Army Research Institute of Environmental Medicine (US Army)
A R I P	Automatic Rocket Impact Predictor
A R I S	Advanced Range Instrumentation Ship
A R L	Aeronautical Research Laboratory
	Aerospace Research Laboratory
	Average Run Length
A R L I S	Arctic Research Laboratory Ice Station
A R M	Anti-Radiation Missile
A R M M S	Automated Reliability and Maintainability Measurement System
A R M S	Aerial Radiological Measuring Survey
	Amateur Radio Mobile Society
A R N M D	Association for Research in Nervous and Mental Disease (USA)
A R O	Army Research Office (US Army)
A R O - D	Army Research Office—Durham (US Army)
A R O D	Airborne Radar Orbital Determination
A R P	Aeronautical Recommended Practice (series issued by SAE)
	Airborne Radar Platform
A R P A	Advanced Research Projects Agency (USDOD)
A R Q	Automatic Repeat Request
A R R L	Amateur Radio Relay League (USA)
A R R S	Aerospace Rescue and Recovery Service (USAF)

A R S	Agricultural Research Service (USDA)
	American Radium Society (USA)
	American Rocket Society (USA) (later merged with Institute of Aerospace Sciences)
A R S P	Aerospace Research Support Program (USAF)
A R S R	Air Route Surveillance Radar
A R T	Advanced Reactor Technology
	Airborne Radiation Thermometer
A R T C C	Air Route Traffic Control Centre
A R T E	Admiralty Reactor Test Establishment (MOD)
A R T O C	Army Tactical Operations Central
A R T R A C	Advanced Range Testing, Reporting and Control
A R T S	Advanced Radar Traffic-control System
A S	prefix to Standards issued by SAA
A S A	American Standards Association (now USASI)
	American Statistical Association (USA)
A S A E	Advanced School of Automobile Engineering
	American Society of Agricultural Engineers (USA)
	American Society of Association Executives (USA)
A S A P	Army Scientific Advisory Panel
A S B	Association of Shell Boilermakers
A S B C	American Standard Building Code
A S B D	Advanced Sea-Based Deterrent
A S B I	Advisory Service for the Building Industry
A S C	Automatic System Controller
A S C A	Automatic Science Citation Alerting
A S C A T S	*Apollo* Simulation Checkout and Training
A S C C	Air Standardization Coordinating Committee
A S C E	American Society of Civil Engineers (USA)
A S C I I	American Standard Code for Information Interchange
A S C O	Automatic Sustainer Cut-Off
A S C P	American Society of Clinical Pathologists (USA)
A S C S	Agriculture Stabilization and Conservation Service (USDA)
A S D	Aerospace Systems Division (USAF)
A S D I C	Anti-Submarine Detection and Identification Committee
A S D F	Air Self Defence Force (Japan)
A S E A	Allmanna Svenska Elektriska Aktiebolaget (Sweden)
A S E E	American Society for Engineering Education (USA)

A S F I R	Active Swept Frequency Interferometer Radar
A S F T S	Airborne Systems Functional Test Stand
A S G	Advanced Study Group
	Aeronautical Standards Group
A S H R A E	American Society of Heating, Refrigerating and Air-conditioning Engineers (USA)
A S H S	American Society for Horticultural Science (USA)
A S I	United States of America Standards Institute
A S I I	American Science Information Institute (USA)
A S I R C	Aquatic Sciences Information Retrieval Center (of University of Rhode Island, USA)
A S I S	Abort Sensing and Instrumentation System
A S K A	Automatic System for Kinematic Analysis
A S K S	Automatic Station Keeping System
A S L E	American Society of Lubrication Engineers (USA)
A S L O	American Society of Limnology and Oceanography (USA)
A S M	Advanced Surface-to-air Missile
	American Society for Metals (USA)
A S M C	Association of Stores and Materials Controllers
A S M E	American Society of Mechanical Engineers (USA)
	Association for the Study of Medical Education
A S M I	Airfield Surface Movement Indication
A S M P	American Society of Magazine Photographers (USA)
A S M S	Advanced Surface Missile System
A S N	Average Sample Number
A S O D D S	ASWEPS Submarine Oceanographic Digital Data System
A S O S	Antimony Sulfide-Oxysulfide
A S P	Aerospace Plane
	American Selling Price
	American Society of Photogrammetry (USA)
	Attached Support Processor
	Automatic Synthesis Programme
A S P A	American Society for Personnel Administration (USA)
A S P B	Assault Support Patrol Boat
A S P M	Armed Services Procurement Manual (USDOD)
A S P O	American Society of Planning Officials (USA)
A S P P	American Society of Plant Physiologists (USA)
A S P Q	Association Suisse pour la Promotion de la Qualite (Switzerland) (Association for Quality Improvement)

A S P R	Armed Services Procurement Regulations (USDOD)
A S P T	American Society of Plant Taxonomists (USA)
A S Q	Deutsche Arbeitsgemeinschaft fur Statistische Qualitatskontrolle (Germany) (German Society for Statistical Quality Control)
A S Q C	American Society for Quality Control (USA)
A S R	Automatic Send-Receive
A S R C T	Applied Scientific Research Corporation of Thailand (Thailand)
A S R E	American Society of Refrigeration Engineers (now ASHRAE)
A S R L	Aeroelastic and Structures Research Laboratory (of Massachusetts Institute of Technology) (USA)
A S R O C	Anti-Submarine Rocket
A S R W P M	Association of Semi-Rotary Wing Pump Manufacturers
A S S E S S	Analytical Studies of Surface Effects of Submerged Submarines
A S S E T	Aerothermodynamic-aerothermoelastic Structural Systems Environmental Test
A S T D	American Society for Training and Development (USA)
A S T I A	Armed Services Technical Information Agency (now DDC) (USDOD)
A S T M	American Society for Testing and Materials (USA)
A S T M E	American Society of Tool and Manufacturing Engineers (USA)
A S T R A	Automatic Scheduling with Time-integrated Resource Allocation
A S T R A C	*Arizona* Statistical Repetitive Analog Computer
A S T R A L	Assurance and Stabilization Trends for Reliability by Analysis of Lots
A S T S	Association Suisse pour la Technique du Soudage (Switzerland) (Swiss Association for the Technique of Welding)
A S V I L M E T	Associazione Italiana per lo Sviluppo degli Studi Sperimentali sulla Lavorazione dei Metalli (Italy) (Italian Association for the Promotion of Metalworking Research)
A S W	Anti-Submarine Warfare
A S W E P S	Anti-Submarine Warfare Environmental Prediction Service (USN)

A T	Atomic Time
A T A	Air Transport Association
A T A C	Army Tank-Automotive Command (US Army)
A T C	Air Traffic Control
	Alloy-Tin Couple
	Automatic Train Control
A T C E U	Air Traffic Control Evaluation Unit (of BOT)
A T C R B S	Air Traffic Control Radar Beacon System
A T D	Aerospace Technology Division (of Library of Congress, USA)
A T D A	Augmented Target Docking Adaptor
A T D S	Airborne Tactical Data System
A T E	Automatic Test Equipment
A T E N	Association Technique pour la production et l'utilisation de l'Energie Nucleaire (France)
A T I	Association of Technical Institutions
A T I S	Automatic Terminal Information Service
A T L	Analogue-Threshold Logic
	Appliance Testing Laboratories (of the Electricity Council)
A T L B	Air Transport Licensing Board
A T L I S	Army Technical Library Improvement Studies (US Army)
A T M	*Apollo* Telescope Mount
	Atmospheric Structure Advisory Committee (of ESRO)
A T O L L	Acceptance, Test, or Launch Language
A T O M S	Automated Technical Order Maintenance Sequences
A T P	Adenosine Triphosphate
A T R	Attenuated Total Reflection
A T S	Administrative Terminal System
	Advanced Technological Satellite
	Air Traffic Service (FAA)
	Air Traffic System
	Applications Technology Satellite
	Auxiliary Tug Service
A T S I T	Automatic Techniques for the Selection and Identification of Targets
A T T C	American Towing Tank Conference
A T T I	Arizona Transportation and Traffic Institute (USA)

A T V	Abwassertechnische Vereinigung (Germany) (Sewage Technical Research Association)
	Akademiet for de Tekniske Videnskaber (Denmark) (Academy of Technical Sciences)
A U	Astronomical Unit
	prefix to numbered series of Automobile Standards issued by BSI
A U D R E Y	Audio Reply
A U L	Above Upper Limit
A U N T I E	Automatic Unit for National Taxation and Insurance
A U T O D I N	Automatic Digital Network (of USDOD)
A U T O D O C	Automated Documentation
A U T O M A S T	Automatic Mathematical Analysis and Symbolic Translation
A U T O S A T E	Automated Data Systems Analysis Technique
A U T O S C R I P T	Automated System for Composing, Revising, Illustrating and Phototypesetting
A U T O S T A T I S	Automatic Statewide Auto Theft Inquiry (California, USA)
A U T O S T R A D	Automated System for Transportation Data
A U T O V O N	Automatic Voice Network
A U W	All-Up-Weight
A U W E	Admiralty Underwater Weapons Establishment (MOD)
A V A	Aerodynamische Versuchanstalt (Germany) (Aerodynamics Experimental Station)
A V B L	Armoured Vehicle Bridge Launcher
A V C	Automatic Volume Control
A V C S	Advanced Vidicon Camera System
A V E C	Amplitude Vibration Exciter Control
A V F	Azimuthally Varying Field
A V L A B S	Aviation Laboratories (US Army)
A V M A	American Veterinary Medical Association (USA)
A V O I D	Airfield Vehicle Obstacle Indication Device
A V R	Arbeitsgemeinschaft Versuchkraftwerke (Germany)
A V S	Aerospace Vehicle Simulation
	American Vacuum Society (USA)
A V T A	Automatic Vocal Transaction Analysis
A W A	Anomalous Winter Absorption
A W A C S	Airborne Warning and Control System
A W A D S	All Weather Aerial Delivery System
A W L S	All-Weather Landing System

A W N	Automated Weather Network (USAF)
A W O P	All-Weather Operations Panel (of ICAO)
A W P A	American Wood Preservers Association (USA)
A W P B	American Wood Preservers Bureau (USA)
A W R E	Atomic Weapons Research Establishment (UKAEA)
A W S	American Welding Society (USA)
A W S G	Army Work Study Group (MOD)
A W V	Ausschus fur Wirtschafliche Verwaltung (Germany) (Committee for Efficiency in Administration)
A W W A	American Water Works Association (USA)
A W W V	Abeitsgemeinschaft der Wasserwirtschafsverbaende (Germany) (Water Utilisation Research Association)
A X	Attack Experimental
A Z A S	Adjustable Zero Adjustable Span

B

B A	Booksellers Association of Great Britain and Ireland
	British Association for the Advancement of Science
B A A	British Acetylene Association
B A C A N	British Association for the Control of Aircraft Noise
B A C I E	British Association for Commercial and Industrial Education
B A D G E	Base Air Defence Ground Environment
B A I T	Bacterial Automated Identification Technique
B A M	Bundesanstalt fur Materialprufung (Germany) (Federal Institute for Materials Testing)
B A M I R A C	Ballistic Missile Radiation Analysis Center (University of Michigan) (USA)
B A M T M	British Association of Machine Tool Merchants
B A R T D	Bay Area Rapid Transit District (USA)
B A S	British Acoustical Society
B A S E E F A	British Approvals Service for Electrical Equipment in Flammable Atmospheres (MINTECH)
B A S I C	Biological Abstracts-Subjects-In-Context
B A S J E	Bolivian Air Shower Joint Experiment
B A S R A	British Amateur Scientific Research Association
B A T C	British Amateur Television Club
B B C	British Broadcasting Corporation

B B E A	Brewery and Bottling Engineers Association
B B I R A	British Baking Industries Research Association
B B M R A	British Brush Manufacturers Research Association
B C	Bathyconductograph
	Bottom Contour
B C A R	British Civil Airworthiness Requirement
B C A S	British Compressed Air Society
B C C	British Colour Council
B C C F	British Cast Concrete Federation
B C D	Binary Coded Decimal
	Burst Cartridge Detection
B C G L O	British Commonwealth Geographical Liaison Office
B C I R A	British Cast Iron Research Association
B C I S C	British Chemical Industrial Safety Council (of CIA)
B C M	Beyond Capability of Maintenance
B C M N	Bureau Central de Mesures Nucleaires (Belgium) (Central Office for Nuclear Measures)
B C P M A	British Chemical Plant Manufacturers Association
B C R	Bituminous Coal Research, Inc (USA)
B C R A	British Ceramic Research Association
	British Coke Research Association
B C R U	British Committee on Radiological Units (now BCRUM)
B C R U M	British Committee on Radiation Units and Measurements
B C S	British Computer Society
B C S A	British Constructional Steelwork Association
B C U R A	British Coal Utilisation Research Association
B C W M A	British Clock and Watch Manufacturers Association
B D A	British Dental Association
B D H I	Bearing, Distance and Heading Indicator
B D I A C	Battelle Defender Information Analysis Center (BMI)
B D L I	Bundesverband der Deutschen Luft- und Raumfahrtindustrie (Germany)
B D S A	Business and Defense Services Administration (of Dept of Commerce (USA))
B E A	British European Airways

B E A B	British Electrical Approvals Board for Domestic Appliances
B E A C O N	British European Airways Computer Network
B E A I R A	British Electrical and Allied Industries Research Association
B E A M A	British Electrical and Allied Manufacturers Association
B E C T O	British Electric Cable Testing Organisation
B E D	Bridge-Element Delay
B E E C	Binary Error-Erasure Channel
B E L V A C	Societe Belge de Vacuologie et de Vacuotechnique (Belgium) (Belgian Society for Vacuum Science and Technology)
B E M A	Business Equipment Manufacturers Association (USA)
B E M A C	British Export Marketing Advisory Committee
B E M S	Bakery Equipment Manufacturers Society
B E N	Bureau d'Etudes Nucleaires (Belgium) (Nuclear Studies Bureau)
B E P C	British Electrical Power Convention
B E P O	British Experimental Pile Operation
B E S	Biological Engineering Society
B E S R L	Behavioral Science Research Laboratory (US Army)
B E S T	Business EDP System Technique
B E T	Best Estimate of Trajectory
B E T A	Business Equipment Trade Association
B E U C	Bureau Europeen des Unions Consommateurs (Bureau of European Consumer Organisations)
B F M I R A	British Food Manufacturing Industries Research Association
B F O	Beat Frequency Oscillator
B F S	Bundesastalt fur Flugsicherung (Germany) (Air-Traffic Control Authority)
B G A	British Gliding Association
B G I R A	British Glass Industry Research Association
B G M A	British Gear Manufacturers Association
B G R R	*Brookhaven's* Graphite Research Reactor (BNL)
B G W F	British Granite and Whinstone Federation
B H C	Benzine Hexachloride
B H R A	British Hydromechanics Research Association
B H W	Boiling Heavy Water
B I A C	Bio-Instrumentation Advisory Council (of AIBS)

29

BIB	Berliner Institut fur Betriebsfuhrung (Germany) (Berlin Business Management Institute)
BIBRA	British Industrial Biological Research Association
BIC	Bureau International des Containers (International Bureau of Containers)
	Bureau of International Commerce (of Dept. of Commerce, USA)
BICEMA	British Internal Combustion Engine Manufacturers Association
BICERA	British Internal Combustion Engine Research Association
BICERI	British Internal Combustion Engine Research Institute
BIFA	British Industrial Film Association (now part of BISFA)
BIH	Bureau International de l'Heure
BILA	*Battelle Institute* Learning Automation (BMI)
BILG	Building Industry Libraries Group
BIM	British Institute of Management
BIMCAN	British Industrial Measuring and Control Apparatus Manufacturers Association
BIMRAB	BuWeps-Industry Material Reliability Advisory Board (USN)
BINA	Bureau International des Normes de l'Automobile (International Bureau of Automobile Standards)
BIOS	Biological Investigations of Space
	British Intelligence Objectives Sub-committee
BIOSIS	Bio-Science Information Service of Biological Abstracts (USA)
BIP	Balanced In Plane
BIPM	Bureau International des Poids et Mesures (International Bureau of Weights and Measures)
BIR	British Institute of Radiology
BIRDIE	Battery Integration and Radar Display Equipment
BIRPI	Bureaux Internationaux Reunis pour la Protection de la Propriete Intellectuelle (United International Bureaux for the Protection of Intellectual Property)
BIS	British Interplanetary Society
BISF	British Iron and Steel Federation
BISFA	British Industrial and Scientific Film Association

B I S I T S	British Iron and Steel Industry Translation Service (of Iron and Steel Institute, BISRA, and the industry)
B I S R A	British Iron and Steel Research Association
B I T	Binary digit
B I T A	British Industrial Truck Association
B I T O	British Institution of Training Officers
B L A D E S	*Bell Laboratories* Automatic Design System
B L C	British Lighting Council
B L E U	Blind Landing Experimental Unit (of RAE)
B L I P	Background Limited Infrared Photoconductor
B L L	Below Lower Limit
B L M	Bureau of Land Management (US Dept. of the Interior)
B L M R A	British Leather Manufacturers Research Association
B L O D I B	Block Diagram Compiler B
B L S	Bureau of Labor Statistics (USA)
B L W A	British Laboratory Ware Association
B M	British Museum
	Bureau of Mines (USA)
B M A	British Medical Association
B M E C	British Marine Equipment Council
B M E W S	Ballistic Missile Early Warning System
B M I	Battelle Memorial Institute (USA)
B M I C	Bureau of Mines Information Circular (series issued by BOM)
B M R	*Brookhaven's* Medical Reactor (BNL)
B M T A	British Mining Tools Association
B M T F A	British Malleable Tube Fittings Association
B M T P	Bureau of Mines Technical Paper (series issued by BOM)
B N C M	British National Committee on Materials
B N C O R	British National Committee for Oceanographic Research
B N C S	British Numerical Control Society
B N C S R	British National Committee on Space Research
B N E C	British National Export Council
B N F C	British National Film Catalogue (now part of BISFA)
B N F R M A	British Non-Ferrous Metals Research Association
B N L	Brookhaven National Laboratory (USAEC)
B N X	British Nuclear Export Executive

B O A	British Optical Association
B O B	Bureau of the Budget (USA)
B O B M A	British Oil Burner Manufacturers Association
B O D	Biological Oxygen Demand
B O L D	Bibliographic On-Line Display
	Bibliographic On-line Library Display
B O C S	*Bendix* Optimum Configuration Satellite
B O P	Basic Oxygen Process
B O R A M	Block Oriented Random Access Memories
B O S	Basic Oxygen Steel
B P A	Biological Photographic Association (USA)
B P B I R A	British Paper and Board Industry Research Association (now PIRA)
B P C	British Productivity Council
B P C F	British Precast Concrete Federation
B P F	British Plastics Federation
	Bottom Pressure Fluctuation
B P G M A	British Pressure Gauge Manufacturers Association
B P I C A	Bureau Permanent International des Constructeurs d'Automobiles (Permanent International Agency of Motor Manufacturers)
B P K T	Basic Programming Knowledge Test
B P M A	British Photographic Manufacturers Association
	British Printing Machinery Association
	British Pump Manufacturers Association
Б P O	British Post Office
B P P M A	British Power Press Manufacturers Association
B P R	Bureau of Public Roads (USA)
B P U	British Powerboating Union
B P W R	Burnable Poison Water Reactor
B R	Boil Resistant
	British Rail
	prefix to numbered series of publications issued by Ministry of Defence (Navy Department)
B R A	Bee Research Association
	British Refrigeration Association
B R A S T A C S	Bradford Scientific, Technical and Commercial Service
B R B M A	Ball and Roller Bearing Manufacturers Association
B R E M A	British Radio Equipment Manufacturers Association

32

B R G M	Bureau de Recherches Geologiques et Minieres (France) (Bureau of Geological and Mining Research)
B R I	Building Research Institute (Japan)
B R L	Ballistics Research Laboratory (US Army)
B R S	Building Research Station (MINTECH)
B R V M A	British Radio Valve Manufacturers Association
B S	Biochemical Society
	prefix to numbered series of British Standards issued by BSI
B S A	Bund Schweizer Architekten (Switzerland) (Federation of Swiss Architects)
B S C R A	British Steel Castings Research Association
B S D A	British Spinners and Doublers Association
B S I	British Standards Institution
B S I R A	British Scientific Instrument Research Association
B S M M A	British Sugar Machinery Manufacturers Association
B S N D T	British Society for Non-Destructive Testing
B S P M A	British Sewage Plant Manufacturers Association
B S R A	British Ship Research Association
B T	Bathythermograph
B T C	British Transport Commission
B T D B	British Transport Docks Board
B T E	Battery Terminal Equipment
B T I	Bridged Tap Isolator
B T M A	British Typewriter Manufacturers Association
B T T P	British Towing Tank Panel
B U	Binding Unit
BuAer	Bureau of Aeronautics (USN) (later BuWeps)
B U I C	Back-Up Interceptor Control
Bull	Bulletin
BuMed	Bureau of Medicine and Surgery (USN)
BuOrd	Bureau of Ordnance (USN) (later BuWeps)
BuPers	Bureau of Naval Personnel (USN)
BuSandA	Bureau of Supply and Accounts (USN)
BuShips	Bureau of Ships (USN) (now NSSC)
BuWeps	Bureau of Naval Weapons (USN) (now NOSC)
B V A	British Veterinary Association
B V D T	Brief Vestibular Disorientation Test
B V M A	British Valve Manufacturers Association
B W	Biological Warfare
B W A	British Waterworks Association

B W B	British Waterways Board
B W M A	British Woodwork Manufacturers Association
B W M B	British Wool Marketing Board
B W O	Backward Wave Oscillator
B W P A	British Wood Preserving Association
B W R	Boiling Water Reactor
B W R A	British Welding Research Association

C

C & M S	Consumer and Marketing Service (USDA)
C & M S - S R A	C&MS—Service and Regulatory Announcement (USDA)
C A	Consumers Association
C A Form	Civil Aviation Form (numbered series issued by Civil Aviation Dept., BOT)
C A A	Central African Airways Corporation
	Civil Affairs Agency (USA)
C A A R C	Commonwealth Advisory Aeronautical Research Council
C A A S	Ceylon Association for the Advancement of Science (Ceylon)
C A B	Captive Air Bubble
	Cellulose Acetate Butyrate
	Civil Aeronautics Board (USA)
	Commonwealth Agricultural Bureaux
C A C A	Canadian Agricultural Chemicals Association (Canada)
C A C P	Cartridge-Actuated Compaction Press
C A D	Computer Aided Design
C A D C	Central Air Data Computer
C A D E T	Computer-Aided Design Experimental Translator
C A D F	Cathode-ray tube Automatic Direction Finding
C A D F I S S	Computation And Data Flow Integrated Sub-Systems
C A D I G	Coventry and District Information Group
C A D O	Central Air Documents Office (USAF)
C A D R E	Current Awareness and Document Retrieval for Engineers
C A E	Compagnie Europeene d'Automatisme Electronique (France)
C A E S	Canadian Agricultural Economics Society (Canada)
C A E T	Corrective Action Evaluation Team

C A F U	Civil Aviation Flying Unit (of BOT)
C A G	Canadian Association of Geographers (Canada)
C A I S	Central Abstracting and Indexing Service
	Computer Aided Instruction
C A L	Conversational Algebraic Language
	Cornell Aeronautic Laboratory (USA)
C A L M	Collected Algorithms for Learning Machines
C A M	Content Addressed Memory
	Cybernetic Anthropomorphous Machine
C A M E R A	Co-operating Agency Method for Event Reporting and Analysis
C A M E S A	Canadian Military Electronics Standards Agency
C A M I	Civil Aeromedical Institute (USA)
C A N D U	Canadian Deuterium Uranium
C A N T A T	Transatlantic Cable
C A N T R A N	Cancel in Transmission
C A N T V	Compania Anonima Nacional Telefonos de Venezuela (Venezuela)
C A O R E	Canadian Army Operational Research Establishment
C A P	Canadian Association of Physicists (Canada)
	Civil Air Patrol (USA)
	Civil Air Publication (numbered series issued by Civil Aviation Dept. BOT)
	Cryotron Associative Processor
C A P E R T S I M	Computer Assisted Programme Evaluation Review Technique Simulation
C A P R I	Computerized Advance Personnel Requirements and Inventory
C A P S	*Courtauld's* All Purpose Simulator
C A R D	Compact Automatic Retrieval Device (*or* Display)
C A R D A N	Centre d'Analyses et de Recherche Documentaires pour l'Afrique Noire (France) (Documentary Analysis and Research Centre for Black Africa)
C A R D E	Canadian Armament Research and Development Establishment (of DRB)
C A R M R A N D	Civilian Application of the Results of Military Research and Development
C A R T O N E X	Conference for the Carton and Case Making Industry

35

C A S	Centre for Administrative Studies (of HM Treasury)
	Chemical Abstracts Service (American Chemical Society)
	Collision Avoidance System
C A S E V A C	Casualty Evacuation
C A S I	Canadian Aeronautics and Space Institute (Canada)
C A S P A R	*Cambridge* Analog Simulator for Predicting Atomic Reactions
C A T	Clear Air Turbulence
	College of Advanced Technology
	Computer-Aided Translation
	Controlled Attenuator Timer
C A T C	Circular-Arc-Toothed Cylindrical
	Commonwealth Air Transport Council
C A T I B	Civil Air Transport Industry Training Board
C A T R A	Cutlery and Allied Trades Research Association
C A T S	Chicago Area Transportation Study (USA)
C A T V	Community Antenna Television
C B A	Cost-Benefit Analysis
C B A T	Central Bureau for Astronomical Telegrams
C B B	Centre Belge du Bois (Belgium) (Belgian Timber Research Centre)
C B E	Council of Biology Editors (USA)
C B I	Confederation of British Industry
C B I S	Computer-Based Instructional System
C B M P E	Council of British Manufacturers of Petroleum Equipment
C B P	County Business Patterns (series issued by Census Bureau, Dept of Commerce, USA)
C B R	California Bearing Ratio
	Chemical, Biological, Radiological
C B R A	Chemical Biological Radiological Agency (USA)
C B S	Canadian Biochemical Society (Canada)
	Centraal Bureau voor de Statistiek (Netherlands) (Central Statistical Bureau)
C C	Control Computer
C C & S	Central Computer and Sequencing
C C A	Cement and Concrete Association
C C A M	Canadian Congress of Applied Mechanics
C C B	Configuration Control Board
C C F M	Cryogenic Continuous-Film Memory
C C G T	Closed-Cycle Gas Turbine

C C I R	Comite Consultatif International des Radio-communications (of ITU) (International Tele-communications Consultative Committee)
C C I S	Command Control Information System
C C I T T	Comite Consultatif International Telegraphique et Telephonique (of ITU) (International Tele-graph and Telephone Consultative Committee)
C C L	Coating and Chemical Laboratory
C C M A	Canadian Council of Management Association (Canada)
C C M D	Continuous Current Monitoring Device
C C O	Current-Controlled Oscillator
C C P M O	Consultative Council of Professional Manage-ment Organisations
C C P S	Consultative Committee for Postal Studies (of UPU)
C C R S T	Comite Consultatif de la Recherche Scientifique et Technique (France) (Consultative Committee for Scientific and Technical Research)
C C S T	Center for Computer Sciences and Technology (of NBS)
C C T	Comite de Coordination des Telecommunications (France)
	Correlated Colour Temperature
	Creosote Coal Tar
C C T V	Closed Circuit Television
C D	Contracting Definition
C D A	Canadian Dental Association (Canada)
	Command and Data Aquisition
	Copper Development Association
C D C	Centro de Documentacao Cientifica (Portugal) (Scientific Documentation Centre)
	Combat Development Command (US Army)
C D C R	Center for Documentation and Communication Research (of Western Reserve University, USA)
C D D C	Comision de Documentacion Cientifica (Argen-tina) (Science Documentation Centre)
C D E E	Chemical Defence Experimental Establishment (MOD)
C D F	Confined Detonating Fuse
C D R A	Committee of Directors of Research Associations
C E	Carbon Equivalent

C E A	Combustion Engineering Association
	Commissariat a l'Energie Atomique (France)
	Communications-Electronics Agency (USA)
	Confederation Europeenne de l'Agriculture (European Confederation of Agriculture)
C E A R C	Computer Education and Applied Research Centre
C E B	Comite Electrotechnique Belge (Belgium) (Belgian Electrotechnical Committee)
C E B E D E A U	Centre Belge d'Etude et de Documentation des Eaux (Belgium) (Belgian Water Study and Documentation Centre)
C E B E L C O R	Centre Belge d'Etude de la Corrosion (Belgium) (Belgian Corrosion Study Centre)
C E B E R E N A	Centre Belge de Recherches Navales (Belgium) (Belgian Marine Research Centre)
C E B T P	Centre Experimental de Recherches et d'Etudes du Batiment et des Travaux Publics (France) (Test Centre of Building and Public Works Research and Studies)
C E C	Co-ordinating European Council for the Development of Performance Tests for Lubricants and Engine Fuels
	Commonwealth Engineering Conference
C E C A	Communaute Europeenne du Charbon et de l'Acier (European Coal and Steel Community)
C E C E	Centre d'Etude et d'Exploitation des Calculateurs Electroniques (Belgium) (Centre for the Study and Use of Electronic Computers)
C E C E D	Conceil Europeen de la Construction Electro-Domestique (European Council for the Manufacture of Domestic Electrical Equipment)
C E C I O S	Conseil Europeene de la Comite International de l'Organisation Scientifique (European Council of the International Committee of Scientific Management)
C E D	Carbon-Equivalent-Difference
C E C M	Commission pour l'Etude de la Construction Metallique (Belgium) (Commission for the Study of Metal Building)
C E D O C	Centre Belge de Documentation et d'information de la Construction (Belgium) (Belgian Documentation and Information Centre for Building)

C E D R I C	Centre d'Etudes, de Documentation et de Recherches pour l'Industrie du Chaufage, du Conditionnement d'Air et des Branches Connexes (Belgium) (Centre for Research Studies and Documentation on Heating and Air Conditioning)
C E E	Commission Internationale de Reglementation en veu de l'Approbation de l'Equipement Electrique (International Commission on Rules for the Approval of Electrical Equipment)
C E F B	Centre d'Etudes des Fontes de Batiment (France) (Research Centre for Cast Iron in Building)
C E G B	Central Electricity Generating Board
C E I	Commission Electrotechnique International (International Electrotechnical Commission)
	Contract End Item
	Council of Engineering Institutions
C E I F	Council of European Industrial Federations
C E L	Carbon-Equivalent, Liquidus
	Centre d'Essais des Landes (France)
C E L C	Commonwealth Education Liaison Committee
C E L M E	Centro Sperimentale Lavorazione Metalli (Italy) (Research Institute for Metalworking)
C E M	Compagnie Electro-Mecanique (France)
C E M A	Conveyor Equipment Manufacturers Association (USA)
C E M B U R E A U	Cement Statistical and Technical Association (headquarters are in Sweden)
C E M U	Centro Sperimentale per le Macchine Utensili (Italy) (Research Institute for Machine Tools)
C E N	Centre d'Etude de l'Energie Nucleaire (Belgium) (Nuclear Research Centre)
	Comite Europeen de Coordination des Normes (European Standards Coordination Committee)
C E N - Ca	Centre d'Etudes Nucleaires de Cadarache (of CEA) (France) (Cadarache Nuclear Research Centre)
C E N - F A R	Centre d'Etudes Nucleaires de Fontenany-Aux-Roses (of CEA) (France) (Fontenany-Aux-Roses Nuclear Research Centre)
C E N - G	Centre d'Etudes Nucleaires de Grenoble (of CEA) (France) (Grenoble Nuclear Research Centre)
C E N - S	Centre d'Etudes Nucleaires de Saclay (of CEA) (France) (Saclay Nuclear Research Centre)

C E N A T R A	Centre National d'Assistance Technique et Recherche Appliquee (Belgium) (National Centre for Technical Assistance and Applied Research)
C E N I D	Centro Nacional de Informacion y Documentacion (Chile) (National Centre for Information and Documentation)
C E N T E X B E L	Centre Scientifique et Technique de l'Industrie Textile Belge (Belgium) (Scientific and Technical Centre for the Belgian Textile Industry)
C E N T O	Central Treaty Organisation
C E P	Centre d'Etudes des Matieres Plastiques (Belgium) (Research Centre for Plastic Materials)
	Circular Error Probability
	Cylinder Escape Probability
C E P A L	Comision Economica para America Latina (of UNO) (Economic Commission for Latin America)
C E P E	Central Experimental and Proving Establishment (Royal Canadian Air Force)
C E P S	Cornish Engines Preservation Society
C E P T	Conference Europeenne des Administrations des Postes et des Telecommunications (European Conference on Postal and Telecommunications Administration)
C E R	Civil Engineering Report
	Cost Estimating Relationship
C E R A	Civil Engineering Research Association (now CIRIA)
C E R B O M	Centre d'Etudes et de Recherches de Biologie et d'Oceanographie Medicale (France) (Study and Research Centre for Medical Biology and Oceanography)
C E R C	Coastal Engineering Research Center (US Army)
C E R C A	Compagnie pour l'Etude et la Realisation de Combustibles Atomiques (France)
C E R C H A R	Centre d'Etudes et Recherche des Charbonnages de France (France) (Study and Research Centre of the French National Coal Industry)
C E R C O L	Centre de Recherches Scientifiques et Techniques des Conserves de Legumes et des Industries Connexes (Belgium) (Scientific and Technical Research Centre for the Vegetable Canning and Allied Industries)

C E R E S	Centre d'Essais et de Recherches d'Engins Speciaux (France) (Centre for Test and Research of Special Engines)
C E R F	Centre d'Etudes et de Recherches en Fonderies (Belgium) (Foundries Study and Research Centre)
C E R L	Central Electricity Research Laboratories
C E R M O	Centre d'Etudes et de Recherches de la Machine-Outil (France) (Machine Tool Research and Study Centre)
C E R N	Organisation Europeene pour la Recherche Nucleaire (European Organisation for Nuclear Research) (formerly ' Centre Europeen de Recherches Nucleaires ')
C E R P H O S	Centre d'Etudes et de Recherches des Phosphates Mineraux (France) (Study and Research Centre on Mineral Phosphates)
C E S	Constant Elasticity of Substitution
C E T	Corrected Effective Temperature
C E T A	Centro des Estudos Technicos de Automocion (Spain) (Centre for Technical Studies on Automation)
C E T E H O R	Centre Technique de l'Industrie Horlogere (France) (Clock and Watch Industry Technical Centre)
C E T I E F	Centre Technique des Industries de l'Estampage de la Forge (France) (Drop Forging and Forging Industries Technical Centre)
C E T I S	Centre de Traitement de l'Information Scientifique (of EURATOM) (Scientific Information Processing Centre)
C E T O P	Comite Europeene des Transmissions Oelohydrauliques et Pneumatiques (European Oil-Hydraulic and Pneumatic Committee)
C E T S	Conference Europeene Telecommunications Spatiales
	Conference on European Telecommunications Satellites
C E V	Centre d'Essais en Vol (France) (Flight Test Centre)
C F	Context Free
C F A	Council of Ironfoundry Associations
	Cross-Field Amplifier

C F A R	Constant False Alarm Rate
C F B S	Canadian Federation of Biological Societies (Canada)
C F C	Capillary Filtration Coefficient
	Consolidated Freight Classification
C F E	Chlorotrifluoroethylene
C F F	Chemins der Fer Federaux (Switzerland) (Swiss Federal Railways)
C F L	Context-Free Language
C F O	Central Forecasting Office (of the Meteorological Office)
C F R	Co-ordinating Fuel Research
C F S G	Cometary Feasibility Study Group (of ESRO)
C F S T I	Clearinghouse for Federal Scientific and Technical Information (Dept of Commerce, USA)
C F T	Compagnie Francaise de Television (France)
C F T H	Compagnie Francaise Thomson-Houston (France)
C G A	Compressed Gas Association (USA)
C G L I	City and Guilds of London Institute
C G O U	Coast Guard Oceanographic Unit (US Coast Guard)
C G P M	Conference Generale des Poids et Mesures (General Conference on Weights and Measures)
C G R A	Canadian Good Roads Association (Canada)
C G S B	Canadian Government Specifications Board
C H A B A	Committee on Hearing and Bio-Acoustics (USA)
C H A D	Code to Handle Angular Data
C H E C	Channel Evaluation and Call
C H F	Critical Heat Flux
C H I L D	Computer Having Intelligent Learning and Development
C H P A E	Critical Human Performance And Evaluation
C H S	Canadian Hydrographic Service (Canada)
C I	Chemical Inspectorate (MOD)
C I A	Central Intelligence Agency (USA)
	Chemical Industries Association
C I A I	Conference Internationale des Associations d'Ingenieurs (International Federation of Engineering Associations)
C I A M	Congres Internationaux d'Architecture Moderne (International Congresses for Modern Architecture)

C I B	Conseil International du Batiment pour la recherche, l'etude et la documentation (International Council for Building Research, Studies and Documentation)
C I C	Centre d'Information de la Couler (France) (Colour Information Centre)
	Chemical Institute of Canada
C I C A	Confederation Internationale du Credit Agricole (International Confederation for Agricultural Credit)
C I C P	Committee to Investigate Copyright Problems (USA)
C I C R I S	West London Commercial and Technical Library Service (formerly ' Co-operative Industrial and Commercial Reference and Information Service ')
C I D	Centre for Information and Documentation (EURATOM)
C I D A	Centre International de Developpement d'Aluminium (International Centre for the Development of Aluminium)
	Comite Interamericano de Desarrollo Agricola (Inter-American Committee for Agricultural Development)
C I D B	Centre d'Information et de Documentation du Batiment (France) (Building Information and Documentation Centre)
C I D E	Centro Informativo de la Edificacion (Spain) (Information Centre on Building)
C I D S	Chemical Information and Data System (US Army)
C I E	Commission Internationale de l'Eclairage (International Commission on Illumination)
C I E S M	Commission Internationale pour l'Exploration Scientifique de la Mediterranee (International Commission for the Scientific Exploration of the Mediterranean Sea)
C I G	Comite International de Geophysique (International Geophysics Committee)
C I G B	Commission Internationale des Grands Barrages de la Conference Mondiale de l'Energie (International Commission of Large Dams of the World Power Conference)
C I G F T	Central Inertial Guidance Test Facility

C I G R	Commission Internationale du Genie Rural (International Commission of Rural Engineering)
C I G R E	Conference Internationale des Grands Reseaux Electriques (International Conference on Large Electric Systems)
C I H M	Commission International d'Histoire Maritime (International Commission of Maritime History)
C I I	Compagnie Internationale pour l'Informatique (France)
C I M	Continuous Image Microfilm
C I M A C	Congres International des Machines a Combustion (International Congress on Combustion Engines)
C I M M	Canadian Institute of Mining and Metallurgy (Canada)
C I M R S T	Comite Interministeriel de la Recherche Scientifique et Technique (France)
C I N S	CENTO Institute of Nuclear Science
C I O M S	Council for International Organisations of Medical Sciences
C I O S	Comite International de l'Organisation Scientifique (International Committee for Scientific Management)
	Combined Intelligence Sub-Committee
C I P	Current Injection Probe
C I P A S H	Committee on International Programs in Atmospheric Sciences and Hydrology (of NAS/NRC)
C I P M	Council for International Progress in Management (USA)
C I R	Canada India Reactor
	Cost Information Report
C I R C	Centralized Information Reference and Control
C I R C A L	Circuit Analysis
C I R F S	Comite International de la Rayonne et des Fibres Synthetiques (International Rayon and Synthetic Fibres Committee)
C I R I A	Construction Industry Research and Information Association
C I R I E C	Centre Internationale de Recherches et d'Information sur l'Economie Collective (International Centre of Research and Information on Public and Cooperative Economy)

C I R M	Comite International Radio-Maritime (International Maritime Radio Committee)
C I S	Centre International d'Information de Securite et d'Hygiene due Travail (International Occupational Safety and Health Information Centre)
	Cue Indexing System
	Current Information Selection
C I S I R	Ceylon Institute of Scientific and Industrial Research (Ceylon)
C I S P R	Comite International Special des Perturbations Radioelectriques (Special International Committee on Radio Interference)
C I S R	Center for International Systems Research (State Dept, USA)
C I T	California Institute of Technology (USA)
	Carnegie Institute of Technology (USA)
	Comite International des Transports par chemins de fer (International Railway Transport Committee)
	Compagnie Industrielle des Telephones (France)
C I T B	Construction Industry Training Board
C I T C	Construction Industry Training Centre
C I T E	Compression—Ignition—and Turbine Engine
C I T E C	Contractor Independent Technical effort
	Compagnie pour l'Information et les Techniques Electroniques de Controle (France)
C I U M R	Commission Internationale des Unites et Mesures Radiologiques (Internal Commission of Radiological Units and Measures)
C K M T A	Cape Kennedy Missile Test Annex (of NASA)
C L A	Centre Line Average
	Communication Link Analyzer
C L A I R A	Chalk Lime and Allied Industries Research Association (now WHRA)
C L A M	Chemical Low-Altitude Missile
C L A O	Consejo Latino Americano de Oceanografia (Uruguay) (Latin-American Council on Oceanography)
C L A R C	Consejo Latino-Americano de Radiacon Cosmica (Bolivia) (Latin-American Council on Cosmic Radiation)
C L A R A	*Cornell* Learning and Recognizing Automaton

C L A S P	Closed Line Assembly for Single Particles
	Consortium of Local Authorities Special Programme
C L A S S	Closed Loop Accounting for Stores Sales
	Computer-based Laboratory for Automated School Systems
C L C R	Controlled Letter Contract Reduction
C L D	Central Library and Documentation branch (of ILO)
C L E M	Composite for the Lunar Excursion Module
C L E O	Clear Language for Expressing Orders
C L F	Capacitive Loss Factor
C L R	Co-ordinating Lubricants Research
	Council on Library Resources (USA)
C L R U	Cambridge Language Research Unit
C L T	Communications Line Terminals
C M A	Canadian Medical Association (Canada)
C M A S	Confederation Mondiale des Activites Subaquatiques (France) (World Underwater Federation)
C M C	Carboxmethyl Cellulose
	Code for Magnetic Characters
C M C L T	Current Mode Complementary Transistor Logic
C M C R	Continuous Melting, Casting and Rolling
C M E R I	Central Mechanical Engineering Research Institute (India)
C M G	Control Moment Gyro
C M I	Christian Michelsen's Institute (Norway)
	Commonwealth Mycological Institute
C M M	Commission for Maritime Meteorology (of WMO)
C M M A	Concrete Mixer Manufacturers Association
C M M P	Commodity Management Master Plan
cmnd	Command Paper (numbered series authorised by Parliament and published by HMSO)
C M V P C B	California Motor Vehicle Pollution Control Board (USA)
C N	Coordination Number
C M R	Committee on Manpower Resources
	Common-Mode Rejection
C N A	Canadian Nuclear Association (Canada)
	Center for Naval Analyses (USN)
	Cosmic Noise Absorption
C N A A	Council for National Academic Awards

C N B O S	Comite National Belge de l'Organisation Scientifique (Belgium) (Belgian National Committee for Scientific Management)
C N E E M A	Centre National d'Etudes et d'Experimentation de Machinisme Agricole (France) (National Design and Experimental Centre for Agricultural Machinery)
C N E N	Comitato Nazionale per l'Energia Nucleare (Italy) (National Atomic Energy Authority)
C N E R A	Centre National d'Etudes et de Recherches Aeronautiques (Belgium) (National Centre for Aeronautical Studies and Research)
C N E S	Centre National d'Etudes Spatiales (France) (National Centre for Space Studies)
C N E T	Centre National d'Etudes des Telecommunications (France) (National Centre of Telecommunication Studies)
C N E X O	Centre National d'Exploitation des Oceans (France) (National Centre for Oceanographic Research)
C N F R O	Comite National Francaise de Recherche Oceanique (France) (National Committee for Oceanographic Research)
C N G A	California Natural Gas Association (USA)
C N I E	Comision Nacional de Investigaciones Especiales (Argentine) (National Commission for Space Research)
C N O F	Comite National de l'Organisation Francaise (France) (French National Committee for Management)
C N O S	Comitato Nazionale per l'Organizzazione Scientifica (Italy) (National Committee for Scientific Administration)
C N P	Comitato Nazionale per la Produttivita (Italy) (National Council for Productivity)
C N P I O	Comissao Nacional Portuguesa para Investigacao Oceanografico (Portugal) (Portuguese National Committee for Oceanographic Research)
C N R	Canadian National Railways Carrier-to-Noise Ratio Consiglio Nazionale delle Recherche (Italy) (National Research Council)

C N R A	Centre National de Recherches Agronomiques (France) (National Rural Economy Research Centre)
C N R M	Centre National de Recherches Metallurgiques (Belgium) (National Metallurgical Research Centre)
C N R S	Centre National de la Recherche Scientifique (France) (National Scientific Research Centre)
C O A	College of Aeronautics
C O B E L D A	Compagnie Belge d'Electronic et d'Automation (Belgium)
C O B L O C	Codap Language Block-Oriented Compiler
C O B O L	Common Business Oriented Language
C O C	Combat Operations Center (of NORAD)
C O D	Carrier-Onboard Delivery
C O D A G	Combined Diesel And Gas
C O D A S Y L	Conference on Data System Languages
C O D A T A	Committee on Data for Science and Technology (of ICSU)
C O D C	Canadian Oceanographic Data Centre (Canada)
C O D E D	Computer Oriented Design of Electronic Devices
C O D O G	Combined Diesel or Gas
C O D S I A	Council of Defense and Space Industry Associations (USA)
C O E C	Comite Central d'Oceanographie et d'Etudes des Cotes (France) (Central Committee of Oceanography and Coastal Studies)
C O E D	Char Oil Energy Development
C O G A G	Combined Gas And Gas
C O G E N T	Compiler and Generalised Translator
C O G O	Coordinated Geometry
C O G S	Continuous Orbital Guidance Sensor
CO I D	Council of Industrial Design
C O I N S	Computer and Information Sciences Counter-Insurgency
C O M A C	Continuous Multiple Access Collator
C O M A T	Computer-Assisted Training
C O M E I N D O R S	Composite Mechanised Information and Documentation Retrieval System
C O M E X O	Comite d'Exploitation des Oceans (France)
C O M P A C	Commonwealth Pacific Cable
C O M P A R E	Computerized Performance and Analysis Response Evaluator

C O M P A R E	Console for Optical Measurement and Precise Analysis of Radiation from Electronics
C O M P A S S	Computer Assisted Classification and Assignment System
C O M S A T	Communications Satellite
C O M S O A L	Computer Method of Sequencing Operations for Assembly Lines
C O N A R C	Continental Army Command (US Army)
C O N F	Conference
C O N S O R T	Conversation System with On-line Remote Terminals
C O N U S	Continental United States (USA)
C O P	Commissie Opvoering Productivitiet (Netherlands) (Productivity Centre)
C O R A P R A N	COBELDA Radar Automatic Preflight Analyser
C O R C	*Cornell* Computing language
C O R E C I	Compagnie de Regulation et de Controle Industriel (France)
C O R E S T A	Centre de Cooperation pour les Recherches Scientifiques relatives au Tabac (France) (Co-operative Centre for Scientific Research on Tobacco)
C O R G	Combat Operations Research Group
C O R S	Canadian Operational Research Society (Canada)
C O S	Cosmic Rays and Trapped Radiation Committee (of ESRO)
C O S A G	Combination of Steam And Gas
C O S A N O S T R A	Computer Oriented System And Newly Organised Storage-to-Retrieval Apparatus
C O S A T I	Committee on Scientific And Technical Information (of FCST)
C O S I	Committee on Scientific Information (USA)
C O S I N E	Committee on Computer Science in Electrical Engineering Education (of Association for Computing Machinery, USA)
C O S I P	College Science Improvement Program (of National Science Foundation, USA)
C O S M I C	Computer Programmes Information Center (University of Georgia, USA)
C O S M O S	Consortium of Selected Manufacturers Open System
C O S P A R	Committee on Space Research (of the International Council of Scientific Unions)

C O S P U P	Committee on Science and Public Policy (of National Academy of Sciences, USA)
C O S R I M S	Committee on Research in the Mathematical Sciences (of National Academy of Sciences, USA)
C O S T I C	Comite Scientifique et Technique de l'Industrie du Chauffage, de la ventilation et du conditionnement d'air (France) (Heating, Ventilating and Air Conditioning Scientific and Technical Committee)
C P	Conference Paper
	Current Paper
	prefix to numbered series of Codes of Practice issued by BSI
C P B	Centraal Planbureau (Netherlands) (Central Planning Bureau)
C P A	Canadian Pharmaceutical Association (Canada)
	Canadian Psychological Association (Canada)
	Closest Point of Approach
	Critical Path Analysis
C P E A	Cooperative Program for Educational Administration (USA)
C P C	Card Programmed Calculator
C P E	Centre de Prospective et d'Evaluation (France) (Feasibility and Evaluation Centre)
C P E M	Conference on Precision Electromagnetic Measurements (USA)
C P F F	Cost Plus Fixed Fee
C P I A	Chemical Propulsion Information Agency
C P I L S	Correlation Protection Integrated Landing System
C P M	Critical Path Method
C P P	Civilian Personnel Pamphlet (numbered series issued by US Army)
C P P A	Canadian Pulp and Paper Association (Canada)
	Coal Preparation Plant Association
C P R	Committee on Polar Research (of NAS/NRC)
	Continuing Property Record
C P U	Central Processing Unit
	Collective Protection Unit
C R	Chemical Report
	Conference Report
	Contract Report
	Contractor Report
	Control Relay

CRA	California Redwood Association (USA)
CRAC	Careers Research and Advisory Centre
CRAD	Committee for Research into Apparatus for the Disabled
CRAFT	Computerized Relative Allocation of Facilities Technique
CRAM	Card Random Access Memory
	Computerized Reliability Analysis Method
	Conditional Relaxation Analysis Method
CRC	Centre de Recherches techniques et scientifiques industries de la tannerie, de la chaussure, de la pantoufle et des autres industries transformatrices du Cuir (Belgium) (Technical and Scientific Research Centre for the Tannery, Shoe, Slipper, and other Leather-Working Industries)
	Co-ordinating Research Council (USA)
	Cumulative Results Criterion
CRCP	Continuously Reinforced Concrete Pavement
CRDL	Chemical Research and Development Laboratories (US Army)
CRDME	Committee for Research into Dental Materials and Equipment
CRDSD	Current Research and Development in Scientific Documentation (numbered series issued by National Science Foundation, USA)
CREO	Centre de Recherches et d'Etudes Oceanographiques (France) (Centre of Oceanographic Research and Studies)
CRESS	Computerised Reader Enquiry Service System
CRESS/AU	Center for Research in Social Systems of the American University (USA)
CRESTS	*Courtauld's* Rapid Extract, Sort and Tabulate System
CRF	Capital Recovery Factor
CRG	Centre de Recherches de Gorsem (Belgium) (Gorsem Research Centre)
CRIC	Centre de Recherches de l'Industrie Belge de la Ceramique (Belgium) (Belgian Ceramic Industry Research Centre)
	Centre de Recherches Industrielles sur Contrats (France) (Industrial Research Centre on Contracts)

C R I F	Centre de Recherches et techniques de l'Industrie Fabrications metalliques (Belgium) (Scientific and Technical Research Centre for the Metals Manufacturing Industry)
C R I P E	Centre de Recherches et techniques pour l'Industrie des Produits Explosifs (Belgium) (Scientific and Technical Research Centre for the Explosives Industry)
C R I S	Command Retrieval Information System
	Current Research Information System
C R L L B	Center for Research on Language and Language Behavior (of University of Michigan, USA)
C R M	Control and Reproducibility Monitor
C R M E	Centre Regional de Mouvements d'Energie (France)
C R N L	Chalk River Nuclear Laboratories (Canada)
C R O	Cathode Ray Oscilloscope
C R P	Centre de Recherche Physique (France) (Physics Research Centre)
C R P L	Central Radio Propagation Laboratory (USA) (now Institute for Telecommunication Sciences and Aeronomy (of ESSA))
C R R	Centre de Recherches Routieres (Belgium) (Road Research Centre)
C R R E L	Cold Regions Research and Engineering Laboratory (US Army)
C R S I M	Centre de Recherches Scientifiques, Industrielles et Maritimes (France) (Scientific, Industrial and Maritime Research Centre)
C S	Commercial Standard (numbered series issued by NBS, USA)
	Computer Science
	prefix to numbered series issued by Central States Forest Experiment Station (Forest Service, USDA)
C S A	Canadian Standards Association (Canada)
	Ceskoslovenske Aerolinie (Czechoslovakia)
C S A E	Canadian Society of Agricultural Engineering (Canada)
C S D	Ceskolovenske Statne Drahy (Czechoslovakia) (Czechoslovak State Railway)
	Constant Speed Drive
	Controlled-Slip Differentials
C S E	Containment Systems Experiment

C S F	Canadian Standard Freeness
	Compagnie Generale de Telegraphie sans Fil (France)
C S I R	Council for Scientific and Industrial Research (South Africa)
	Council of Scientific and Industrial Research (India)
C S I R O	Commonwealth Scientific and Industrial Research Organisation (Australia)
C S K	Co-operative Study of the Kuroshio and adjacent region
C S L	Control and Simulation Language
	Current Switch Logic
C S M M F R A	Cotton, Silk and Man-Made Fibres Research Association
C S P	Continuous Sampling Plan
	Council for Scientific Policy
C S S B	Compatible Single-Sideband
C S S S	Canadian Soil Science Society (Canada)
C S T B	Centre Scientifique et Technique du Batiment (France) (Building Science and Technology Centre)
C S T C	Centre Scientique et Technique de la Construction (Belgium) (Scientific and Technical Research Centre for the Construction Industry)
C T A	California Trucking Association (USA)
	Conurbation Transport Authority
C T B	Centre Technique de Bois (France) (Wood Research Centre)
C T C	Central Training Council
C T D H	Command and Telemetry Data Handling
C T E B	Council of Technical Examining Bodies
C T F M	Continuous-Transmission Frequency-Modulated
C T H	Chalmers Tekniska Hogskola (Sweden) (Chalmers University of Technology)
C T I F	Centre Techniques des Industries de la Fonderie (France) (Foundry Industries Technical Centre)
C T L	Cincinnati Testing Laboratories (USA)
	Complementary Transistor Logic
	Constant Time Loci
C T O	Charge Transforming Operator
C T B	Charge Transforming Parameter
C T P B	Carboxyl-Terminated Polybutadiene Binder
C T R A	Coal Tar Research Association

C T S	Cab Tyred Sheathed
C T S I B V	Centre Technique et Scientifique de l'Industrie Belge du Verre (Belgium) (Belgian Glass Industry Technical and Scientific Centre)
C T S S	Compatible Time Shared System
C U	Columbia University (USA)
C U D O S	Continuously Updated Dynamic Optimizing Systems
C U M M	Council of Underground Machinery Manufacturers
C U R	Commissie voor Uitvoering van Research (Netherlands) (Committee for Performing Research)
C U R T S	Common User Radio Transmission System
C U R V	Cable-controlled Underwater Research Vehicle
C U S P	Central Unit for Scientific Photography (of RAE)
C U W	Committee on Undersea Warfare (USDOD)
C V D	Co-ordination of Valve Development
	Coupled Vibration-Dissociation
	Current-Voltage Diagram
C V D V	Coupled Vibration-Dissociation-Vibration
C V M A	Canadian Veterinary Medical Association (Canada)
C W	Carrier *or* Composite *or* Continuous Wave
	Chemical Warfare
C W A R	Continuous Wave Acquisition Radar
C W A S	Contractor Weighted Average Share
C W B	Canadian Welding Bureau (Canada)
C W I T	Concordance Words In Titles
C W S	Canadian Welding Society (Canada)

D

D A A D	Deutscher Akadernischer Austauschienst (German Academic Exchange System)
D A C	Design Augmented by Computer
	Digital to Analogue Converter
D A C O R	Data Correction
D A D	Drum And Display
D A D E E	Dynamic Analog Differential Equation Equalizer
D A F	van Doorne's Automobiel-fabriek (Holland)
D A F C	Digital Automatic Frequency Control

54

D A I	Deutscher Architekten und Ingenieurverband (Germany) (German Architecture and Engineering Society)
D A F M	Discard-At-Failure Maintenance
D A G K	Deutschen Arbeitsgemeinschaft Kybernetic (Germany) (German Study Group on Cybernetics)
D A I R	Driver Air, Information, and Routing
D A I S	Defence Automatic Integrated Switching system
D A M	Data Addressed Memory
D A P H N E	DIDO and PLUTO Handmaiden for Nuclear Experiments
D A P S	Direct Access Programming System
D A R E	Document Abstract Retrieval Equipment
	Doppler Automatic Reduction Equipment
D A R E S	Data Analysis and Reduction System
D A R L I	Digital Angular Readout by Laser Interferometry
D A R S	Digital Adaptive Recording System
D A R T	Daily Automatic Rescheduling Technique
	Dynamic Acoustic Response Trigger
	Dual Axis Rate Transducer
D A S	Data Acquisition System
	Data Automation System
	Digital Analogue Simulator
	District Auditors Society
D A S A	Defense Atomic Support Agency (USDOD) (formerly Armed Forces Special Weapons Project)
D A S H	Drone Anti-Submarine Helicopter
D A S H E R	Dynamic Analysis of Shells of Revolution
D A T A N	Data Analysis
D A T A R	Digital Auto Transducer and Recorder
D A T I C O	Digital Automatic Tape Intelligence Check-out
D A V I	Dynamic Anti-resonant Vibration Isolator
D A W	Deutscher Arbeitskreis Wasserforschung (Germany) (German Water Research Association)
D B	Deutsche Budesbahn (Germany) (German Federal Railway)
D B A	Deutsche Bauakademie (Germany) (German Building Academy)
D B M	Data Buffer Module
D B R	Division of Building Research (of National Research Council, Canada)
D B V	Deutscher Betoverein (Germany) (German Concrete Association)
D C	Data Classifier

D C A	Defense Communications Agency (USDOD)
D C A S	Defense Contract Administration Service (USDOD)
D C A S A	Dyers and Colourists Association of South Africa
D C A S R	Defense Contract Administrative Service Region (USDOD)
D C B	Decimal Currency Board (Australia)
D C B R L	Defence Chemical, Biological, and Radiation
D C C A	Laboratories (of DRB) (now DCBRE)
	Design Change Cost Analysis
D C D M A	Diamond Core Drill Manufacturers Association (USA)
D C F	Discounted Cash Flow
D C S	Defence Communications System
	Digital Command System
D C S C	Defense Construction Supply Center (USDOD)
D C T L	Direct Coupled Transistor Logic
D D A	Digital Differential Analyzer
	Dynamics Differential Analyzer
D D A S	Digital Data Acquisition System
D D C	Deck Decompression Chamber
	Defense Documentation Center (USDOD)
	Direct Digital Control
D D D	Direct Distance Dialling
D D F	Design Disclosure Format
D D I	Depth Deviation Indicator
D D M	Data Demand Module
D D N P	Diazodinitrophenol
D D R & E	Directorate of Defense Research and Engineering (USDOD)
D D S	Deep-Diving System
	Deployable Defence System
	Digital Dynamics Simulator
D D T	Deflagration to Detonation Transition
	Dichlorodiphenyltrichlorethane
	Dynamic Debugging Technique
D E A	Dairy Engineers Association
	Department of Economic Affairs
D E A C O N	Direct English Access and Control
D E C H E M A	Deutsche Gesellschaft für Chemisches Apparate-wesen (Germany) (German Society for Chemical Apparatus)
D E C U S	Digital Equipment Computer Users Society
D E D U C O M	Deductive Communicator
D E E	Digital Events Evaluator

D E F	prefix to numbered series of Defence Specifications issued by the Ministry of Defence and published by HMSO
D E L F I C	Department of Defense Land Fallout Prediction System
D E R V	Diesel Engine Road Vehicle
D E S	Department of Education and Science
D E S C	Defense Electronics Supply Center (USDOD)
D E U	Data Exchange Unit
D E U A	Diesel Engines and Users Association
D E U C E	Digital Electronic Universal Computing Engine
D E W	Distant Early Warning
D E X A N	Digital Experimental Airborne Navigator
D F	Decontamination Factor
	Direction Finding
D F B	Distribution Fuse Board
D F G	Deutsche Forschungsgmeinschaft (German Research Association)
D F I K	Dansk Forening for Industriel Kvalitetskontrol (Denmark) (Danish Society for Industrial Quality Control)
D F L	Deutsche Forschungsanstalt fur Luftfart (Germany) (German Aeronautical Research Institute)
D F P	Diisopropylflurophosphate
D F R	Decreasing Failure Rate
	Dounreay Fast Reactor
D F R A	Drop Forging Research Association
D G	prefix to numbered series of Defence Guides issued by the Ministry of Defence
D G F	Deutsche Gesellschaft fur Flugwissenschaften (Germany) (German Society for Aeronautical Sciences)
D G G	Deutsche Gesellschaft fur Galvanotechnik (Germany) (German Society for Electroplating)
	Deutsche Glastechnische Gesellschaft (Germany) (German Society for Glass Technology)
D G K	Deutsche Geodatisch Kommission (Germany) (German Geodetic Commission)
D G M	Deutsche Gesellschaft fur Metallkunde (Germany) (German Metallography Society)
D G M K	Deutsche Gesellschaft fur Mineralolwissenschaft und Kohlechemie (Germany) (German Society of the Science of Petroleum and the Chemistry of Coal)

D G N	Direccion General de Normas (Mexico) (Standards Institute)
D G P H	Deutsche Gesellschaft fur Photographie (Germany) (German Photographic Society)
D G R R	Deutsche Gesellschaft fur Raketentechnik und Raumfart (Germany) (German Society for Rocket and Space Technology)
D H I	Deutsches Hydrographisches Institut (Germany) (Germany Hydrographic Institute)
D H R	Division of Housing Research (USA)
D I	Deutsches Industrieinstitut (Germany) (German Industrial Institute)
D I A	Drug Information Association (USA)
D I A C	Defense Industry Advisory Council (USA)
D I A N	Digital Analogue
D I B	Deutsches Institut fur Betriebswirtschaft (Germany) (German Institute for Business Studies)
D I F	Deutsches Institut fur Forderung des Industriellen Fuhrungsnachwuchses (Germany) (German Institute for Industrial Management Development)
D I M A T E	Depot Installed Maintenance Automatic Test Equipment
D I M P L E	Deuterium Moderated Pile Low Energy
D I N	Deutsche Industrie-Norm (German Industrial Standard)
D I N A	Diesel Nacional (Mexico)
D I P	Dual-in-line Package
D I P E C	Defense Industrial Plant Equipment Center (USDOD)
D I S A C	Digital Simulator and Computer
D I T R A N	Diagnostic FORTRAN
D L	Diode Logic
	prefix to series of Defence Lists issued by the Ministry of Defence
D L C	Direct Lift Control
D L H	Deutsche Lufthansa (Germany)
D L I R	Depot Level Inspection and Repair
D L T	Depletion-Layer Transistor
D L W	Diesel Locomotive Works (India)
D M	Delta Modulation
	Design Manual
	Design Memorandum
D M A P N	Dimethylaminoproionitrile
D M C	Dough Moulding Compound

D M E	Distance Measuring Equipment
D M P E	Dimethoxphenylethylamine
D M S	Documentation of Molecular Spectroscopy
D M T R	*Dounreay* Materials Testing Reactor
D M T S	Department of Mines and Technical Surveys (Canada)
D M U	Dual Manoeuvring Unit
D N A	Deoxy-ribonucleic Acid
	Deutscher Normenausschuss (Germany) (German Standards Institute)
D N B	Departure from Nucleate Boiling
D N J	Det Norske Justervesen (Norway) (Norwegian Bureau of Weights and Measures)
D O A E	Defence Operational Analysis Establishment (MOD)
D O C	Direct Operating Costs
D O C U S	Display-Orientated Computer Usage System
D O D *or* D O D	Department of Defense (USA)
D O D D A C	Department of Defense Damage Assessment Center
D O D G E	Department of Defense Gravity Experiment
D O D I S	Distribution of Oceanographic Data at Isentropic Levels
D O F I C	Domain Originated Functional Integrated Circuit
D O F L	Diamond Ordnance Fuze Laboratories (now HDL) (US Army)
D O M	Digital Ohmmeter
D O T	Deep Ocean Technology
	Department of Transport (Canada)
	Department of Transportation (USA)
D O V A P	Doppler Velocity And Position
D O W B	Deep Operating Work Boat
D P C M	Differential Pulse Code Modulation
D P H	Diamond Pyramid Hardness
D P M A	Data Processing Management Association
D R	Dead Reckoning
	Deutsche Reischbahn (Germany) (German State Railway)
D R A I	Dead Reckoning Analogue Indicator
D R B	Defence Research Board (Canada)
D R C	Damage Risk Criterion
D R I	Denver River Institute (USA)
D R I F T	Diversity Receiving Instrumentation For Telemetry

D R M	Digital Ratiometer
D R M E	Direction des Recherches et Moyens d'Essais (France) (Defence Agency for the Coordination of Research)
D R M L	Defence Research Medical Laboratories (of DRB) (now DRET)
D R O	Destructive Readout
D R O D	Delayed Readout Detector
D R P	Deutsches Reichs Patent (German State Patent)
D R P A	Delaware River Port Authority (USA)
D R S	Digital Radar Simulator
D R T	Dead Reckoning Tracer
D R T C	Documentation Research and Training Centre (India)
D R T E	Defence Research Telecommunications Establishment (of DRB)
D S	Dansk Standardiseringsraad (Denmark) (Danish Standards Institute)
D S A	Defence Supply Agency (USDOD) Dial Service Assistance
D S B	Defense Science Board (USA)
D S I	Dairy Science International
D S I F	Deep Space Instrumentation Facility (of NASA)
D S I R	Department of Scientific Research (disbanded 1965)
D S I S	Directorate of Scientific Information Services (of DRB)
D S L C	Defense Logistics Services Center (USDOD)
D S N	Deep Space Network
D S R	Discriminating Selector Repeater
D S R V	Deep Submergence Rescue Vehicle
D S S P	Deep Submergence Systems Project (USN)
D S S R G	Deep Submergence Systems Research Group (USN)
D S S V	Deep Submergence Search Vehicle
D S T V	Deutscher Stahlbau-Verband (Germany) (German Steel Construction Association)
D T A	Differential Thermal Analysis
D T D	prefix to numbered series of Specifications issued by MINTECH and published by HMSO
D T D S	Digital Television Display System
D T L	Diode Transistor Logic
D T M B	David Taylor Model Basin (USN)
D T P	Directory Tape Processor

D T P L	Domain Tip Propagation Logic
D U M S	Deep Unmanned Submersibles
C U N C	Deep Underwater Nuclear Counter
D V A	Dynamic Visual Acuity
D V E O	Department of Defense Value Engineering Services (USDOD)
D V G	Deutsche Volkswirtschaftliche Gesellschaft (Germany) (German Economics Association)
D V L	Deutsche Versuchsanstalt fuer Luftfart (Germany) (German Aviation Experimental Centre)
D V M	Deutscher Verband fuer Material-pruefung (Germany) (German Association for Materials Testing)
	Digital Voltmeter
D V N I G M I	Dal'nevostochnyy Nauchno-Issledovatel'skiy Gidrometeorologicheski (USSR) (Far Eastern Scientific Research Hydro-meteorological Institute)
D V S	Deutscher Verband fuer Schweisstechnik (Germany) (German Welding Technology Association)
D V S T	Direct View Storage Tube
D V T W V	Deutscher Verband Technisch-Wissenschaftlicher Verbands (Germany) (German Association of Technological Societies)
D V W	Deutscher Verein fuer Vermessungswesen (Germany) (German Association for Surveying)
D V W G	Deutche Verkehrswissen-Schaftliche Gesellschaft (Germany) (German Transportation Society)
D W B A	Distorted-Wave Born Approximation
D W I C A	Deep Water Isotopic Current Analyzer
D W S M C	Defense Weapons Systems Management Center (USDOD)
D Y S T A C	Dynamic Storage Analogue Computer

E

E A	Edgewood Arsenal (US Army)
E A A C	East African Airways Corporation (Kenya)
E A A P	European Association for Animal Production
E A B R D	Electrically Actuated Band Release Device
E A C	Electro-Agricultural Centre (of the Electricity Council)
E A C C	Error Adaptive Control Computer
E A C S O	East Africa Common Services Organization

E A E C	European Airlines Electronic Committee
E A E S	European Atomic Energy Society
E A F	Electron Arc Furnace
E A M	Electronic Accounting Machine
E A N D C	European-American Nuclear Data Committee
E A N D R O	Electrically Alterable NDRO
E A R	Employee Attitude Research
E A R C	Extraordinary Administrative Radio Conference
E A S	Extensive Air Shower
E A S L	Engineering Analysis and Simulation Language
E A S Y	Engine Analyzer System
E A W	Equivalent Average Words
E B	Electron Beam
E B R	Electron Beam Remelting
	Experimental Breeder Reactor
E B U	European Broadcasting Union
E B W	Exploding Bridgewire
E B W R	Experimental Boiling Water Reactor
E C A	Economic Commission for Africa (of UNO)
	Electrical Contractors Association
	European Confederation of Agriculture
E C A C	Electromagnetic Compatibility Analysis Center (USDOD)
E C A F E	Economic Commission for Asia and the Far East (of UNO)
F C A P	Electronic Circuit Analysis Programme
E C C	Electronic Calibration Center (of NBS Radio Standards Laboratory)
E C C M	Electronic Counter-Countermeasures
E C D M	Electrochemical and Electrical Discharge Machining
E C E	Economic Commission for Europe (of UNO)
	Engineering Capacity Exchange
E C F A	European Committee for Future Accelerators
E C G	Electrocardiogram
E C L	Electronics Components Laboratory
E C L A	Economic Commission for Latin America (of UNO)
E C M	Electrochemical Machining
	Electronic Countermeasures
E C M A	European Computer Manufacturers Association
E C M C	Electric Cable Makers Confederation
E C M S A	Electronics Command Meteorological Support Agency (US Army)

E C M T	European Conference of Ministers of Transport
E C O M	Electronics Command (US Army)
E C O N O M A N	Effective Control of Manpower
E C O S O C	Economic and Social Council (of UNO)
E C P D	Engineers Council for Professional Development (USA)
E C R C	Electronic Components Reliability Center (USA)
E C S	Enable Control System
	Environmental Control System
E C S C	European Coal and Steel Community
E C U	Environmental Control Unit
E D A	Economic Development Administration (USA)
	Electrical Development Advisory Division (of the Electricity Council)
	Electrical Development Association
E D C	Economic Development Committee
	Education and training of Chemists
E D D	Electronic Data Display
E D E	Emitter Dip Effect
E D F	Electricite de France (France)
E D I A C	Electronic Display of Indexing Association and Content
E D I C T	Engineering Document Information Collection Technique
E D I S	Engineering Data Information System
E D M	Electrodischarge Machining
E D P	Electronic Data Processing
E D P E	Electronic Data Processing Equipment
E D P S	Electronic Data Processing System
E D S	Emergency Detection System
E D S A C	Electronic Delay Storage Automatic Calculator
	Electronic Discrete Sequential Automatic Computer
E D T A	Ethylenediamine Tetra-acetic Acid
	European Dialysis and Transplant Association
E D U	Experimental Diving Unit
E D U C O M	Interuniversity Communications Council (USA)
E D V A C	Electronic Discrete Variable Automatic Computer (*or* Calculator)
E E	Electrical Engineering
E E A	Electronic Engineering Association
E E C	EUROCONTROL Experimental Centre
	European Economic Community
E E C L	Emitter-Emitter Coupled Logic

E E D	Electro-Explosive Device
E E G	Electro-encephalograph
E E M	Electronic Equipment Monitoring
	Emission Electron Microscope
E E M J E B	Electrical and Electronic Manufacturers Joint Education Board
F E R	Explosive Echo Ranging
E E R L	Electrical Engineering Research Laboratory
E E S	Engineering Experiment Station
E E U A	Engineering Equipment Users Association
E F C	European Federation of Corrosion
E F D A S	Epsylon Flight Data Acquisition System
E F I	Elektrisitetsforsyningens Forskningsinstitutt (Norway) (Electricity Supply Research Institute)
E F L C	Engineers Foreign Language Circle
E F P W	European Federation for the Protection of Waters
E F S	Electronic Frequency Selection
E F T	Earliest Finish Time
E F T A	European Free Trade Association
E G D	Electrogasdynamics
E G O	Eccentric Orbiting Geophysical Observatory
E G T	Exhaust Gas Temperature
E H D	Electrohydrodynamic
E H F	Extra *or* Extremely High Frequency
	Experimental Husbandry Farm (or MAFF)
E H S	Experiment Horticulture Station (of MAFF)
E I A	Engineering Industries Association
	Electronic Industries Association (USA)
E I B	Economisch Instituut voor de Bouwnijverheid (Netherlands) (Building Industry Economic Institute)
E I C	Engineering Institute of Canada
	Equipment Identification Code
E I D	Electrical Inspection Directorate (MINTECH)
E I L	Electron Injection Laser
E I M	Excitability Inducing Material
E I M O	Electronic Interface Management Office (of USN)
E I P	Educational Investing and Planning Programme
E I S	Economic Information System
E I T B	Engineering Industry Training Board
E J C	Engineers Joint Council (USA)
E J C C	Eastern Joint Computer Conference (USA)
E L	Electro-Luminescence
	Electronics Laboratory

E L C D	Evaporative Loss Control Device
E L D	Economic Load Dispatching
E L D O	European Launcher Development Organisation
E L E C	European League for Economic Cooperation
E L F A	Electric Light Fittings Association
E L I	Extra-Low Interstitial
E L I P	Electrostatic Latent Image Photography
E L M I A	European Agricultural and Industrial Fair
E L O I S E	European Large Orbiting Instrumentation for Solar Experiments
E L R	Engineering Laboratory Report
E L R O	Electronics Logistics Research Office (US Army)
E L S I	*Esso* Lubrication Service to Industry
E L S I E	Electronic Signalling and Indicating Equipment
E L S S	Extravehicular Life Support System
E M	Extensible Machine
	Engineering Manual
	Engineering Memorandum
E M A	Extended Mercury Autocode
	Excavator Makers Association
E M A T S	Emergency Mission Automatic Transmission Service
E M B E T	Error Model Best Estimate of Trajectory
E M B O	European Molecular Biology Organization
E M C	Electro-Magnetic Compatibility
E M D	Extractive Metallurgy Division (of the Metallurgical Society of AIME)
E M D I	Energy Management Display Indicator
E M E C	Electronic Maintenance Engineering Center (US Army)
E M E T F	Electromagnet Environmental Test Facility (US Army)
E M I	Electromagnetic Interference
E M K O	Ethyl Michler's Ketone Oxime
E M L	Engineering Mechanics Laboratory (of NBS)
E M M	Electromagnetic Measurement
E M M A	Electron Microscopy and Microanalysis
E M O S	Earth's Mean Orbital Speed
E M P	Electromagnetic Pulse
E M P I R E	Early Manned Planetary-Interplanetary Round-trip Expedition
E M R I C	Educational Media Research Information Center (USA)
E M S A	Electron Microscope Society of America (USA)

65

E M U	Extravehicular Mobility Unit
E N D O R	Electron Nuclear Double Resonance
E N E A	European Nuclear Energy Agency (of OECD)
E N E L	Ente Nazional per l'Energia Elettrica (Italy)
E N I	Ente Nazionale Idrocarburi (Italy)
E N I A C	Electronic Numerical Integrator And Calculator
E N I K M Ash	Eksperimental'nyy Nauchno Issledovatel'skiy Institut Kuznechno pressovogo Mashinostroyeniya (USSR) (Experimental Scientific Research Institute of Forging-Pressing-Machine Construction)
E N I M S	Eksperimental'nyy Nauchno Issledovatel'skiy Institut Metallorezhushchikh Stankov (USSR) (Experimental Scientific Research Institute for Machine Tools)
E N I P P	Eksperimental'nyy i Nauchno Issledovatel'skiy Institut Podshipnikovoy Promyshlennosti (USSR) (Experimental and Scientific Research Institute of the Bearing Institute)
E N O	Comite Hellenique de Normalisation (Greece) (Standards Organisation)
E N R	Equivalent Noise Resistance
E N T	Equivalent Noise Temperature
E N T A C	Engine-Teleguide Anti-Char
E O D D	Electro-Optic Digital Deflector
E O G	Electro-oculograph
E O Q	Economic Order Quantity
E O Q C	European Organisation for Quality Control
E O S	Electro-Optical Systems
E P A M	Elementary Perceiver and Memorizer
E P I C	Earth-Pointing Instrument Carrier
	Electronic Photochromic Integrating Cathode ray tube
E P P	European Pallet Pool
E P P O	European and Mediterranean Plant Protection Organisation
E P R	Electron Paramagnetic Resonance
	Ethylene and Propylene Rubber
E P S	Expandable Polystyrene
E P T	Electrostatic Printing Tube
	Ethylene Propylene Terpolymer
E P T A	Expanded Programme of Technical Assistance (of UNO)

E P U L	Ecole Polytechnique de l'Universite de Lausanne (Switzerland) (Institute of Technology of the University of Lausanne)
E Q U A L A N T	Equatorial Atlantic
E Q U I P	Equipment Usage Information Programme
E R A	Electrical Research Association
E R A P	Entreprise de Recherches Petrolieres (France)
E R B M	Extended Range Ballistic Missile
E R C	Electronics Research Center (of NASA)
	Equatorial Ring Current
E R C R	Electronic Retina Computing Reader
E R D A	Electronics Research and Development Activity (US Army)
E R D	Emergency Return Device
E R D E	Explosives Research and Development Establishment (MINTECH)
E R F	Epoxy Resins Formulators Division (of SPI, USA)
E R G S	En-Route Guidance System
E R I C	Educational Research Information Center (USOE)
	Energy Rate Input Controller
E R M	Earth Re-entry Module
E R N O	Entwicklungsring Nord (Germany) (Northern Development Centre)
E R O P	Extensions and Restrictions of Operators
E R O S	Earth Resources Observation Satellite
E R P	Effective Radiated Power
	Environmental Research Paper
E R P L D	Extended-Range Phased-Locked Demodulator
E R S	Economic Research Service (USDA)
	Environmental Research Satellite
	Extremal Regulation System
E R S R	Equipment Reliability Status Report
E R S S	Earth Resources Survey Satellite
E R W	Electric Resistance Welding
E S	Experiment *or* Experimental Station
E S A	Ecological Society of America (USA)
E S A R S	Earth Surveillance and Rendezvous Simulator
E S B	Electrical Simulation of the Brain
	Electrical Standards Board (of USASI)
E S C	Engineering Society of Cincinnati (USA)
	Entomological Society of Canada
E S C A	Electron Spectroscopy for Chemical Analysis
E S D	Electronic Systems Division (USAFSC)
E S D A C	European Space Data Centre (of ESRO)

E S E	Ecole Superieure d'Electricite (France)
	Electrical Support Equipment
E S G	Electrically Suspended Gyroscope
E S H	Equivalent Standard Hours
E S L	Expected Significance Level
E S L A B	European Space (Research) Laboratory (of ESRO)
E S L O	European Satellite Launching Organisation
E S M	Elastomeric Shield Material
E S N E	Engineering Societies of New England (USA)
E S O	European Southern Observatory
E S O M A R	European Society for Opinion Surveys and Market Research
E S P	Extra Sensory Perception
E S R	Electron Spin Resonance
	Electro-Slag Refining
E S R A N G E	European Space (Sounding-Rocket Launching) Range (of ESRO)
E S R I N	European Space Research Institute (of ESRO)
E S R O	European Space Research Organisation
E S S	Electronic Switching System
	Emplaced Scientific Station
E S S A	Environmental Science Services Administration (of Dept of Commerce, USA)
E S S G	Engineer Strategic Studies Group (US Army)
E S T	Earliest Start Time
	Electrolytic Sewage Treatment
E S T E C	European Space Research Technical Centre (of ESRO)
E S T R A C K	European Space Satellite Tracking and Telemetry Network (of ESRO)
E S W L	Equivalent Single Wheel Load
E T	Ephemeris Time
F T C	European Translations Centre
E T C A	Etudes Techniques et Constructions Aerospatiales (Belgium)
E T L	Electro Technical Laboratory (Japan)
E T P	Effluent Treatment Plant
E T R	Engineering Test Reactor
F U C E P A	European Liaison Committee for Cellulose and Paper
E U M - A F T N	European Mediterranean Aeronautical Fixed Telecommunications Network
E U R A T O M	European Atomic Energy Community
E U R E X	Enriched Uranium Extraction

E U R O C A E	European Organisation of Civil Aviation Electronics
E U R O C O N T R O L	European Organisation for the Safety of Air Navigation
F U R O D O C	Joint Documentation Service of ESRO, EUROSPACE and the European Organisation for the Development and Construction of Space Vehicle Launchers
E U R O S P A C E	European Industrial Space Research Group
E U S E C	Conference of Engineering Societies of Western Europe and the USA
E V	Efficient Vulcanization
E V A	Electronic Velocity Analyser
	Ethylene Vinyl Acetate
	Extravehicular Activity
E V A T M I	European Vinyl Asbestos Tile Manufacturers Institute
E V K I	Europaische Vereinigung der Keramik-Industrie (European Federation of the Electro-Ceramic Industry)
E V O P	Evolutionary Operation
E W F	Electrical Wholesalers Federation
E W R C	European Weed Research Council
E W S F	European Work Study Federation
E X A M E T N E T	Experimental Meteorological Sounding Rocket Research Network
F X T E R R A	Extraterrestrial Research Agency (US Army)

F

F A	Frankford Arsenal (US Army)
F A A	Federal Aviation Agency (USA)
F A A R	Forward Area Alerting Radar
F A C E	Field Artillery Computer Equipment
F A C E J	Forges et Ateliers de Construction Electrique de Jeumont (France)
F A C E T	Fluid Amplifier Control Engine Test
F A C I	First Article Configuration Inspection
F A C M T A	Federal Advisory Council on Medical Training Aids (USA)
F A C S	Federation des Amis des Chemins de Fer Secondaires (France) (Federation of the Friends of Light Railways)
	Fine Attitude Control System

F A C S I	Fast Access Coded Small Images
F A D A C	Field Artillery Digital Automatic Computer
F A G S	Federation of Astronomical and Geophysical Services (of IAPO)
F A H Q M T	Fully-Automatic High Quality Machine Translation
F A I	Federation Aeronautique Internationale (International Aeronautical Federation)
F A I R	Fast Access Information Retrieval
F A I R S	*Federal Aviation* Information Retrieval System
F A M E M	Federation of Associations of Mining Equipment Manufacturers
F A N T A C	Fighter Analysis Tactical Air Combat
F A O	Food and Agriculture Organisation (of UNO)
F A P I G	First Atomic Power Industry Group (Japan)
F A R	Flight Aptitude Rating
F A R A D A	Failure Rate Data
F A R E T	Fast Reactor Test
F A S	Federation des Architectes Suisses (Switzerland) (Federation of Swiss Architects)
	Foreign Agriculture Service (USDA)
F A S E	Fundamentally Analyzable Simplified English
F A S E B	Federation of American Societies for Experimental Biology
F A S T	*Fluor* Analytical Scheduling Technique
	Friction Assessment Screening Test
F A S T - V A L	Forward Air Strike Evaluation
F A T E	Fuzing and Arming Test Evaluation
F B C R	Fluidized-Bed Control Rod
F B F M	Frequency Feedback Frequency Modulation
F B I	Federation of British Industries (now CBI)
F B M	Fleet Ballistic Missile
F B P	Final Boiling Point
F B R	Fast Burst Reactor
F C A	Frequency Control and Analysis
F C C	Federal Communications Commission (USA)
F C D	Failure-Correction Decoding
F C I M	Farm, Construction and Industrial Machinery
F C M I	Federation of Coated Macadam Industries
F C S T	Federal Council for Science and Technology (USA)
F D A	Food and Drug Administration (USA)

F D L	prefix to numbered series of Fish Disease Leaflets issued by Fish and Wildlife Service, Department of the Interior, USA
F D L S	Fast Deployment Logistics Ship
F D M	Frequency Division Multiplex
F D S	Frame Difference Signal
F E	Further Education
F E A N I	Federation Europeen d'Associations Nationales d'Ingenieurs (European Federation of National Associations of Engineers)
F E A T	Frequency of Every Allowable Term
F E B	Functional Electronic Block
F E B S	Federation of European Biochemical Societies
F E C	Forward Error Correction
F E D C	Federation of Engineering Design Consultants
F E F	prefix to numbered series of leaflets Fixed Equipment of the Farm issued by MAFF
F E F C O	Federation Europeene des Fabricants de Carton Ondule (European Federation of Corrugated Container Manufacturers)
F E I	Financial Executives Institute (USA)
F E M	Federation Europeene de la Manutention (European Federation of Materials Handling)
F E P	Fluorinated Ethylene-Propylene
F E P A P	Federation of European Producers of Abrasives
F E P E M	Federation of European Petroleum Equipment Manufacturers
F E R D	Fuel Element Rupture Detector
F E S	Fundamental Electrical Standards
F E T	Field Effect Transistor
F F A	Free Fatty Acid
F F A G	Fixed-Field Alternating-Gradient
F F T F	Fast Flux Test Facility (of USAEC)
F G A F	Fraunhofer-Gessellschaft zur Forderung der Angewandten Forschung (Germany) (Fraunhofer Society for the Promotion of Applied Research)
F G W	Forschunsgellschaft fur den Wohnungsbau (Austria) (Housing Research Association)
F H A	Federal Housing Administration (USA)
F I A	Flame Ionization Analysis
F I A R	Fabbrica Italiana Apparechi Radio (Italy)

F I A T	Field Information Agency, Technical (USA)
F I A T A	Federation Internationale des Associations de Transitaires et Assimiles (International Federation of Forwarding Agents Associations)
F I B T P	Federation Internationale du Batiment et des Travaux Publics (International Federation of Building and Public Works)
F I C S	Forecasting and Inventory Control System
F I D	Federation International de la Documentation (International Documentation Federation)
	Flame Ionization Detector
F I D A C	Film Input to Digital Automatic Computer
F I D A S E	Falkland Islands and Dependencies Aerial Survey Expedition
F I D I C	Federation Internationale des Ingenieurs Conseil (International Federation of Consulting Engineers)
F I D O R	Fibre Building Board Development Organisation
F I E N	Forum Italiano dell Energia Nucleare (Italy)
F I E R	Foundation for Instrumentation Education and Research (of Instrument Society of America)
F I F O	First In First Out
F I G	Federation Internationale des Geometres (International Federation of Surveyors)
F I J P A	Federation Internationale des Journalistes Professionnels de l'Aeronautique (International Federation of Writers on Aeronautics)
F I L T E C H	International Filtration and Separation Exhibition and Conference
F I M	Field Ion Microscope
F I N D	File Interrogation of *Nineteen-Hundred* Data
F I P A	Federation Internationale des Producteurs Agricoles (International Federation of Agricultural Producers)
F I P P	Federation Internationale de la Presse Periodique (International Federation of the Periodical Press)
F I R	Flight Information Region
FireRO	Joint Fire Research Organisation
F I R M	Financial Information for Resource Management
F I R S T	Fabrication of Inflatable Re-entry Structures for Test

F I S I T A	Federation Internationale des Societies d'Ingenieurs et de Techniciens de l'Automobile (International Federation of Automobile Engineering Societies)
F I S T	Fault Isolation by Semi-automatic Techniques
F I T	Federation International des Traducteurs (International Federation of Translators)
F I T A P	Federation Internationale des Transports Aeriens Prives (International Federation of Independent Air Transport)
F J C C	Fall Joint Computer Conference (USA)
F L A P	*Flores* Assembly Programme
F L I P	Film Library Instantaneous Presentation
	Flight Launched Infrared Probe
	Floated Instrument Platform
	Floated Lightweight Inertial Platform
	Floating Instrument Platform
F L I R	Forward Look Infrared
F L O O D	Fleet Observation of Oceanographic Data (USN)
F L S C	Flexible Linear-Shaped Charge
F M	Field Manual
	Franklin and Marshall College (USA)
	Frequency Modulation
F M D	Foot and Mouth Disease
F M C E	Federation of Manufacturers of Construction Equipment
F M E A	Failure Mode and Effects Analysis
F M B F	Frequency-Modulation Feedback
F M F M	prefix of numbered series of Fleet Marine Force Manuals issued by US Marine Corps
F M I C	Frequency Monitoring and Interference Control
F M L S	Full-Matrix Least Squares
F N I E	Federation Nationale des Industries Electroniques (France) (Electronic Industries National Federation)
F N W F	Fleet Numerical Weather Facility (USN)
F O A	Forsvarets Forskningsanstalt (Sweden) (National Defence Research Institute)
F O I R	Field of Interest Register
F O P T	Fibre-Optics Photon Transfer
F O R A C S	Fleet Operational Readiness Accuracy Check Site (USN)
F O R A T O M	Forum Atomique Europeen

73

F O R B L O C	FORTRAN - compiled Block - oriented simulation programme
F O R D	Floating Ocean Research Development station
F O R M A C	Formula Manipulation Compiler
F O R M A T	FORTRAN Matrix Abstraction Techniques
F O R T R A N	Formula Translation
F O S	Fuel-Oxygen Scrap
F O S D I C	Film Optical Sensing Device for Input to Computers
F P A	Fire Protection Association
	Formacion Professional Acelerada (Spain) (Centre for the Accelerated Training of Craftsmen)
F P C	Federal Power Commission (USA)
F P H S	Fall-out Protection in Homes
F P L	Forest Products Laboratory (USA)
F P P S	Flight Plan Processing System
F P R C	Flying Personnel Research Committee (of Royal Air Force Institute of Aviation Medicine)
F P R L	Forest Products Research Laboratory (MINTECH)
F P S	Focus Projection and Scanning
F R A M A T O M E	Societe Franco-Americaine de Constructions Atomiques (France)
F R C	File Research Council
	Flight Research Center (of NASA)
	Functional Residue Capacity
F R C T F	Fast Reactor Core Test Facility (USAEC)
F R I	Food Research Institute (of Agricultural Research Council)
F R P	Fibre Reinforced Plastic
F R S	Festiniog Railway Society
	Fire Research Station
F S	Ferrovie dello Stato-Italia (Italian State Railways)
F S C	Federal Supply Classification (USA)
F S H	Follicle Stimulating Hormone
	prefix to numbered series of pamphlets issued by MAFF
F S K	Frequency Shift Keying
F S L	Formal Semantic Language
F S P T	Federation of Societies for Paint Technology
F S R	Feedback Shift Register
F S T C	Foreign Science and Technology Center (US Army)
F S U C	Federal Statistics Users Conference (USA)
F T	Frequency and Time

F T C	Federal Trade Commission (USA)
	Flight Test Centre
F T D	Foreign Technology Division (of USAFSC)
F T E S A	Foundry Trades Equipment and Supplies Association
F T F E T	Four-Terminal Field-Effect Transistor
F T S	Federal Telecommunications System (USA)
F U D R	Failure and Usage Data Report
F V P R A	Fruit and Vegetable Preservation Research Association
F V R D E	Fighting Vehicles Research and Development Establishment (MOD)
F W A	Fluorescent Whitening Agent
F W	Filament Wound
F W H M	Full Width at Half Maximum
F W P C A	Federal Water Pollution Control Administration (USA)

G

G A A A	Groupement Atomique Alsacienne Atlantique (France)
G A C	Geological Association of Canada
G A L C I T	Guggenheim Aeronautical Laboratory of California Institute of Technology (USA)
G A M I S	Graphic Arts Marketing and Information Service (of PIA)
G A M L O G S	Gamma-ray Logs
G A M M	Gesellschaft fur Angewandte Mathematik und Mechanik (Germany) (Association for Applied Mathematics and Mechanics)
G A N	Generalized Activity Network
G A O	General Accounting Office (USA)
	Glavnaya Astronomicheskaya Observatoriya (USSR) (Main Astronomical Observatory)
G A P	General Assembly Programme
G A R P	Global Atmospheric Research Programme
G A S	Group Apprenticeship Scheme
G A S P	General Activity Simulation Programme
G A T	*Georgetown* Automatic Translation
G A T A C	General Assessment Tridimensional Analogue Computer
G A T F	Graphic Arts Technical Foundation (USA)

G A T N I P	Graphic Approach to Numerical Information Processing
G A T T	General Agreement on Tariffs and Trade (of UNO)
G C A	Ground Control Approach
G C F R	Gas Cooled Fast Reactor
G C F R E	Gas Cooled Fast Reactor Experiment
G C H Q	Government Communications Headquarters
G C M S	Gas Chromatography and Mass Spectroscopy
G C R	General Component Reference
G C S	Gate Controlled Switch
G D C	Gesellschaft Deutscher Chemiker (Germany) (Society of German Chemists)
	Generalised Dynamic Charge
G D M B	Gesellschaft Deutscher Metallhutten-und Bergleute (Germany) (German Research Association for Metalworking and Mining)
G D O P	Geometric Dilution of Precision
G E B C O	General Bathymetric Chart of the Oceans
G E B E C O M A	Groupement Belge des Constructeurs de Materiel Aerospatial (Belgium)
G E C O S	General Comprehensive Operating Supervisor
G E E S E	*General Electric* Electronic Systems Evaluator
G E I S H A	Geodetic Inertial Survey and Horizontal Alignment
G E K	Geomagnetic Electrokinetograph
G E M	General Epitaxial Monolith
	Ground Effect Machine
G E M S	*General Electric* Manufacturing Simulator
G E M S I P	*Gemini* Stability Improvement Programme
G E N D A	General Data Analysis and Simulation
G E O N	Gyro Erected Optical Navigation
G E O S	Geodetic Earth Orbiting Satellite
G E P A C	*General Electric* Programmeable Automatic Comparator
G E R E C	Groupement pour l'Etude et la Realisation d'Ensembles Controle-Commande (France)
G E R S I S	*General Electric* Range Safety Instrumentation System
G E R T	Graphical Evaluation and Review Technique
G E R T S	*General Electric* Remote Terminal System
G E T	Ground Elapsed Time
G E T O L	Ground Effect Take-Off and Landing

G F	prefix to numbered series of Governmental Finances issued by Dept of Commerce, USA
G F C M	General Fisheries Council for the Mediterranean
G F F S A	German Federal Flight Security Agency
G F R P	Glass Fibre Reinforced Plastic
G F W	Glass Filament Wound
G G I	Gosudarstvennyy Girdrologicheskiy Institut (USSR) (State Hydrological Institute)
G G U	Gor'kovskiy Gosudarstvennyy Universitet (USSR)
G G T S	Gravity Gradient Test Satellite
G H	Growth Hormone
G H A	Greenwich Hour Angle
G H O S T	Global Horizontal Sounding Technique
G I	Geodesic Isotensoid
	Government Initiated
G I A T	Groupement d'Industries Atomiques (France)
G I F T I	Gor'kovskiy Nauchno Issledovatel'skiy Fiziko-Teknicheskiy Institut (USSR) (Gor'kiy Physical-Technical Scientific Research Institute)
G I I N	Groupe Intersyndical de l'Industrie Nucleaire (France)
G I I V T	Gor'kovskiy Institut Inzhenerov Vodnogo Transporta (USSR) (Gor'kiy Water Transportation Engineers Institute)
G I K I	Gosudarstvennyy Isseldovatel'skiy Keramicheskiy Institut (USSR) (State Ceramics Research Institute)
G I M R A D A	Geodesy Intelligence and Mapping Research and Development Agency (US Army)
G I R L S	Generalised Information Retrieval and Listing System
G I S	Generalized Information System
G K I A E	Gosudarstvennyy Komitet po Ispolzovaniyu Atomnoi Energi (USSR) (State Committee for the Utilization of Atomic Energy)
G L C	Gas-Liquid Chromatography
	Greater London Council
G L E E P	Graphite Low Energy Experimental Pile
G L O M E X	Global Meteorological Experiment
G L O P A C	Gyroscopic Lower Power Attitude Controller
G L O T R A C	Global Tracking network
G L V	*Gemini* Launch Vehicle
G N I	Generation of New Ideas
G N P	Gross National Product

G O C I	General Operator-Computer Interaction
G O E	Ground Operating Equipment
G O I	Gosudarstvennyy Opticheskiy (USSR) (State Optical Institute)
G O I N	Gosudarstvennyy Okeanograficheskiy Institute (USSR) (State Oceanographic Institute)
G O R	Gained Output Ratio
	Gas Oil Ratio
	General Operations Requirement
G O R I D	Ground Optical Recorder for Intercept Determination
G O S S	Ground Operational Support System
G O S T	Gosudarstvennyy Obshchesoguznyy Standart (USSR) (State All-Union Standard)
G P A	Graphical PERT Analogue
G P A T S	General Purpose Automatic Test System
G P C	Groupements de Producteurs de Ciment (Belgium)
G P D S	General Purpose Display System
G P C P	Generalized Process Control Programming
G P I S	*Gemini* Problem Investigation Status
G P O	General Post Office
	Government Printing Office (USA)
G P S	General Problem Solver
G P S S	General Purpose System Simulation
	General Purpose Systems Simulator
G P T	Gas Power Transfer
G R A	Gesellschaft fur Rechnergesteuerte Analagen (Germany)
G R A C E	Graphic Arts Composing Equipment
G R A D	General Recursive Algebra and Differentiation
G R A F	Graphic Addition to FORTRAN
G R A M P A	General Analytical Model for Process Analysis
G R A P E	Gamma-Ray Attenuation Porosity Evaluator
G R A P H D E N	Graphic Data Entry
G R A S P	Generalized Retrieval and Storage Programme
	Graphic Service Programme
G R B	Geophysical Research Board (of National Research Council, USA)
G R E D	Generalized Random Extract Device
G R P	Glass Reinforced Plastic
G R S C S W	Graduate Research Center of the Southwest (USA)
G S	Glaciological Society

G S A	General Services Administration (USA)
	Genetics Society of America (USA)
G S C	Gas-Solid Chromatography
	Genetics Society of Canada (Canada)
G S E	Ground-based Support Equipment
G S N	Groupement des Soufflantes Nucleaires (France)
G S P I	Gosudarstvennyy Soyuznyy Proyektnyy Institut (USSR) (State All-Union Planning Institute)
G S S	Graphic Service System
G T C	Government Training System
G T I S	Gloucestershire Technical Information Service
G T M A	Gauge and Tool Makers Association
	Georgia Textile Manufacturers Association (USA)
G U H A	General Unary Hypotheses Automaton
G U I D E	Guidance for Users of Integrated Data Equipment

H

H A	Hydraulic Association
H A D I S	Huddersfield and District Information Service
H A D S	Hypersonic Air Data Sensor
H A F	High Abrasion Furnace
	High Altitude Fluorescence
H A M	Hardware Associative Memory
H A N E	High Altitude Nuclear Effects
H A O S S	High Altitude Orbital Space Station
H A P D A R	Hard Point Demonstration Array Radar
H A R A C	High Altitude Resonance Absorption Calculation
H A R C O	Hybolic Area Coverage
H A R P	High Altitude Research Project (*or* Probe)
H A R T R A N	*Harwell Atlas* FORTRAN
H A S	Hellenic Astronautical Society (Greece)
H A S L	Health and Safety Laboratory (USAEC)
H A S P	High Altitude Sampling Programme
H A T R A	Hosiery and Allied Trades Research Association
H A T R I C S	Hampshire Technical Research Industrial Commercial Service
H A Y S T A Q	Have You Stored Answers to Questions?
H A Z	Heat Affected Zone
H C E	Hollow-Cathode Effect
H C I T B	Hotel and Catering Industry Training Board

H D D R	High Density Digital Recording
H D L	Harry Diamond Laboratories (US Army)
	High Density Lipoproteins
H D M R	High Density Moderated Reactor
H D S T	High Density Shock Tube
H E A T	High-Explosive Anti-Tank
H E C T O R	Heated Experimental Carbon Thermal Oscillator Reactor
H E D	Horizontal Electric Dipole
H E L E N	Hydrogenous Exponential Liquid Experiment
H E O S	High Excentricity Orbit Satellite
H E P	High-Explosive Penetrating
H E P C	Hydro-Electric Power Commission (Canada)
H E P C A T	Helicopter Pilot Control And Training
H E P L	High Energy Physics Laboratory (Stanford University, USA)
H E R A L D	Highly Enriched Reactor *Aldermaston*
H E R C U L E S	Helicopter Remote Classification and Localization System
H E R F	High Energy Rate Forming
H E R M E S	Heavy Element and Radioactive Material Electromagnetic Separator
H E R O	Hot Experimental Reactor of O (ie ' Zero ') power
H E R T I S	Hertfordshire Technical Information Service
H E T	Heavy Equipment Transporter
H E V A C	Heating, Ventilating and Air Conditioning Manufacturers Association
H E W	Health, Education and Welfare Department (US Education Office)
H F B R	High Flux Beam Reactor
H F I R	High Flux Isotope Reactor
H F G	Heavy Free Gas
H F I M	High Frequency Instruments and Measurements
H F S	Hyper-Fine Structure
H I	Hydraulic Institute (USA)
H I F A R	High Flux Australian Reactor
H I B E X	High-G Boost Experiment
H I L	High-Intensity Lighting
H I P A R	High Power Acquisition Radar
H I V O S	High Vacuum Orbital Simulation
H L G	Ministry of Housing and Local Government
H M N A O	Her Majesty's Nautical Almanac Office
H M P A	Hexamethyl Phosphoramide

H M S O	Her Majesty's Stationery Office
H O D R A L	*Hokushin* Data Reduction Algorithm Language
H O R A C E	H_2O Reactor *Aldermaston* Critical Experiment
H P A	Hospital Physicists Association
H P D	*Hough-Powell* Device
H R	House of Representatives (USA)
H R B	Highways Research Board (USA)
H R C	High Rupturing Capacity
H R I R	High Resolution Infrared Radiometer
H R S	Hydraulics Research Station (MINTECH)
H R U	Hydrological Research Unit
H S D	High Speed Displacement
H S D A	High Speed Data Acquisition
H S G T	High Speed Ground Transport
H S M	High Speed Memory
H S T	Hypersonic Transport
H T G C R	High Temperature Gas Cooled Reactor
H T G R	High Temperature Gas-cooled Reactor
H T M	Hypothesis Testing Model
H T M A E W	Home Timber Merchants Association of England and Wales
H T O	High Temperature Oxidation
H T P	High Test Peroxide
H T S S	*Hamilton* Test Simulation System
H T U	Heat Transfer Unit
H U D	Department of Housing and Urban Development (USA)
	Head-Up Display
H U L T I S	Hull Technical Interloan Scheme
Hum R R O	Human Resources Research Office, George Washington University (USA)
H V A R	High-Velocity Airborne Rocket
H V C A	Heating and Ventilating Contractors Association
H V R A	Heating and Ventilating Research Association
H W C T R	Heavy Water Components Test Reactor
H W O C R	Heavy Water Organic Cooled Reactor
H Y - B A L L	Hydraulic Ball
H Y B L O C	Hybrid computer Block-oriented Compiler
H Y F E S	Hypersonic Flight Environmental Simulator
H Y P S E S	Hydrographic Precision Scanning Echo Sounder
H Y S T A D	Hydrofoil Stabilization Device
H Y T R E S S	High Test Recorder and Simulator System

I

I A A	Instituto Antartico Argentino (Argentina) (Argentine Antarctic Institute)
	International Academy of Astronautics
I A A C	International Agriculture Aviation Centre
I A A L D	International Association of Agriculture Libraries and Documentalists
I A B	Industrial Advisors to the Blind
I A B A	International Association of Aircraft Brokers and Agents
I A B S E	International Association for Bridge and Structural Engineering
I A C	Information Analysis Centre
I A C S	Inertial Attitude Control System
	Integrated Armament Control System
I A D	Integrated Automatic Documentation
I A D B	Inter-American Development Bank
I A D R	International Association for Dental Research
I A E	Integral Absolute Error
I A E A	International Atomic Energy Agency (of UNO)
I A E E	International Association of Earthquake Engineering
I A E S T E	International Association for the Exchange of Students for Technical Experience
I A F	International Astronautical Federation
I A G	International Association of Geodesy
	IFIP Administrative Data Processing Group
I A G A	International Association of Geomagnetism and Aeronomy
I A G C	Instantaneous Automatic Gain Control
I A G S	Inter-American Geodetic Survey (USA)
I A H R	International Association for Hydraulic Research
I A I A S	Inter-American Institute of Agricultural Sciences
I A L A	International Association of Lighthouse Authorities
I A M	Institute of Aviation Medicine
I A M A P	International Association of Meteorology and Atmospheric Physics
I A M C	Institute for Advancement of Medical Communication (USA)
I A M S	International Association of Microbiological Societies

I A M T C T	Institute of Advanced Machine Tool and Control Technology
I A N E C	Inter-American Nuclear Energy Commission (USA)
I A P	Institute of Animal Physiology (of the Agricultural Research Council)
I A P O	International Association of Physical Oceanography
I A R I G A I	International Association of Research Institutes for the Graphic Arts Industry
I A R U	International Amateur Radio Union
I A S	Immediate Access Store
	Institute of Advanced Studies (US Army)
	Institute of Aerospace-Sciences (USA)
	Integrated Analytical System for global range planning
	International Association of Sedimentology
I A S A	International Air Safety Association
I A S C	International Association of Seed Crushers
I A S H	International Association of Scientific Hydrology
I A S I	Inter-American Statistical Institute
I A S L I C	Indian Association of Special Libraries and Information Centres (India)
I A S P E I	International Association of Seismology and Physics of the Earth's Interior
I A T	Institut Avtomatiki Telemekhaniki (USSR) (Automation and Remote Control Institute)
	Institute for Applied Technology (of NBS)
I A T A	International Air Transport Association
I A T U L	International Association of Technical University Libraries
I A U	International Association of Universities
	International Astronomical Union
I A V	International Association of Volcanology
I B A M	Institute of Business Administration and Management (Japan)
I B B D	Instituto Brasileiro de Bibliografia e Documentacao (Brazil) (Brazilian Institute of Bibliography and Documentation)
I B C C	International Building Classification Committee
I B E	Institute Belge de l'Emballage (Belgium) (Belgian Packaging Institute)
I B F	Institute of British Foundrymen

I B G	Internationales Buro fur Gebirgsmechanik (International Bureau for Rock Mechanics)
I B H P	Institute Belge des Hautes Pressions (Belgium) (Belgian Institute for High Pressures)
I B I S	Intense Bunched Ion Source
I B M	Instytut Budownictwa Mieszkaniowego (Poland) (Institute of House Building)
I B N	Institut Belge de Normalisation (Belgium) (Belgian Standards Institute)
I B P	Initial Boiling Point
	International Biological Programme
I B P A	International Business Press Associates
I B R	Integral Boiling Reactor
I B R D	International Bank for Reconstruction and Development (of UNO)
I B S	Institut Belge de la Soudure (Belgium) (Belgian Institute of Welding)
	Institute for Basic Standards (of NBS)
I B S A C	Industrialized Building Systems and Components
I B W M	International Bureau of Weights and Measures
I C	Integrated Circuit
I C A	International Cartographic Association
	International Council on Archives
I C A F	Industrial College of the Armed Forces (USA)
	International Committee on Aeronautic Fatigue
I C A I	International Commission for Agricultural Industries
I C A I T I	Instituto Centroamericano de Investigacion y Technologia Industrial (Central American Research Institute for Industrial Technology)
I C A N	International Committee of Air Navigation
I C A O	International Civil Aviation Organisation (of UNO)
I C A P	International Congress of Applied Psychology
I C A R V S	Interplanetary Craft for Advanced Research in the Vicinity of the Sun
I C B M	Inter-Continental Ballistic Missile
I C B O	International Conference of Building Officials
I C C	International Chamber of Commerce
	Interstate Commerce Commission (USA)
I C C P	International Conference on Cataloguing Principles
I C E	Institution of Civil Engineers
	Integrated Cooling for Electronics

I C E S	Integrated Civil Engineering System
	International Conference of Engineering Societies
	International Council for the Exploration of the Sea
I C E T K	International Committee of Electrochemical Thermodynamics and Kinetics
I C F C	Industrial and Commercial Finance Corporation
I C H C A	International Cargo Handling Co-ordination Association
I chem E	Institution of Chemical Engineers
I C I	Investment Casting Institute (USA)
I C I D	International Commission on Irrigation and Drainage
I C I R E P A T	International Co-operation in Information Retrieval among Examining Patent Offices
I C I T A	International Co-operative Investigations of the Tropical Atlantic (of UNESCO)
I C L A	International Commission on Laboratory Animals
I C M	Improved Capability Missile
I C M M P	International Committee on Military Medicine and Pharmacy
I C N A F	International Commission for the Northwest Atlantic Fisheries
I C N D T	International Conference on Non-Destructive Testing
I C N V	International Committee for the Nomenclature of Viruses
I C O	Inter-agency Committee on Oceanography (*now* Interagency Committee on Marine Research Facilities and Education)
	International Coffee Organisation
	International Commission for Optics
I C O G R A D A	International Council of Graphic Design Associations
I C O L D	International Congress on Large Dams
I C O R	Intergovernmental Conference on Oceanic Research (UNESCO)
I C P P	Idaho Chemical Processing Plant (USAEC)
I C P S	International Conference on the Properties of Steam
	International Congress of Photographic Science
I C R H	Institute for Computer Research in the Humanities (of New York University, USA)

I C R P	International Commission on Radiological Protection
I C R U	International Commission on Radiological Units
I C S	Institute of Computer Science
	International Chamber of Shipping
	International College of Surgeons
I C S C	Interim Communications Satellite Committee (of INTELSAT)
	Inter-ocean Canal Study Commission (USA)
I C S E M S	International Commission for the Scientific Exploration of the Mediterranean Sea
I C S I	International Conference on Scientific Information
I C S U	International Council of Scientific Unions
I C W	Interrupted Continuous Wave
I C W M	International Committee of Weights and Measures
I C Y	International Co-operation Year
I C Z N	International Commission on Zoological Nomenclature
I D	Inside Diameter
	Intermediate Description
I D A	Institute for Defense Analysis (USA)
	Ionospheric Dispersion Analysis
	International Development Association (of UNO)
I D A M I	Istituto Documentazione Associazione Meccanica Italiana (Italy) (Documentation Institute of the Italian Mechanical Association)
I D A S T	Interpolated Data and Speech Transmission
I D B T	Industrial Development Bank of Turkey
I D C	Image Dissector Camera
I D D R G	International Deep-Drawing Research Group
I D E A S	Integrated Design and Engineering Automated System
I D E E A	Information and Data Exchange Experimental Activities (US Army)
I D E P	Interservice Data Exchange Program (USDOD)
I D E X	Initial Defence Experiment
I D F	International Dairy Federation
	International Dental Federation
	International Diabetes Federation
I D I	Improved Data Interchange

86

I D I C T	Instituto de Documentacion e Informacion Cientifica y Tecnica (Cuba) (Scientific and Technical Documentation and Information Institute)
I D O C	Inner Diameter of Outer Conductor
I D T	Isodensitracer
I D T S	Instrumentation Data Transmission System
I D U	Industrial Development Unit
I E A	Instituto de Energia Atomica (Brazil) (Atomic Energy Institute)
I E C	International Electrotechnical Commission
I E C P S	International Electronic Packaging Symposium
I E D	Individual Effective Dose
I E E	Institution of Electrical Engineers
I E E E	Institute of Electrical and Electronic Engineers (USA)
I E E T E	Institution of Electrical and Electronics Technician Engineers
I E G	Information Exchange Group
I E I	Institution of Engineering Inspection
I E I C	Iowa Educational Information Center (University of Iowa, USA)
I E M	Institut Elektromekhaniki (USSR) (Institute of Electromechanics)
I E R	Institutes for Environmental Research (of ESSA)
I E R E	Institution of Electronic and Radio Engineers
I E S	Illuminating Engineering Society
	Institute of Environmental Sciences (USA)
	Institut Elektrosvarki (USSR) (Electric Welding Institute)
	Integral Error Squared
	Intrinsic Electric Strength
I E S C	International Executive Service Corps
I E S S	Institution of Engineers and Shipbuilders in Scotland
I F A	Institut Fiziki Atmosfery (USSR) (Atmospheric Physics Institute)
	Institutt For Atomenergi (Norway) (Atomic Energy Institute)
I F A C	International Federation for Automatic Control
I F A P	International Federation of Agricultural Producers
I F A T C A	International Federation of Air Traffic Controllers Associations
I F B	Invitation For Bid

I F C	International Finance Corporation (of UNO)
	International Formulation Committee (*of* International Conference on the Properties of Steam)
I F C A T I	International Federation of Cotton and Allied Textile Industries
I F C E	Institut Francaise des Combustibles et de l'Energie (France) (French Institute of Fuels and Energy)
I F C S	In-Flight Checkout System
I F E M S	International Federation of Electron Microscopes Societies
I F F	Identification Friend or Foe
I F F J P	International Federation of Fruit Juice Producers
I F G O	International Federation of Gynaecology and Obstetrics
I F H P	International Federation for Housing and Planning
I F I P	International Federation of Information Processing
I Fire E	Institution of Fire Engineers
I F Kh	Institut Fizicheskoy Khimii (USSR) (Physical Chemistry Institute)
I F L A	International Federation of Library Associations
I F M	Institut Fiziki Metallov (USSR) (Physics of Metals Institute)
I F M A	International Federation of Margarine Associations
I F M E	International Federation of Medical Electronics
I F O R S	International Federation of Operational Research Societies
I F P	Institut Francaise du Petrole (France) (French Petroleum Institute)
I F R	Increasing Failure Rate
	Institute of Fisheries Research (University of North Carolina, USA)
	Instrument Flight Rules
I F R B	International Frequency Registration Board (of ITU)
I F R F	International Flame Research Foundation
I F S	International Federation of Surveyors
I F T	Institute of Food Technologists (USA)
I F T C	International Federation of Thermalism and Climatism
	International Film and Television Council
I F V M E	Inspectorate of Fighting Vehicles and Mechanical Equipment (MOD)

I F Z	Institut Fiziki Zemli (USSR) (Institute of Physics of the Earth)
I G	Instructor's Guide
I G C	International Geophysical Committee
I G D	Institut Gornogo Dela (USSR) (Institute of Mining)
I G E	Institution of Gas Engineers
I G F E T	Insulated Gate Field Effect Transistor
I G I	Institut Goryuchikh Iskopayemykh (USSR) (Institute of Mineral Fuels)
I G O R	Intercept Ground Optical Recorder
I G P A I	Inspeccao-Geral dos Produtes Agricolas e Industriais (Portugal) (Inspectorate of Agricultural Products and Manufactured Goods)
I G P P	Institute of Geophysics and Planetary Physics (of SIO)
I G S	Inertial Guidance System
I G U	International Gas Union
	International Geographical Union
I G Y	International Geophysical Year
I H	Industrialized Housing
I H A S	Integrated Helicopter Avionics System
I H B	International Hydrographic Bureau
I H C	Interstate Highway Capability
I H D	International Hydrological Decade
I H E	Institution of Highway Engineers
I H F	International Hospital Federation
I H I	Ishkawajima Harima Heavy Industries (Japan)
I H T U	Interservice Hovercraft Trials Unit (MOD)
I I A S	International Institute of Administrative Services
I I C	International Institute of Communications
I I C A	Instituto Interamericano de Ciencias Agricolas (Costa Rica) (Inter-American Institute of Agricultural Science)
I I L S	International Institute for Labour Studies (of ILO)
I I O E	International Indian Ocean Expedition
I I R	International Institute of Refrigeration
I I R S	Institute for Industrial Research and Standards (Eire)
I I S	Institute of Industrial Supervisors
	Institute of Information Scientists
I I S O	Institution of Industrial Safety Officers
I I T	Illinois Institute of Technology (USA)
I I T R A N	*Illinois Institute of Technology* Translator

I I T R I	Illinois Institute of Technology Research Institute (USA)
I I W	International Institute of Welding
I K	Institut Kristallografii (USSR) (Institute of Crystallography)
I Kh	Institut Khimii (USSR) (Institute of Chemistry)
I K O	Institut voor Kernphysisch Ondersoek (Netherlands) (Institute for Nuclear Physics Research)
I L A	Institute of Landscape Architects
I L A A S	Integrated Light Attack Avionic System
I L A F A	Instituto Latinoamericano del Fierro y el Acero (Latin-American Iron and Steel Institute)
I L A R	Institute of Laboratory Animal Resources (USA)
I L A S	Inter-related Logic Accumulating Scanner
I L C	International Labelling Centre (of the Consumer Council)
I L E C	Institut de Liaisons d'Etudes des Industries de Consommation (France)
I L F	Inductive Loss Factor
I L I R	In-House Laboratories Independent Research
I L M A C	International Congress and Exhibition of Laboratory Measurement and Automation Techniques in Chemistry
I L O	Industrial Liaison Officer
	International Labour Office (of the International Labour Organization)
	International Labour Organization (of UNO)
I L S	Ideal Liquidus Structures
	Instrument Landing System
I L T S	Institute of Low Temperature Science (Japan)
I L U	Illinois University (USA)
I L W	Intermediate-Level Wastes
I M A	Industrial Medical Association (USA)
	International Mineralogical Association
	Irish Medical Association (Eire)
I M A G	Institut de Mathematiques de Grenoble (France) (Grenoble Institute of Mathematics)
I Mar E	Institute of Marine Engineers
I M A S	Industrial Management Assistance Survey
I Mash	Institut Mashinovedeniya (USSR) (Institute of Machine Science)
I M C	Instrument Meteorological Conditions
	Integrated Maintenance Concept

I M C O	Intergovernmental Maritime Consultative Organization (of UNO)
I M E	Institute of Mining Engineers
I M E A	Institut d'etudes Metallurgiques et Electroniques Appliquees (Switzerland) (Institute of Studies in Applied Metallurgy and Electronics)
I Mech E	Institute of Mechanical Engineers
I M E Kh	Institut Mekhaniki (USSR) (Institute of Mechanics)
I M E K O	International Measurement Congress
I M E T	Institut Metallurgii (USSR) (Institute of Metallurgy)
I M F	International Monetary Fund (of UNO)
I M F I	Industrial Mineral Fiber Institute (USA)
I M H	Institute of Materials Handling
I M I	Irish Management Institute (Eire)
I M M	Institute of Mining and Metallurgy
	Integrated Maintenance Management
I M M S	International Material Management Society (USA)
I M O	Industrial Medical Officer
I M P	Interplanetary Monitoring Platform
	Inter-industry Management Programme
I M P A C T	Inventory Management Programme And Control Technique
I M P A T T	Impact Avalanche and Transit Time
I M P I	International Microwave Power Institute
I M P S	Integrated Master Programming and Scheduling System
I M R	Institute for Materials Research (of NBS)
I M S	Institute of Marine Science (USA)
I M U	Inertial Measuring Unit
	International Mathematical Union
I M W	International Map of the World
I N A C	Instituto Nazionale per le Applicazioni del Calco (Italy) (National Institute for Computer Applications)
I N A C H	Instituto Antartico Chileno (Chile) (Antarctic Institute of Chile)
I N A C O L	Institut National pour l'Amelioration des Conserves des Legumes (Belgium) (National Institute for the Improvement of Vegetable Preserves)
I N A N T I C	Instituto Nacional de Normas Tecnicas Industriales y Certificacion (Peru) (Standards Institute)
I N A S	Inertial Navigation and Attack Systems

INAT	Institut National d'Assistance Technique (Belgium) (National Institute of Technical Assistance)
INCAP	Institute of Nutrition of Central America and Panama
INCO	International Chamber of Commerce
INCOR	Indian National Committee on Oceanic Research (India)
	Intergovernmental Conference on Oceanographic Research
	Israeli National Committee for Oceanographic Research (Israel)
INCOSPAR	Indian National Committee for Space Research (India)
INDEX	Inter-NASA Data Exchange
INDITECNOR	Instituto Nacional de Investigaciones Tecnologicas y Normalizacion (Chile) (National Institute for Technical Research and Standardisation)
INEL	International Exhibition of Industrial Electronics
ING	Intense Neutron Generator
INGO	International Non-Governmental Organisation
INI	Instituto Nacional de Industria (Spain) (National Institute of Industry)
INICHAR	Institut National de l'Industrie Charbonniere (Belgium) (National Institute of the Coal Industry)
INIS	International Nuclear Information System (of IAEA)
INKhP	Institut Neftekhimicheskikh Protsessov (USSR) (Institute of Petrochemical Processes)
INORCOL	Instituto de Normas Colombiana (Colombia) (Standards Institute)
INOSHAC	Indian Ocean and Southern Hemisphere Analysis Centre
INP	Inert Nitrogen Protection
INPFC	International North Pacific Fisheries Commission
INSA	Institut National des Sciences Appliquees (France) (National Institute of Applied Sciences)
INSDOC	Indian National Scientific Documentation Centre (India)
INSERM	Institut National de la Sante et de la Recherche Medicale (France) (National Institute of Health and Medical Research)
INSJ	Institute for Nuclear Study, Tokyo University (Japan)

I N S P E C	Information Service in Physics, Electrotechnology and Control (of IEE)
I N S P E X	Engineering Inspection and Quality Control Conference and Exhibition
I N S T A R S	Information Storage And Retrieval Systems
Inst F	Institute of Fuel
I N S T N	Institut National des Sciences et Techniques Nucleaires (France) (National Institute of Nuclear Science and Technology)
I N T	Interior
	prefix to series issued by the Intermountain Forest and Range Station (of the Forest Service, USDA)
I N T A	Instituto Nacional de Tecnica Aerospacial (Spain) (National Institute of Aerospace Technology)
I N T A P U C	International Association of Public Cleansing
I N T E L S A T	International Telecommunications Satellite Consortium
I N T E R G A L V A	International Galvanizing Conference
I N T E R K A M A	International Congress for Measurement and Automation
I N T E R M A G	International Magnetics Conference
I N T E R P L A S	International Plastics Exhibition and Conference
I N T O P	International Operations Simulation
I N T R E X	Information Transfer Experiments
I O C	Indirect Operating Costs
	Intergovernmental Oceanographic Commission (of UNESCO)
I O C U	International Organisation of Consumers Unions
I O F	International Oceanographic Foundation
I O M B	Instytut Organizacji i Mechanizacji Budownictwa (Poland) (Institute for the Organisation and Mechanisation of Building)
I O M T R	International Office for Motor Trades and Repairs
I O N	Ionosphere and Aural Phenomena Advisory Committee (of ESRO)
I O N Kh	Institut Obshchey i Neorganicheskoy Khimii (USSR) (Institute of General and Inorganic Chemistry)
I O O C	International Olive Oil Council
I O P	Instytut Obroki Plastycznej (Poland) (Materials Forming Institute)
I O P M	Instytut Organizacjo Przemysiu Maszcynowego (Poland) (Institute for the Organisation of Mechanical Engineering)

I O S	Instytut Obrobki Skrawanien (Poland) (Metal Cutting Institute)
I O U B C	Institute of Oceanography, University of British Columbia (Canada)
I O V S T	International Organisation for Vacuum Science and Technology
I P	Initial Phase
	Institute of Petroleum
	Institut Poluprovodnikov (USSR) (Institute of Semiconductors)
I P A	Information Processing Association (Israel)
	International Psycho-analytical Association
I P C	Information Processing Code
I P C E A	Insulated Power Cable Engineers Association (USA)
I P F C	Indo-Pacific Fisheries Council (Thailand)
I P F M	Integral Pulse Frequency Modulation
I P H C	International Pacific Halibut Commission (USA)
I P L	Information Processing Language
I P M	Institute of Personnel Management
	Interference Prediction Model
I P O E E	Institution of Post Office Electrical Engineers
I P P F	International Planned Parenthood Federation
I P P J	Institute of Plasma Physics, Japan
I P P S	Institute of Physics and the Physical Society
I P R E I G	Institut Professionnel de Recherches et d'Etudes des Industries Graphiques (France) (Professional Research Institute for the Printing Industry)
I P S F C	International Pacific Salmon Fisheries Commission (Canada)
I P S C	Instytut Przemyslu Skla i Ceramiki (Poland) (Glass and Ceramics Industries Institute)
I P S T	International Practical Scale of Temperature
I Q C	International Quality Centre (of EOQC)
I Q S Y	International Quiet Sun Year
I R	Information Retrieval
	Infrared
	Infrared Radiation
I R & D	Independent Research and Development
I R A B A	Institut de Recherche Appliquee du Beton Arme (France) (Applied Research Institute for Reinforced Concrete)
I R A B O I S	Institut de Recherche Appliquee du Bois (France) (Applied Research Institute for Wood)

I R A D	Institute for Research on Animal Diseases (of the Agricultural Research Council)
I R A M	Institut de Recherche Appliquee du Metal (France) (Applied Research Institute for Metal)
	Instituto Argentino de Racionalizacion de Materiales (Argentina) (Standards Institute)
I R A T E	Interim Remote Air Terminal Equipment
I R A T R A	Instituto Nacional de Racionalizacion del Trabjo (Spain) (Standards Institute)
I R B M	Intermediate Range Ballistic Missile
I R C	Industrial Reorganisation Corporation
I R C H A	Institut National de Recherche Chimique Appliquee (France) (National Institute of Applied Chemistry Research)
I R E	Institute of Radio Engineers (now IEEE) (USA)
	Institut Radiotekhniki i Elektroniki (USSR) (Institute of Radio and Electronic Engineering)
I R F	International Road Federation
I R H D	International Rubber Hardness Degrees
I R H O	Institut de Recherches des Huiles et Oleagineaux (France) (Oil Research Institute)
I R I	Industrial Research Institute (USA)
	Institution of the Rubber Industry
	Instituto per la Ricostruzione Industriale (Italy) (Industrial Reconstruction Institute)
I R I A	Institute Recherche d'Information et d'Automatique (France) (Research Institute of Information and Automatic Processing)
I R I G	Inter-Range Instrumentation Group (USDOD)
I R I S	Infrared Interferometer Spectrometer
	Integrated Reconnaissance Intelligence System
I R L S	Interrogation, Recording of Location Subsystem
I R M	Intermediate Range Monitor
I R M A	Information Revision and Manuscript Assembly
I R O D	Instantaneous Read-Out Detector
I R P A	Institut Radioveshchatel'nogo Priyema i Akustiki (USSR) (Radio Reception and Acoustics Research Institute)
	International Radiation Protection Association
I R R D	International Road Research Documentation (of OECD)
I R S	Internal Revenue Service (USA)
	Isotope Removal System

I R S I A	Institut pour l'encouragement de la Recherche Scientifique dans l'Industrie et l'Agriculture (Belgium) (Institute for the Encouragement of Industrial and Agricultural Scientific Research)
I R T	Institute of Reprographic Technology
I R T E	Institute of Road Transport Engineers
I R U	Inertial Reference Unit
I S	Information Science
	Iowa State University of Science and Technology (USA)
	prefix to Standards issued by Indian Standards Institute
I S A	Instrument Society of America
	International Society of Acupuncture
I S A R	Information Storage and Retrieval
I S B	International Society of Biometeorology
I S B B	International Society of Bioclimatology and Biometeorology
I S C	Instruction Staticizing Control
	International Sericulture Commission
	International Sugar Council
I S C A N	Inertialess Steerable Communication Antenna
I S C C	Inter-Society Color Council (USA)
I Sc T	Institute of Science Technology
I S D	Induction System Deposit
	International Subscriber Dialling
I S E	Institution of Structural Engineers
I S I	Indian Standards Institution (India)
	Institute for Scientific Information (USA)
	International Statistical Institute
	Iron and Steel Institute
	Israel Standards Institute (Israel)
I S I S	International Satellites for Ionospheric Studies
	International Science Information Service (USA)
I S L I C	Israel Society for Special Libraries and Information Centres (Israel)
I S M	Institute of Supervisory Management
I S M A	International Superphosphate Manufacturers Association
I S M C M	Institut Superieur des Materiaux et de la Construction Mecanique (France) (Advanced Institute of Materials and Construction Mechanics)
I S M E S	Instituto Sperimentale Modelli e Structure (Italy) (Models and Structures Experimental Institute)

96

I S N	International Society for Neurochemistry
I S O	International Standardization Organization
I S O C	Individual System/Organisation Cost
I S P	International Society of Photogrammetry
I S P E M A	Industrial Safety (Personal Equipment) Manu-facturers Association
I S P O	International Statistical Programs Office (Dept of Commerce, USA)
I S R	Information Storage and Retrieval
	Intersecting Storage Ring
I S S	Ideal Solidus Structures
I S S A	International Social Security Agency
I S S C	International Ship Structures Congress
I S S C T	International Society of Sugar Cane Technology
I S S S	International Society of Soil Science
I S T	Integrated System Transformer
I S T P M	Institut Scientifique et Technique des Peches Maritimes (France) (Sea Fisheries Scientific and Technical Institute)
I S T S	International Symposium on Space Technology and Science
I S U	International Society of Urology
I S W I M	If you See What I Mean
I T A	Industrial Transport Association
	Institut du Transport Aerien (Institute of Air Transport)
	Institut Teoreticheskoy Astronomii (USSR) (Insti-tute of Theoretical Astronomy)
	International Typographic Association
I T B	Industrial Training Board
	Instytut Techniki Budowlanej (Poland) (Institute of Building Research)
I T B T P	Institut Technique du Batiment et des Travaux Publics (France) (Building and Public Works Technical Institute)
I T C	Instytut Techniki Cieplnej (Poland) (Institute of Heating)
	International Tea Council
	International Tin Council
	Ionic Thermoconductivity
I T C A	Inter-American Technical Council of Archives
I T D	Instytut Technologii Drewna (Poland) (Timber Technology Institute)
I T E	Institute of Traffic Engineers (USA)

I T L	Integrate-Transfer-Launch
	Isotoptekniska Laboratoriet (Sweden) (Isotopes Techniques Laboratory)
I T M	Instituto di Tecnologia Meccanica (Italy) (Institute of Mechanical Technology)
I T R C	International Tin Research Council
I T S	Industrial Training Service
I T S A	Institute for Telecommunication Sciences and Aeronomy (of ESSA) (formerly CRPL of NBS) (USA)
I T T	Instituut voor Tuinbowtechneik (Netherlands) (Institute of Agricultural Engineering)
I T T C	International Towing Tank Conference
I T U	International Telecommunications Union (of UNO)
I U A	International Union of Architects
I U A P P A	International Union of Air Pollution Prevention Associations
I U B	International Union of Biochemistry
I U B S	International Union of Biological Sciences
I U C	International University Contact for Management Education
I U C N	International Union for the Conservation of Nature and Natural Resources
I U Cr	International Union of Crystallography
I U F R O	International Union of Forest Research Organisations
I U G G	International Union of Geodesy and Geophysics
I U G S	International Union of Geological Sciences
I U H P S	International Union for the History and Philosophy of Science
I U L C S	International Union of Leather Chemists Societies
I U M P	International Upper Mantle Project
I U N S	International Union of Nutritional Sciences
I U P A C	International Union of Pure and Applied Chemistry
I U P A P	International Union of Pure and Applied Physics
I U P S	International Union of Physiological Sciences
I U R	International Union of Railways
I U T A M	International Union of Theoretical and Applied Mechanics
I U V S T A	International Union for Vacuum Science Techniques and Applications

98

I U W D S	International Ursigrams and World Days Service (UNESCO)
I V A	Ingeniors Vetenskaps Akademein (Sweden) (Academy of Engineering Societies)
I V D S	Independent Variable Depth Sonar
I V I C	Instituto Venezolano de Investigaciones Cienticas (Venezuela) (Venezuelan Institute of Scientific Research)
I V M U	Inertial Velocity Measurement Unit
I W A H M A	Industrial Warm Air Heater Manufacturers Association
I W C	International Whaling Commission
	International Wheat Council
I W C S	Integrated Wideband Communications System
I W M	Institution of Works Managers
I W S	Industrial Welfare Society
	Institute of Work Study (incorporated into IWSP)
I W S A	International Water Supply Association
I W SC	Institute of Wood Science
I W S P	Institute of Work Study Practitioners

J

J A C C	Joint Automatic Control Conference
J A E C	Japan Atomic Energy Commission (Japan)
J A E R I	Japan Atomic Energy Research Institute (Japan)
J A F C	Japan Atomic Fuel Corporation (Japan)
J A I F	Japan Atomic Industrial Forum (Japan)
J A L	Japan Air Lines (Japan)
J A M T S	Japan Association of Motor Trade and Service (Japan)
J A N A I R	Joint Army Navy Aircraft Instrument Research (USDOD)
J A N S	Joint Army-Navy Specification (USDOD)
J A P CO	Japan Atomic Power Company (Japan)
J A S D F	Japan Air Self-Defence Force (Japan)
J C A E	Joint Committee on Atomic Energy (USA)
J C A M	Joint Commission on Atomic Masses
J C A R	Joint Commission on Applied Radioactivity
J C C	Joint Computer Conference
J C T F I	Joint Committee for Training in the Foundry Industry
J D A	Japan Defence Agency (Japan)
J D S	Job Data Sheet

J E B M	Jet Engine Base Maintenance
J E B M - R R	Jet Engine Base Maintenance Return Rate
J C A E	Joint Economic Committee (of the United States Congress)
J E D E C	Joint Electron Device Engineering Councils (USA)
J E I D A	Japan Electronic Industry Development Association (Japan)
J E I P A C	JICST Electronic Information Processing Automatic Computer
J E N	Junta de Energia Nuclear (Spain) (Nuclear Energy Authority)
J E R C	Joint Electronic Research Committee (of the BPO and industry)
J H U	Johns Hopkins University (USA)
J I C	Joint Industrial Council
J I C S T	Japan Information Centre of Science and Technology (Japan)
J I E	Junior Institution of Engineers
J I L A	Joint Institute for Laboratory Astrophysics (University of Colorado, USA)
J I M A	Japan Industrial Management Association (Japan)
J I O A	Joint Intelligence Objectives Agency
J I S	prefix to Standards issued by JISC
J I S C	Japan Industrial Standards Committee (Japan)
J M A	Japan Meteorological Agency (Japan)
J M E D	Jungle Message Encoder-Decoder
J O I D E S	Joint Oceanographic Institution's Deep Earth Sampling
J O S S	Johnniac Open-Shop System
J O V I A L	Jules' Own Version of an International Algorithmic Language
J P D R	Japan Power Demonstration Reactor
J P L	Jet Propulsion Laboratory (of NASA)
J P P S	Joint Petroleum Products Sub-committee
J P R S	Joint Publications Research Service (USA)
J R A T A	Joint Research And Test Activity
J R I A	Japan Radioisotope Association (Japan)
J S C	Japan Science Council (Japan)
J S E M	Japan Society of Electrical Discharge Machining (Japan)
J S H S	Junior Science and Humanities Symposium
J S M E	Japan Society of Mechanical Engineers (Japan)
J S T U	Joint Services Trials Unit
J T B	Joint Transportation Board (USA)

JTI	Jydsk Teknologisk Institut (Denmark) (Jutland Technological Institute)
JTRU	Joint-services Tropical Research Unit (Australia)
JUDGE	Judged Utility Decision Generator
JUSE	Union of Japanese Scientists and Engineers (Japan)
JZS	Jugoslovenski Zavod za Standardizacija (Yugoslavia) (Standards Institute)

K

KALDAS	*Kidsgrove* ALGOL Digital Analogue Simulation
KAO	Krymskaya Astrofizicheskaya Observatoriya (USSR) (Crimea Astrophysical Observatory)
KDD	Kokusia Denshim Denwa Company (Japan)
KDI	Stichting Kwaliteitsdienst voor de Industrie (Holland) (Society for Industrial Quality Control)
KEMA	Keuring van Electrotechnische Materialen (Netherlands) (Testing Institute for Electrotechnical Materials)
KIFIS	*Kollsman* Integrated Flight Instrumentation System
KIVI	Koninklij Instituut van Ingenieurs (Netherlands) (Royal Institution of Engineers)
KIWA	Keurings Instituut voor Waterleiding-Artikelen (Netherlands) (Institute for Testing Waterworks Equipment)
KLM	Koninklije Luchtvaart Maatschappij (Netherlands)
KNMI	Koninklijk Nederlands Meteorologisch Instituut (Netherlands) (Royal Netherlands Meteorological Institute)
KORSTIC	Korea Scientific and Technological Information Centre (Korea)
KPIC	Key Phrase In Context
KSC	John F Kennedy Space Center (of NASA)
KTH	Kungl Tekniska Hogskolań (Sweden) (Royal Institute of Technology)
KTSA	*Kahn* Test of Symbol Arrangement
KWIC	Keyword In Context
KWIT	Keyword In Title
KWOC	Keyword Out of Context

L

L A	Library Association
	Los Alamos Scientific Laboratory (USA)
L A A V	Light Airborne ASW Vehicle
L A C B W R	La Crosse Boiling Water Reactor
L A C E S	Los Angeles Council of Engineering Societies (USA)
L A D A P T	Lookup Dictionary Adaptor Programme
L A D S I R L A C	Liverpool and District Scientific, Industrial and Research Library Advisory Council
L A E D P	Large Area Electronic Display Panel
L A F B	Lockland Air Force Base (USAF)
L A F T A	Latin American Free Trade Association (Headquarters in Uruguay)
L A H	Logical Analyzer of Hypothesis
L A I	Leaf Area Index
L A M A	Locomotive and Allied Manufacturers Association
L A M C S	Latin American-American Communications Systems
L A N N E T	Large Artificial Nerve Net
L A P E S	Low Altitude Parachute Extraction System
L A R A	Light Armed Reconnaissance Aircraft
L A R S	Laser Angular Rate Sensor
L A S	Large Astronomical Satellite
L A S A	Large Aperture Seismic Array
L A S E R	Light Amplification by Stimulated Emission of Radiation
L A S I L	Land and Sea Interaction Laboratory (USC & GS)
L A S L	Los Alamos Scientific Library (USA)
L A S R M	Low-Altitude Supersonic Research Missile
LA S S O	Laser Search and Secure Observer
L A T A F	Logistics Activation Task Force
L A T C C	London Air Traffic Control Centre (of BOT)
L A T S	Long-Acting Thyroid Stimulator
L A V A	Linear Amplifier for Various Applications
L C	Library of Congress (USA)
L C A O	Linear Combination of Atomic Orbitals
L C D	List of Chosen Descriptors
L C E	Launch Complex Equipment
L C E S	Least Cost Estimating and Scheduling
L C F	Local Cycle Fatigue

L C I E	Laboratoire Central des Industries Electriques (France)
L C N	Load Classification Number
L C R E	Lithium Cooled Reactor Experiment
L C S	*Lincoln* Calibration Sphere
L D	Letter Description
L D A	Lead Development Association
L D C	LASA Data Center
L D E	Laminar Defect Examination
L D F	Light Distillate Feedstock
L D H	Lactic Dehydrogenase
L D R S	LEM Data Reduction System
L D S	Light Distillate Spirit
L D T	Logic Design Translator
L D X	Long Distance Xerography
L E A N S	*Lehigh* Analog Simulator
L E D T	Limited-Entry Decision Table
L E E D	Laser-Energised Explosive Device
	Low Energy Electron Diffraction
L E L	Lower Explosion Limit
L E M	Lunar Excursion Module
L E M A	Lifting Equipment Manufacturers Association
L E N A	Laboratorio Energia Nucleare Applicata (Italy)
L E S	Launch Escape System
	Lincoln Experimental Satellite
	Louisiana Engineering Society (USA)
L E S S	Least Cost Estimating and Scheduling
L E T	Linear Energy Transfer
	Lincoln Experimental Terminal
L F C	Laminar Flow Control
L F T I	Leningradskiy Fiziko-Technicheskiy Institut (USSR) (Leningrad Physical-Technical Institute)
L G	Letter Gestalts
L G C	Laboratory of the Government Chemist (MIN-TECH)
L G M	Laboratorium voor Grondmechanica (Netherlands) (Soil Mechanics Laboratory)
L G O	Lamont Geological Observatory (Columbia University, USA)
L H	Liquid Hydrogen
	Lutenizing Hormone
L H R	Lower Hybrid Resonance
Li	prefix to numbered series issued by the Light Division of NPL

L I A P	Leningradskiy Institut Aviatsionnogo Priborostroyeniya (USSR) (Leningrad Institute of Aviation Instrument Construction)
L I D	Leadless Inverted Device
L I D A R	Laser Intensity Direction And Ranging
	Light Detection And Ranging
L I F O	Last-In, First-Out
L I F T	London (Stratford) International Freight Terminal
L I I V T	Leningradskiy Institut Inzhenerov Vodnogo Transporta (USSR) (Leningrad Institute of Water Transport Engineers)
L I L	Lunar International Laboratory
L I N A C	Linear Accelerator
L I N C	*Lincoln* Laboratory Instrument Computer
L I N C O M P E X	Linked Compressor and Expander
L I N O S C O	Libraries of North Staffordshire in Cooperation
L I R	Line Integral Refractometer
L I R A	Linen Industry Research Association
L I S A	Library Systems Analysis
L I S T	Library and Information Services, Tees-side
L I T	Liquid Injection Technique
L I T R	Low-Intensity Test Reactor
L I T V C	Liquid Injection Thrust Vector Control
L I T E	Legal Information Through Electronics
L L L T V	Low Light Level Television
L L R V	Lunar Landing Research Vehicle
L M C A	Lorry Mounted Crane Association
L L W	Low Level Waste
L M E	London Metal Exchange
L M F	Linear Matched Filter
L M F A	Light Metal Founders Association
L M F B R	Liquid Metal Fast Breeder Reactor
L M S	London Mathematical Society
L M S S	Lunar Mapping and Survey System
L M T	Le Materiel Telephonique (France)
L N B E E	Laboratoire National Belge d'Electrothermie et d'Electrochime (Belgium) (Belgian National Electrothermal and Electrochemical Laboratory)
L N G	Liquefied Natural Gas
L O	Longitudinal Optical
L O B	Line of Balance
L O C	Launch Operations Centre

L O C A T E	Library of Congress Automation Techniques Exchange
L O C I	Logarithmic Computing Instrument
L O C S	Logic and Control Simulator
L O E R Q	Large Orbiting Earth Resources Observatory
L O F	Lowest Operating Frequency
L O F T	Loss of Flow Test
L O G E L	Logic Generating Language
L O G I T	Logical Inference Tester
L O H	Light Observation Helicopter
L O H A P	Light Observation Helicopter Avionics Package
L O L A	Lunar Orbit Landing Approach
L O P A D	Logarithmic Outline Processing system for Analogue Data
L O R	Lunar Orbital Rendezvous
L O R A N	Long Range Navigation
L O R L	Large Orbital Research Laboratory
L O S	Line of Sight
L O S S	Large Object Salvage System
L O X	Liquid Oxygen
L P	Linear Programming
L P A C	Launching Programmes Advisory Committee (of ESRO)
L P D	Language Processing and Debugging
L P G	Liquefied Petroleum Gas
L P G I T C	Liquefied Petroleum Gas Industry Technical Committee
L P R I N T	Lookup Dictionary Print Programme
L P T V	Large Pay-load Test Vehicle
L R A	Lace Research Association
L R B A	Laboratoire de Recherches Balistiques et Aerodynamics (France) (Ballistics and Aerodynamics Research Laboratory)
L R C	Langley Research Center (of NASA)
L R L	Lawrence Radiation Laboratory (University of California, USA)
L R P L	Liquid Rocket Propulsion Laboratory (US Army)
L R S M	Long Range Seismograph Measurements
L R T L	Light Railway Transport League
L R U	Line-Replaceable Unit
L R V	Lunar Roving Vehicle
L S A	Limited Space-Charge Accumulation
L S B R	Large Seed Blanket Reactor
L S C C	Line-Sequential Colour Composite

4*

L S D	Lysergic Acid Diethylamide
L S E C S	Life Support and Environmental Control System
L S F F A R	Low-Spin Folding Fin Aircraft Rocket
L S M R	Landing Ship Medium Rocket
L S R H	Laboratoire Suisse de Recherches Horlogere (Switzerland) (Swiss Laboratory for Horological Research)
L S S M	Local Scientific Survey Module
L S U	Louisiana State University (USA)
L T P	Library Technology Project
L T P D	Lot Tolerance Percentage Defective
L T V	Long Tube Vertical
L U C I D	Language for Utility Checkout and Instrumentation Development
L U F	Lowest Usable Frequency
L U T	Launcher Umbilical Tower
L V D	Low Velocity Detonation
L V D A	Launch Vehicle Data Adapter
L V D C	Launch Vehicle Digital Computer
L V D T	Linear Variable Differential Transformer
L V H V	Low Volume High Velocity
L W B R	Light-Water Breeder Reactor
L W L	Limited War Laboratory
L W R	Light Water Reactor
L Y R I C	Language for Your Remote Instruction by Computer

M

M A	Maritime Administration (Dept of Commerce, USA)
M A A	Mathematical Association of America (USA)
	Motor Agents Association
M A A G	Military Assistance Advisory Group (USDOD)
M A A R C	Magnetic Annular Arc
M A C	Machine Aided Cognition
	Maintenance Allocation Chart
	Maximum Allowable Concentration
	Military Aircraft Command (USAF)
	Mineralogical Association of Canada
	Multiple Access Computer
	Multiple Access Computing
M A C S	Media Account Control System
M A C V	Multi-purpose Airmobile Combat-support Vehicle

M A D	Magnetic Anomaly Detection
	Michigan Algorithm Decoder
	Multi-Aperture Device
M A D A M	Moderately Advanced Data Management
M A D A R	Malfunction Analysis Detection And Recording
	Malfunction and Data Recorder
M A D R E	Magnetic Drum Receiving Equipment
M A D R E C	Malfunction Detection and Recording
M A D S	Machine-Aided Drafting System
	Missile Attitude Determination System
M A E S T R O	Machine Assisted Educational System for Teaching by Remote Operation
M A A F	Ministry of Agriculture, Fisheries and Food
M A G I C	Machine for Automatic Graphics Interface to a Computer
M A G I S	Marine Air-Ground Intelligence System (US Marine Corps)
M A G P I E	Machine Automatically Generating Production Inventory Evaluation
M A I	Moskovskiy Aviatsionny Institut (USSR) (Moscow Aviation Institute)
M A I D	Multiple Aircraft Identification Display
M A I D S	Multipurpose Automatic Inspection and Diagnostic System
M A I G	Matsushita Atomic Industrial Group (Japan)
M A L E	Multi-Aperture Logic Element
M A L T	Mnemonic Assembly Language Translator
M A M B A	*Martin* Armored Main Battle Aircraft
M A M B O	Mediterranean Association for Marine Biology and Oceanology (Malta)
M A M O S	Marine Automatic Meteorological Observing Station
M A N D R O	Mechanically Alterable NDRO
M A N O V A	Multivariate Analysis Of Variance
M A P	Macro Assembly Programme
	Message Acceptable Pulse
M A P I	Machinery and Allied Products Institute (USA)
M A P S	Multivariate Analysis and Prediction of Schedules
M A R	Multifunction Array Radar
M A R A D	Maritime Administration (Dept of Commerce, USA)
M A R C	Machine-Readable Cataloguing
M A R C A S	Manoeuvring Re-entry Control and Ablation Studies

MARCEP	Maintainability and Reliability Cost-Effectiveness Programme
MARCIA	Mathematical Analysis of Requirements for Career Information Appraisal
MARS	*Marconi* Automatic Relay System
	Martin Automatic Reporting System
	Multi-Aperture Reluctance Switch
MART	Mean Active Repair Time
MAS	Military Agency for Standardisation (of NATO)
	Multi-Aspect Signalling
MASER	Microwave Amplification by Stimulated Emission of Radiation
MASIS	Management And Scientific Information System
MASK	Manoeuvring and Seakeeping
MASS	*Michigan* Automatic Scanning System
MASTER	Multiple Access Shared Time Executive Routine
MATA	Michigan Aviation Trades Association (USA)
MATE	Multi-system Automatic Test Equipment
MATI	Moskovskiy Aviatsionnyy Teknologicheskiy Institut (USSR) (Moscow Aviation Technology Institute)
MATICO	Machine Applications to Technical Information Centre Operations
MATCON	Microwave Aerospace Terminal Control
MATS	Military Air Transport Service (now Military Airlift Command) (USAF)
MAW	Medium Anti-tank Assault Weapon
MBA	Marine Biological Association
MBIAC	Missouri Basin Inter-Agency Committee (USA)
MBL	Marine Biological Laboratory
MBLE	Manufacture Belge de Lampes et de Materiel Electronique (Belgium)
MBT	Main Battle Tank
	Metal-Base Transistor
MC	Mathematisch Centrum (Netherlands)
	Molded Components
MCA	Manufacturing Chemists Association (USA)
MCAA	Mechanical Contractors Association of America (USA)
MCC-H	Mission Control Center—Houston (of NASA)
MCD	Months for Cyclical Dominance
MCDP	Micro-programmed Communication Data Processor
MCDS	Management Control Data System

M C G	Man-Computer Graphics
M C I S	Maintenance Control Information System
M C L	Mid-Canada Line
M C P	Master Control Programme
M C R	Military Compact Reactor
M C S	Method of Constant Stimuli
	Multiprogrammed Computer System
M C T	Mechanical Comprehension Test
M D A	Multi-Dimensional Analysis
	Multi Docking Adapter
M D C	Maintenance Data Collection
	Maintenance Dependency Chart
M D C S	Maintenance Data Collection System
M D F	Mild Detonating Fuse
M D H	Malic Dehydrogenase
M D H B	Mersey Docks and Harbour Board
M D I	Miss Distance Indicator
M D L	Mine Defense Laboratory (USDOD)
M D S	Maintenance Data System
	Malfunction Detection System
M D S S	Meteorological Data Sounding System
M D T	Mean Time Down
M D W	Measured Daywork
M E	Mechanical Engineering
M E A R	Maintenance Engineering Analysis Report
M E C C A	Mechanised Catalogue
M E D	Mobile Energy Depot
M E D A C	Medical Equipment Display and Conference
M E D I A	*Magnavox* Electronic Data Image Apparatus
M E D L A R S	Medical Literature Analysis and Retrieval System
M E L	Many-Element Laser
	Marine Engineering Laboratory (USN)
	Materials Evaluation Laboratory (of IMR)
M E L B A	Multipurpose Extended Life Blanket Assembly
M E M	Mars Excursion Module
	Minimum Essential Medium
M E R A	Molecular Electronics for Radar Applications
M E R D L	Medical Equipment Research and Development Laboratory (US Army)
M E R M U T	Mobile Electronic Robot Manipulator and Underwater Television
M E R S	Mobility Environmental Research Study
M E S	Manual Entry Subsystem
	Michigan Engineering Society (USA)

M E S A	Manned Environmental System Assessment
M E S G	Maximum Experimental Safe Gap
M E S H	Medical Subject Headings
M E S S	Monitor Event Simulation System
M E S U C O R A	Measurement, Control Regulation and Automation
M E T	Management Engineering Team
	Modified Expansion Tube
M E T A	Maintenance Engineering Training Agency (US Army)
	Methods of Extracting Text Automatically
M E T A P L A N	Methods of Extracting Text Automatically Programming Language
M E T R I C	Multi-Echelon Technique for Recoverable Item Control
M E V	Millions of Electron Volts
M E X E	Military Engineering Experimental Establishment (MOD)
M F	Medium Frequency
	Microfiche
M F B	Mixed Functional Block
M F D	Magnetofluid Dynamics
M F I	Mobile Fuel Irradiator
M F S	Manned Flying System
M F T R S	Magnetic Flight Test Recording System
M G O	Megagauss Oersted
M G U	Moskoviskiy Gosudarstvennyy Universitet (USSR) (Moscow State University)
M H D	Magnetohydrodynamic
M H E A	Mechanical Handling Engineers Association
M H E D A	Material Handling Equipment Distributors Association (USA)
M H R S T	Medical and Health Related Sciences Thesaurus
M H T	Mild Heat Treatment
M I A	Metal Interface Amplifier
M I A C	Minimum Automatic Computer
M I B	Multilayer Interconnection Board
M I C	Minimum Ignition Current
M I C O M	Missile Command (US Army)
M I C R	Magnetic Ink Character Recognition
M I C R O	International Symposium on Microscopy
	Multiple Indexing and Console Retrieval Options
M I C S	Management Information and Control System
	Mineral Insulated Copper Sheathed

M I D A S	Measurement Information Data Analytic System
	Missile Intercept Data Acquisition System
	Modified Integration Digital Analogue Simulator
	Modulator Isolation Diagnostic Analysis System
M I D O R	Miss Distance Optical Recorder
M I D O T	Multiple Interference Determination of Trajectory
M I F I	Moskovskiy Inzhenerno Fizicheskiy Institut (USSR) (Moscow Engineering Physics Institute)
M I G	Metal Inert Gas
M I L	followed by a single capital letter and numbers— Military Specification (USDOD)
M I L - E - C O N	Military Electronics Conference (USA)
M I L - H D B K	Military Handbook (numbered series issued by USDOD)
M I L - S T D	Military Standard (numbered series issued by (USDOD)
M I L A	Merritt Island Launch Area (of NASA)
M I L S	Missile Location System
M I L S T R I P	Military Standard Requisitioning and Issue Procedure (US Army)
M I M	Metal - Insulator - Metal
	Modified Index Method
M I M S	Multi-Item Multi-Source
M I N D A C	Marine Inertial Navigation Data Assimilation Computer
M I N D D	Minimum Due Date
M I N E A C	Miniature Electronic Auto-Collimator
M I N P R T	Miniature Processing Time
M I N S	Miniature Inertial Navigation System
M I N S D	Minimum Planned Start Date
M I N S O P	Minimum Slack time per Operation
M I N T	Materials Identification and New Item Control Technique
M I N T E C H	Ministry of Technology
M I P I R	Missile Precision Instrumentation Radar
M I R A	Motor Industry Research Association
M I R A C O D E	Microfilm Retrieval Access Code
M I R A G E	Microelectronic Indicator for Radar Ground Equipment
M I R D	Medical Internal Radiation Dose
M I R F	Multiple Instantaneous Response File
M I R O S	Modulation Inducing Retrodirective Optical System

M I R R	Material Inspection and Receiving Report
M I R T	Molecular Infrared Track
M I R V	Multiple Independent Re-entry Vehicle
M I S	Management Information System
	Metal-Insulator-Semiconductor
M I S D A S	Mechanical Impact System Design for Advanced Spacecraft
M I S F E T	Metal Insulator Semiconductor Field Effect Transistor
M I S L I C	Mid-Staffordshire Libraries In Co-operation
M I S S	Mechanical Interruption Statistical Summary (series issued by FAA)
	Multi-item, Single-source
M I S S I L	Management Information System Symbolic Interpretive Language
M I S T R A M	Missile Trajectory Measurement
M I T	Massachusetts Institute of Technology (USA)
M I T E	Missile Integration Terminal Equipment
M I T I	Ministry of International Trade and Industry (Japan)
M I T R	*Massachusetts Institute of Technology* Reactor
M K S	Metre Kilogramme Second
M K S A	Metre Kilogramme Second Ampere
M L	Methods of Limits
M L D	Minimum Lethal Dose
M L E	Maximum Likelihood Estimate
M L R G	Marine Life Research Group (of SIO)
M L S	Machine Literature Searching
M L T	Mean Logistical Time
M M	Maintenance Manual
	Materials Measurement
M M C	Maximum Metal Condition
M M F P I T B	Man-Made Fibres Industry Training Board
M M L	Material Mechanics Laboratory
M M P	Multiplex Message Processor
M M P T	Man-Machine Partnership Translation
M M R B M	Mobile Medium Range Ballistic Missile
M M S E	Minimum-Mean-Squared Error
M M U	Modular Manoeuvring Unit
M N D X	Mobile-Non-Director Exchange
M N S	Metal Nitride Semiconductor
M O A	Ministry of Aviation (disbanded 1967)
M O B I D I C	Mobile Digital Computer
M O B U L A	Model Building Language

M O C	Memory Operating Characteristic
M O D	Ministry of Defence
M O D A	Motion Detector and Alarm
M O D E M S	Modulators-Demodulators
M O D I	Modified Distribution method
M O D I C O N	Modulator Dispersed Control
M O E R O	Medium Orbiting Earth Resources Observatory
M O F	Maximum Operating Frequency
M O G A	Microwave and Optical Generation and Amplification
M O L	Manned Orbiting Laboratory
M O L A B	Mobile Lunar Laboratory
M O L D S	Multiple On-line De-bugging System
M O O S E	Manned Orbital Operations Safety Equipment
M O P	Multiple On-line Programming
M O P A	Master Oscillator Power Amplifier
M O P B W	*see* MPBW
M O P T S	Mobile Photographic Tracking Station
M O R L	Manned Orbital Research Laboratory
M O R S	Military Operations Research Symposium
M O S A I C	Metal Oxide Semiconductor Advanced Integrated Circuit
M O S F E T	Metallic Oxide Semiconductor Field Effect Transistor
M O S M	Metal-Oxide—Semi-Metal
M O S T	Management Operation System Technique
	Metal Oxide Semiconductor Transistor
M O T N E	Meteorological Operational Telecommunications Network of Europe
M O T U	Mobile Optical Tracking Unit
M O V E C A P	Movement Capability
M P	Main Phase
	Minimum Phase
	Miscellaneous Paper
	Miscellaneous Publication
M P B E	Molten Plutonium Burnup Experiment
M P B W	Ministry of Public Building and Works
M P D	Magneto-plasmadynamic
M P E P	Manual of Patent Examining Procedure
M P G	Max-Planck-Gesellschaft zur Foederung der Wissenschaften (Germany) (Max Planck Society for the Promotion of Science)
	Miniature Precision Gyrocompass
M P L	Maximum Permissible Level

M P R E	Medium Power Reactor Experiment
M P T A	Municipal Passenger Transport Association
M P W	Modified Plane Wave
M R	Memorandum Report
	Miscellaneous Report
	Monthly Report
	Moisture Resistant
M R . A T O M I C	Multiple Rapid Automatic Test of Monolithic Integrated Circuits
M R A D	Mass Random Access Disc
M R B	Magnetic Recording Borescope
M R B M	Medium Range Ballistic Missile
M R C	Mathematics Research Centre
	Medical Research Council
M R E	Microbiological Research Establishment (MOD)
	Mining Research Establishment
M R I	Meat Research Institute (of the Agricultural Research Council)
	Medical Research Institute (USN)
M R I R	Medium Resolution Infrared Radiometer
M R L	Medical Research Laboratory
M R M	Metabolic Rate Monitor
M R N	Meteorological Rocket Network
M R R	Mechanical Reliability Report (series issued by FAA)
M R T	Modified Rhyme Test
M S	Material Specification
	Machine Selection
	Mass Spectrometry
	Metallurgical Society (USA)
	prefix to Military Standard (numbered series issued by USDOD)
M S & T	Methodical Structures and Textures
M S A	Mechanical Signature Analysis
	Mycological Society of America (USA)
M S C	Manned Spacecraft Center (of NASA)
M S C E	Main Storage Control Element
M S D F	Maritime Self-Defence Force
M S D T	Maintenance Strategy Diagramming Technique
M S F C	Marshall Space Flight Center (NASA)
M S F N	Manned Space Flight Network (of NASA)
M S H	Melanocyte Stimulating Hormone
M S R	Missile Site Radar
M S R E	Molten Salt Reactor Experiment

M S S	Military Supply Standard (USDOD)
M S S R	Mars Soil Sample Return
M S T S	Military Sea Transportation Service (USN)
	Multisubscriber Time Sharing Systems
M T	Machine Translation
M T B F	Mean Time Between Failure
M T B M	Mean Time Between Maintenance
M T C	Maintenance Time Constraint
M T D	Minimal Toxic Dose
M T D R	Machine Tool Design and Research
M T D S	Marine Tactical Data System (US Marine Corps)
M T E	Materiel de Traction Electrique (France)
M T F	Mississippi Test Facility (of NASA)
	Modulation Transfer Function
M T I	Moving Target Indicator
M T I R A	Machine Tool Industry Research Association
M T M	Methods-Time Measurement
M T M T S	Military Traffic Management and Terminal Service (USDOD)
M T O P	Molecular Total Overlap Population
M T O S	Metal Thick Oxide Silicon
M T P	Mechanical Thermal Pulse
M T R	Materials Testing Reactor
	Materials Testing Report
M T S	Maintenance Test Station
	Missile Tracking System
M T S E	Magnetic Trap Stability Experiment
M T S T	Magnetic Tape Selective Typewriter
M T T A	Machine Tool Trades Association
M T T F	Mean Time to Failure
M T T R	Maximum Time To Repair
	Mean Time To Restore
M T V	Marginal Terrain Vehicle
M U F	Maximum Usable Frequency
M U L T I C S	Multiplexed Information and Computing Service
M U M M S	Marine Corps Unified Material Management System (US Marine Corps)
M U R A	Midwestern University Research Association (USA)
M U S T	Medical Unit Self-contained Transportable
M V C	Multiple Variate Counter
M V P	Manpower Validation Programme
M W D D E A	Mutual Weapons Development Data Exchange Programme

M W D P	Mutual Weapons Development Programme
M W (E)	Megawatts (Electrical)
M W (H)	Megawatts (Heat)
M W O	Medicine White Oil

N

N A A	National Association of Accountants (USA)
N A A S	National Agriculture Advisory Service
N A A T S	National Association of Air Traffic Specialists (USA)
N A B	National Association of Broadcasters (USA)
N A B E	National Association for Business Education (now amalgamated with BACIE)
N A C	National Airways Corporation (New Zealand)
N A C A	National Advisory Committee for Aeronautics (now NASA)
	National Agricultural Chemicals Association (USA)
N A C A T S	*North American* Clear Air Turbulence Tracking System
N A C E	National Association of Corrosion Engineers (USA)
N A C E I C	National Advisory Council on Education for Industry and Commerce
N A D	No-Acid Descaling
N A D C	Naval Air Development Center (USN)
N A D G E	NATO Air Defence Ground Environment network
N A D W A R N	Natural Disaster Warning system (USA)
N A E	National Academy of Engineering (USA)
	National Aeronautical Establishment (of National Research Council, Canada)
N A E C	National Aerospace Education Council (USA)
	Naval Air Engineering Center (USN)
N A E C O N	National Aerospace Electronics Conference (USA)
N A E S	Naval Air Experimental Station (USN)
N A E T	National Association of Educational Technicians
N A F E C	National Aviation Facilities Experimental Center (USA)
N A F I	Naval Avionics Facility, Indianapolis (USN)
N A F I N	Nacional Financiera (Mexico)
N A I G	Nippon Atomic Industry Group (Japan)
N A I P R C	Netherlands Automatic Information Processing Research Centre

N A L	National Aeronautical Laboratory (India)
	National Agricultural Library (USA)
N A L C	National Association of Litho Clubs (USA)
N A L M	National Association of Lift Makers
N A M	National Association of Manufacturers (USA)
N A M C	Naval Air Material Center (USN)
	Nihon Aeroplane Manufacturing Company (Japan)
N A M E S	NAVDAC Assembly, Monitor, Executive System
N A M F I	NATO Missile Firing Installation
N A M I	Naval Aerospace Medical Institute (USN)
N A M R A D	Non-Atomic Military Research and Development
N A M R U	Naval Medical Research Unit (USN)
N A M S A	NATO Maintenance and Supply Agency
N A M T C	Naval Air Missile Test Center (USN)
N A N T I S	Nottingham And Nottinghamshire Technical Information Service
N A O	Her Majesty's Nautical Almanac Office
N A P A	National Association of Purchasing Agents (USA)
N A P L	National Association of Photo-Lithographers (USA)
N A P S S	Numerical Analysis Problem Solving System
N A R	Net Assimilation Rate
N A R D I S	Navy Automated Research and Development Information System (USN)
N A R F	Nuclear Aerospace Research Facility
N A R M	National Association of Relay Manufacturers (USA)
N A S	National Academy of Sciences (USA)
N A S / N R C	National Academy of Sciences/National Research Council (USA)
N A S A	National Aeronautics and Space Administration (USA)
N A S A R R	*North American* Search And Range Radar
N A S C A S	NAS/NRC Committee on Atmospheric Sciences (USA)
N A S C O	National Academy of Sciences' Committee on Oceanography (USA)
N A S C O M	NASA Communications
N A S L	Naval Applied Sciences Laboratory (USN)
N A S W	National Association of Science Writers (USA)
N A T	Normal Allowed Time
N A T A	National Association of Testing Authorities (Australia)

N A T C	Naval Air Test Center (USN)
N A T C S	National Air Traffic Control Service (of BOT)
N A T O	North Atlantic Treaty Organisation
N A T T S	Naval Air Test Turbine Station (USN)
N A T U	Naval Aircraft Torpedo Unit (USN)
N A V A I R	prefix to numbered series issued by Naval Air Systems Command (USN)
NAVAIRDEVCEN	Naval Air Development Center (USN)
N A V A P I	*North American* Voltage and Phase Indicator
Nav B I T	Naval Basic Instrument Trainer (USN)
N A V C O S S A C T	Naval Command Systems Support Activity (USN)
N A V D A C	Navigation Data Assimilation Computer
N A V D O C K S	prefix to numbered series issued by Navy Yards and Docks Bureau (USN)
N A V E L E X	Naval Electronics System Command (USN)
N A V M A T	prefix to numbered series issued by Office of Naval Material (USN)
N A V M C	prefix to numbered series issued by the Marine Corps (US Marine Corps)
N A V M E D	prefix to numbered series issued by Naval Aerospace Medical Institute (USN)
N A V S A T	Navy Navigation Satellite
N A V W E P S	prefix to numbered series issued by Bureau of Naval Weapons (USN)
N A V O C E A N O	Naval Oceanographic Office (USN)
N A V O R D	prefix to numbered series issued by NOSC (USN)
N A V P E R S	prefix to numbered series issued by Bureau of Naval Personnel (USN)
N A V S O	prefix to numbered series issued by Navy Industrial Relations Office (USN)
NAVTRADEVCEN	prefix to numbered series issued by Naval Training Device Center (USN)
N B A	National Brassfoundry Association
	National Building Agency
N B A A	National Business Aircraft Association (USA)
N B C	Norwegian Bulk Carrier
N B E R	National Bureau of Economic Research
N B L	Naval Biological Laboratory (USN)
N B N	prefix to Standards issued by IBN
N B O	National Buildings Organization (India)
N B R I	National Building Research Institute (South Africa)

N B S	National Bureau of Standards (of the Dept of Commerce (USA))
N B S R	*National Bureau of Standards* Reactor
N B T	Null-Balance Transmissometer
N B T L	Naval Boiler and Turbine Laboratory (USN)
N C	Numerical Control
N C A R	National Center for Atmospheric Research (USA)
N C B	National Coal Board
N C C	National Computing Centre
N C C A T	National Committee for Clear Air Turbulence (US Dept of Commerce)
N C C C C	Naval Command, Control and Communications Center (USN)
N C E L	Naval Civil Engineering Laboratory (USN)
N C E T	National Council for Educational Technology
N C F	National Clayware Federation
N C F M F	National Committee for Fluid Mechanics Films (USA)
N chem L	National Chemical Laboratory (MINTECH)
N C G G	National Committee for Geodesy and Geophysics (Pakistan)
N C H P R	National Cooperative Highways Research Program (of AASHO)
N C H S	National Center for Health Statistics (USPHS)
N C H V R F E	National College for Heating, Ventilating, Refrigeration and Fan Engineering
N C I C	National Crime Information Center (USA)
N C I P	Comision Nacional de Productividad Industrial (Spain) (National Commission for Industrial Productivity)
N C L	National Central Library
	National Chemical Laboratory (Amalgamated with NPL 1965)
N C M A	National Contract Management Association (USA)
N C O R	National Committee for Oceanographic Research (Pakistan)
N C P E A	National Conference for Professors of Educational Administration (USA)
N C P T W A	National Clearinghouse for Periodical Title Word Abbreviations (of USASI)
N C Q R	National Council for Quality and Reliability
N C R	No Carbon Required
N C R E	Naval Construction Research Establishment

N C R P	National Committee on Radiation Protection (USA)
N C S	National Communications System
N C S E	North Carolina Society of Engineers (USA)
N C S L	National Conference on Standards Laboratories (USA)
N C S O R G	Naval Control of Shipping Organization (USA)
N C S S	National Council of Social Service
N C S U	North Carolina State University (USA)
N C T A	National Community Television Association (USA)
N D I	Numerical Designation Index
N D L	Nuclear Defense Laboratory (US Army)
N D R O	Non-Destructive Read-Out
N D T	Nil-Ductility Transition
	Non-Destructive Testing
N D T A	National Defense Transportation Association (USA)
N D T C	Non-Destructive Testing Centre (at AERE, Harwell)
N E A	National Education Association
N E A C P	National Emergency Airborne Command Post (USDOD)
N E A F C	North East Atlantic Fisheries Commission
N E B S S	National Examinations Board in Supervisory Studies
N E C	National Electrical Code (USA)
	National Electronics Council
N E C I E S	North East Coast Institution of Engineers and Shipbuilders
N E C P A	National Emergency Command Post Afloat (USDOD)
N E C T A	National Electrical Contractors Trade Association
N E D C	National Economic Development Council
	North East Development Council
N E D O	National Economic Development Office
N E E P	Nuclear Electronic Effect Programme
N E F A	Nonesterified Fatty Acids
N E L	National Engineering Laboratory (MINTECH)
	Navy Electronics Laboratory (USN) (reorganised as Navy Undersea Warfare Center *and* Navy Command, Control and Communications Center)

N E L M A	Northeastern Lumber Manufacturers Association (USA)
N E M A	National Electrical Manufacturers Association
N E M I	National Elevator Manufacturing Industry (USA)
N E M O	Naval Edreobenthic Manned Observatory (USN)
N E N	prefix to Standards issued by NNI
N E P T U N E	*North-Eastern* Electronic Peak Tracing Unit and Numerical Evaluator
N E R C	National Electronic Research Council (now National Electronics Council)
	Natural Environment Research Council
N E R E M	Northeast Electronics Research and Engineering Meeting (USA)
N E R O	Na Experimental Reactor of O (' Na ' is chemical symbol for Sodium; ' O ' is Zero)
N E R V A	Nuclear Engine for Rocket Vehicle Application
N E S C	National Environmental Satellite Center (of ESSA)
N E S T	Naval Experimental Satellite Terminal
N E S T O R	Neutron Source Thermal Reactor
N E T F S	National Educational Television Film Service (USA)
N E V A C	Nederlandse Vacuumverenigung (Netherlands) (Netherlands Vacuum Engineering Society)
N E W R A D S	Nuclear Explosion Warning and Radiological Data System
N F	prefix to Standards issued by AFNOR
N F C I T	National Federation of Cold Storage and Ice Trades
N F E A	National Federated Electrical Association
N F E R	National Foundation for Educational Research in England and Wales
N F E T M	National Federation of Engineers' Tools Manufacturers
N F I K	Norsk Forening for Industriell Kvalitetskontroll (Norway) (Norwegian Institute for Quality Control)
N F O	National Freight Organisation
N F P A	National Fire Protection Association (USA)
	National Fluid Power Association (USA)
	National Forest Products Association (formerly NLMA) (USA)
N F S A I S	National Federation of Science Abstracting and Indexing Services (USA)

N F S W M M	National Federation of Scale and Weighing Machine Manufacturers
N G	Nitroglycerine
N G A A	Natural Gasoline Association of America (USA)
N G C	New Galactic Catalogue
N G M	Neutron-Gamma Monte Carlo
N G R S	Narrow Gauge Railway Society
N G T E	National Gas Turbine Establishment (MINTECH)
N G U	Norges Geologiske Underskelse (Norway) (Norwegian Geological Surveying Department)
N H B R C	National House Builders Registration Council
N H K	Nippon Hoso Kyokai (Japan Broadcasting Corporation)
N H L A	National Hardwood Lumber Association (USA)
N H P M A	Northern Hardwood and Pinewood Manufacturers Association (USA)
N I A E	National Institute of Agricultural Engineering
N I A T	Nauchno Issledovatel'skiy Institut Aviatsionnoy Tekhniki (USSR) (Scientific Research Institute of Aviation Technology)
N I C	National Inspection Council
	Negative Impedance Converter
	Nineteen-hundred Indexing and Cataloguing
N I C A P	National Investigations Committee on Aerial Phenomena (USA)
N I C B	National Industrial Conference Board (USA)
N I C E	National Institute of Ceramic Engineers (USA)
N I C E I C	National Inspection Council for Electrical Installation Contracting
N I C O L	*Nineteen hundred* Commercial Language
N I D C	Northern Ireland Development Council
N I D E R	Nederlands Institut voor Documentatie en Registratuur (Netherlands) (Netherlands Institute for Documentation and Filing)
N I D O C	National Information and Documentation Centre (United Arab Republic)
N I E R	National Industrial Equipment Reserve
N I E S R	National Institute for Economic and Social Research
N I F E S	National Industrial Fuel Efficiency Service
N I F T E	Neon Indicating Functional Test Equipment
N I G P	National Institute of Governmental Purchasing (USA)
N I H	National Institutes of Health (USA)

N I I E P	Nauchno Issledovatel'skiy Institut Elektrotekhnicheskoy Promyshlennosti (USSR) (Scientific Research Institute for the Electrical Engineering Industry)
N I I G S M	Nauchno Issledovatel'skiy Institut Goryuchikhi Smazovyka (USSR) (Fuels and Lubricants Scientific Research Institute)
N I I K P	Nauchno Issledovatel'skiy Institut Kabel'noy Promyshlennosti (USSR) (Cable Industry Scientific Research Institute)
N I I L K	Nauchno Issledovatel'skiy Institut Lakorasochnoy Promyshlennosti (USSR) (Paint Industry Scientific Research Institute)
N I I P	National Institute of Industrial Psychology
N I I P M	Nauchno Issledovatel'skiy Institut Plasticheskikh Mass (USSR) (Plastics Scientific Research Institute)
N I I R P	Nauchno Issledovatel'skiy Institut Rezinovoy Promyshlennosti (USSR) (Rubber Industry Scientific Research Institute)
N I I T Avtoprom	Nauchno Issledovatel'skiy Institut Teknologii Avtomobil'noy promyshlennosti (USSR) (Automobile Industry Technological Scientific Research Institute)
N I I T M A Sh	Nauchno Issledovatel'skiy Institut Teknologii Mashinostroyeniya (USSR) (Machine-Building Technological Research Institute)
N I N A	*National Institute* Northern Accelerator
N I N D B	National Institute of Neurological Diseases and Blindness (of NIH, USA)
N I O	National Institute of Oceanography
N I P P M	Nauchno Issledovatel'skiy Institut Polimerizatsionnykh Plasticheskikh Mass (USSR) (Polymerization Plastics Scientific Research Institute)
N I R F I	Nauchno Issledovatel'skiy Radiofizicheskiy Institut (USSR) (Radiophysics Scientific Research Institute)
N I R N S	National Institute for Research in Nuclear Science
N I S C	National Industrial Space Committee
N J A C	National Joint Advisory Council
N L A B S	Natick Laboratories (US Army)
N L G I	National Lubricating Grease Institute (USA)
N L I	Non-Linear Interpolating

N L L	National Lending Library for Science and Technology
N L M	National Library of Medicine (USA)
N L M A	National Lumber Manufacturers Association (now NFPA) (USA)
N L O	Nonlinear Optics
N L O G F	National Lubricating Oil and Grease Federation
N L R	Nationaal Lucht en Ruimtevaartlaboratorium (Netherlands) (National Aeronautics and Astronautics Laboratory)
N L R B	National Labor Relations Board (USA)
N M A	National Microfilm Association (USA)
N M C	National Marketing Council
	National Meteorological Center (USA)
	Naval Material Command (USN)
	Naval Missile Center (USN)
N M C C	National Military Command Center (USDOD)
N M C S	National Military Command System (USDOD)
	Nuclear Materials Control System
N M E R I	National Mechanical Engineering Research Institute (South Africa)
N M F C	National Motor Freight Classification
N M F R L	Naval Medical Field Research Laboratory (USN)
N M R	Nuclear Magnetic Resonance
N M R I	Naval Medical Research Institute (USN)
N M S	Norsk Metallurgisk Selskap (Norway) (Norwegian Metallurgical Society)
N M T B A	National Machine Tool Builders Association (USA)
N N I	Nederlands Normalisatie Institut (Netherlands) (Netherlands Standards Institute)
N O A	National Oceanographic Association (USA)
N O C	Notation Of Content
N O D A C	Naval Ordnance Data Automation Center (USA)
N O D C	National Oceanographic Data Center (USA)
N O F I	National Oil Fuel Institute (USA)
N O H C	National Open Hearth Committee (USA)
N O L	Naval Ordnance Laboratory (USN) (now merged into Naval Weapons Laboratory)
N O M	Norme Italiani per il controllo degli Olii Minerali e derivati (Italy) (Italian Standard for Mineral Oils and Derivatives)
N O M A	National Office Management Association (USA) (now Administrative Management Society)

N O M A D	Naval Oceanographic Meteorological Automatic Device
N O M S S	National Operational Meteorological Satellite System
N O O	Naval Oceanographic Office (USN)
N O R A D	North American Air Defense Command
N O R C	National Opinion Research Center (University of Chicago, USA)
	Naval Ordnance Research Computer
N O R M	Not Operationally Ready Maintenance
N O R S	Not Operationally Ready Supply
N O R V E N	Comision Venezolana de Normas Industriales (Venezuela) (Standards Institute)
N O S	Naval Ordnance Station (USN)
N O S A	National Occupational Safety Association (South Africa)
N O S C	Naval Ordnance Systems Command (USN)
N O T S	Naval Ordnance Test Station (USN) (now merged into Naval Weapons Laboratory)
N P	Naval Publication (numbered series issued by MOD (Navy Dept))
N P A	National Petroleum Association (USA)
	National Planning Association (USA)
	Numerical Production Analysis
N P A C I	National Production Advisory Council on Industry
N P C	National Ports Council
N P D	National Power Demonstration
N P F O	Nuclear Power Field Office (US Army)
N P G	Naval Proving Ground (USN)
N P L	National Physical Laboratory (MINTECH)
N P P S O	Navy Publications and Printing Services Office (USN)
N P R	Noise Power Ratio
N P R A	Naval Personnel Research Activity (USN)
N P R C G	Nuclear Public Relations Contact Group
N P S H	Net Positive Suction Head
N P T	Network Planning Technique
N R A B	National Railroad Adjustment Board (USA)
N R A C	Naval Research Advisory Council (USA)
N R A O	National Radio Astronomy Observatory (USA)
N R B	National Roads Board (New Zealand)
N R C	National Research Council (Canada *and* USA)
N R Cd	National Reprographic Centre for documentation

N R C M A	National Ready Mixed Concrete Association
N R C S T	National Referral Center for Science and Technology (USA)
N R D C	National Research Development Council
N R D L	Naval Radiological Defense Laboratory (USN)
N R D S	Nuclear Rocket Development Station (of NASA)
N R E	Naval Research Establishment (of Defence Research Board, Canada) (now Defence Research Establishment Atlantic)
N R E C	National Resource Evaluation Centre (USA)
N R L	National Reference Library for Science and Invention
	Naval Research Laboratory (USN)
N R L M	National Research Laboratory of Metrology (Japan)
N R M	Natural Remanent Magnetization
N R P R A	Natural Rubber Producers Research Association
N R T S	National Reactor Testing Station (USA)
N R U	National Research Universal
N R X	National Research X-perimental
N R Z	Non-Return to Zero
N S	Nederlandsche Spoorwegen (Netherlands) (Netherlands Railways)
N S A	National Security Agency (USDOD)
N S A M	Naval School of Aviation Medicine (USN)
N S B	National Science Board (USA)
	Norges Statsbauer (Norway) (Norwegian State Railways)
N S C	National Safety Council (USA)
	National Steel Corporation
	Nutrition Society of Canada (Canada)
N S C A	National Safety Council of Australia
N S F	National Science Foundation (USA)
	Norges Standardiserings-Forbund (Norway) (Standards Institute)
N S F S	Net Section Fracture Strength
N S H E B	North of Scotland Hydro-Electric Board
N S I A	National Security Industrial Association (USA)
N S M C	Naval Submarine Medical Center (USN)
N S O D C C	North Sumatra Oil Development Corporation Company (Japan)
N S O E A	National Stationery and Office Equipment Association (USA)
N S P E	National Society of Professional Engineers (USA)

N S P I	National Society for Programmed Instruction (USA)
N S P P	Nuclear Safety Pilot Plant (ORNL)
N S R D S	National Standard Reference Data System (of OSRD)
N S S	National Sample Survey
N S S C	Naval Ships System Command (USN)
N S T I C	Naval Scientific and Technical Information Centre
N S T P	Nuffield Science Teaching Project
N S V V	Nederlandse Stichting voor Verlichtingskunde (Netherlands) (Netherlands Foundation for Illumination)
N T A	National Tuberculosis Association (USA)
N T D C	Naval Training Device Center (USN)
N T D S	Naval Tactical Data System (USN)
N T G	Nachrichten-Technische Gesellschaft im VDE (Germany) (Association of Telecommunications Engineers within the German Association of Electrical Engineers)
N T H	Norges Tekniske Hogskole (Norway) (Technical University of Norway)
N T N F	Norges Teknisk-Naturvitenskapelige Forsknings- rad (Norway) (Norwegian Council for Scientific and Industrial Research)
N T P	Normal Temperature and Pressure
N T R L	Navy Training Research Laboratory (USN)
N T S	Nevada Test Site (of NASA)
N T S C	National Television Systems Committee (USA)
N T T	Nippon Telegraph and Telephone Public Cor- poration (Japan)
N T T A	National Traders Traffic Association
N U C L E X	International Nuclear Industrial Fair and Tech- nical Meetings
N U D A C	Nuclear Data Centre (India)
N U D E T S	Nuclear Detection System
N U O S	Naval Underwater Ordnance Station (USN)
N U P A D	Nuclear Powered Active Detection
N U W C	Naval Undersea Warfare Center (USN)
N V G A	National Vocational Guidance Association (USA)
N V L	Nederlandse Vereniging voor Lastechniek (Netherlands) (Netherlands Welding Society)
N W L	Naval Weapons Laboratory (USN)

N W M A	National Woodwork Manufacturers Association (USA)
N W O	Non-Woven Oriented
N W R C	National Weather Records Center (of ESSA)
N W R F	Naval Weather Research Facility (USN)
N W S C	National Weather Satellite Center (USA)
N Y A D S	New York Air Defense Sector (USA)
N Y N S	New York Naval Shipyard (USN)
N Y S U	State University of New York (USA)
N Z D S I R	New Zealand Department of Scientific and Industrial Research
N Z N C O R	New Zealand National Committee on Oceanic Research (New Zealand)
N Z O I	New Zealand Oceanographic Institute (New Zealand)
N Z S I	New Zealand Standards Institute
N Z S R	prefix to Standards issued by NZSI
N Z S S	prefix to Standards issued by NZSI

O

O & M	Organisation and Method
O & M, A	Operation and Maintenance, Army
O A C I	*see* ICAO
O A M S	Orbital Altitude Manoeuvring System
O A O	Orbital *or* Orbiting Astronomical Observatory
O A R	Office of Aerospace Research (USAF)
O A R T	Office of Advanced Research and Technology (of NASA)
O A S	Organization of American States
O A S F	Orbiting Astronomical Support Facility
O B A P	Office Belge pour l'Accroissement de la Productivitie (Belgium) (Belgian Productivity Improvement Office)
O B R	Overseas Business Report (series issued by Dept of Commerce, USA)
O C	Operating Characteristic
O C C A	Oil and Colour Chemists Association
O C D	Office of Civil Defense (USA)
O C D E	*see* OECD
O C E A N	Oceanographic Co-ordination Evaluation and Analysis Network (USN)
O C M A	Oil Companies Material Association
O C R	Optical Character Recognition

O C R - A	Optical Character Recognition—Font A
O C R - B	Optical Character Recognition—Font B
O C R D	Office of the Chief of Research and Development (US Army)
O C S	Office of Commodity Standards (of NBS, USA)
O C T	Office of Critical Tables (of NAS/NRC, USA)
O D	Optical Density
	Outside Diameter
O D D R E	Office of the Director of Defense Research and Engineering (USDOD)
O D L R O	Off-Diagonal Long-Range Order
O D M	Ministry of Overseas Development
O D O P	Offset Doppler
O D P	Original Document Processing
O D P E X	Offshore Drilling and Production Exhibition
O E A S	Organisation Europaischer Aluminium Schmelzhutten (Organisation of European Aluminium Foundries)
O E C D	Organisation for Economic Co-operation and Development
O E C O	Outboard Engine Cut-Off
O E E P E	Organisation Europeene d'Etudes Photogrammetriques Experimentales (European Organisation for Experimental Photogrammetric Research)
O E G	Operations Evaluation Group
O E P P	Organisation Europeene et Mediteraneenne pour la Protection des Plantes (European and Mediterranean Plant Protection Organisation)
O G D B	Oesterreichische Gesellschaft fur Dokumentation and Bibliographie (Austria) (Austrian Association for Documentation and Bibliography)
O G O	Orbiting Geophysical Observatory
O G R C	Office of Grants and Research Contracts (of NASA)
O H P	Oxygen at High Pressure
O I A	Oceanic Industries Association (USA)
O I I	Office of Invention and Innovation (of NBS)
O I S A	Office of International Scientific Affairs (US Dept of State)
O I Ya I	Ob'yedinennyy Institut Yadernykh Issledodovaniy (USSR) (Joint (ie including other nations) Institute for Nuclear Research)
O K A B	Oskarshamnsverkets Kraftgrupp (Sweden)

O K W	Oesterreichische Kuratorium fur Wirtschaftlich-heit (Austria) (Austrian Management Board)
O L R T	On-Line Real-Time
O M E	Office of Minerals Exploration (USA)
O M E F	Office Machines and Equipment Federation
O M E R A	Societe d'Optique, de Mecanique, d'Electricitie et de Radio, Argenteuil (France)
O M K D K	Orszagog Muszaki Konyvtar es Dokumentacios Kozpont (Hungary) (Technical Library and Documentation Centre)
O M P R A	One-Man Propulsion Research Apparatus
O M S F	Office of Manned Space Flight (of NASA)
O M T C	Organisation and Methods Training Council
O M T S	Organizational Maintenance Test Station
O N	Octane Number
O N A	Oesterreichischer Normencusschuss (Austria) (Austrian Standards Organisation)
O N E R A	Office National d'Etudes et de Recherches Aero-spatiales (France) (National Office for Aerospace Studies and Research)
O N O R M	prefix to Standards issued by ONA
O N R	Office of Naval Research (USN)
O N U L P	Ontario New Universities Libraries Project
O P A	Optoelectronic Pulse Amplifier
O P E C	Organisation of Petroleum Exporting Countries
O P E P	Orbital Plane Experimental Package
O P E X	Operational and Executive
O P I	Office of Public Information (of SBA, USA)
O P L E	Omega Position Location Experiment
O P P	Orientated Poly-Propylene
O P P O S I T	Optimisation of a Production Process by an Ordered Simulation and Iteration Technique
O P R	Optical Page Reading
O P S	On-line Process Synthesizer
O P T A	Optimal Performance Theoretically Attainable
O P W	Orthogonalized Plane Wave
O P Z	Oesterreichisches Produktivitats Zentrum (Aus-tria) (Austrian Productivity Centre)
O R	Operational Requirement
	Operational *or* Operations Research
O R B I S	Orbiting Radio Beacon Ionospheric Satellite
O R C	Operational *or* Operations Research Centre
O R D	Once-Run Distillate
	Optical Rotary Dispersion

O R E	Operational Research Establishment (of DRB, Canada) (now Defence Operational Research Establishment)
O R G	Operational *or* Operations Research Group
O R G A L I M E	Organisme de Liaison des Industries Metalliques Europeenes (European Association for Co-operation of the Metal Industry)
O R G D P	*Oak Ridge* Gaseous Diffusion Plant
O R I	Ocean Research Institute (Japan)
O R L	Orbital Research Laboratory
	Ordnance Research Laboratory
O R N L	Oak Ridge National Laboratory (of USAEC)
O R O	Operations Research Office (of Johns Hopkins University, USA)
O R R	*Oak Ridge* Reactor
O R S A	Operations Research Society of America (USA)
O R S T O M	Office de la Recherche Scientifique et Technique Outre-Mer (France) (Office of Overseas Scientific and Technical Research)
O R T A G	Operations Research Technical Assistance Group (US Army)
O R T F	Organisation Radio Television Francaise (France)
O S C A R	Optimum Systems Covariance Analysis Results
	Orbiting Satellite Carrying Amateur Radio
O S D	Office of the Secretary of Defense (USA)
	Operational Sequence Diagram
O S E	Operational Support Equipment
O S I C	Optimization of Subcarrier Information Capacity
O S I S	Office of Science Information Service (of National Science Foundation, USA)
O S O	Orbital Solar Observatory
	Orbiting Satellite Observer
O S R	prefix to numbered series of pamphlets relative to the Offices, Shops and Railway Premises Act issued by the Ministry of Labour and published by HMSO
O S R D	Office of Standard Reference Data (of NBS)
O S S A	Office of Space Science and Applications (of NASA)
O S T	Office of Science and Technology (of PSAC, USA)
O S T A C	Ocean Science and Technology Advisory Committee (of NSIA)

O S T I	Office for Scientific and Technical Information (of DES)
	Organization for Social and Technological Innovation (USA)
O S T S	Office of State Technical Service (of Dept of Commerce, USA)
O S U R F	Ohio State University Research Foundation (USA)
O S W	Office of Saline Water (of the Department of the Interior, USA)
O T J	On The Job
O T S	Office of Technical Services (now CFSTI, USA)
O T U	Office of Technology Utilization (of NASA)
O T U A	Office Technique pour l'Utilisation de l'Acier (France) (Technical Office for Steel Utilisation)
O V	Orbiting Vehicle
O W M	Office of Weights and Measures (of NBS)
O W P R	Ocean Wave Profile Recorder
O W R R	Office of Water Resources Research (of the Dept of the Interior, USA)
O W S	Ocean Weather Station

P

P & E E	Proving and Experimental Establishment
P A	Picatinny Arsenal (US Army)
	Product Analysis
P A B L A	Problem Analysis By Logical Approach
P A B X	Private Automatic Branch Exchange
P A C	Personal Analogue Computer
P A C A F	Pacific Air Force (USAF)
P A C E	Projects to Advance Creativity in Education
P A C E D	Public Accounts Committee
	Programme for Advanced Concepts in Electronic Design
P A C E R	Process Assembly Case Evaluator Routine
P A C S	Pacific Area Communications System
P A C T	Programmed Analysis Computer Transfer
P A D	Post Activation Diffusion
	Propellant Actuated Device
P A D L O C	Passive Active Detection and Location
P A D R E	Patient Automatic Data Recording Equipment
P A E M	Programme Analysis and Evaluation Model
P A G E O S	Passive Geodetic Earth Orbiting Satellite
P A H O	Pan-American Health Organization

P A I G H	Pan-American Institute of Geography and History (Mexico)
P A I S	Public Affairs Information Service
P A K E X	Packaging Exhibition
P A L	Permanent Artificial Lighting
	Phase Alternation Line
	Process Assembler Languages
P A L - D	Phase Alternation Line Delay
P A M	Pole Amplitude Modulation
	Pulse Amplitude Modulation
P A N S	Procedures for Air Navigation Services (series issued by ICAO)
P A N S - M E T	Procedures for Air Navigation Services—Meteorology (series issued by ICAO)
P A N S D O C	Pakistan National Scientific and Technical Documentation Centre (Pakistan)
P A P A	Programmer and Probability Analyzer
P A R	Precision Approach Radar
P A R D	Parts Application Reliability Data
P A R L	Prince Albert Radar Laboratory (of DRTE)
P A R M	Programme Analysis for Resource Management
P A R O S	Passive Ranging On Submarines
P A S E	Power Assisted Storage Equipment
P A S S	Production Automated Scheduling System
P A S S I M	Presidential Advisory Staff on Scientific Information Management (USA)
P A T	Parametric Artificial Talker
	Picric Acid Turbidity
	Programme Aptitude Test
P A T A	Pneumatic All-Terrain Amphibian
P A T I	Passive Airborne Time-difference Intercept
P A T R A	Packaging and Allied Trades Research Association (now PIRA)
P A T T E R N	Planning Assistance Through Technical Evaluation of Relevance Numbers
P A X	Private Automatic Exchange
P B	Precipitation Body
	Publications Board
	prefix to numbered series of Research and Development Reports usually available for purchase from CFSTI
P B P S	Post Boost Propulsion System
P B S	Pacific Biological Station (Canada)
P B T F	Polybromotrifluoroethylene

P B W	Parts By Weight
P C	Photochromic
P C A	Polar Cap Absorption
P C A C	Partially Conserved Axial-vector Current
P C A M	Punched Card Accounting Machine
P C B C	Partially Conserved Baryon Current
P C B S	Positive Control Bombardment System
P C C	Partial Crystal Control
P C E	Punched Card Equipment
P C I	Pilot Controller Integration
P C M	Pulse-Code Modulation
P C M I	Photochromic Micro-Image
P C P	Parallel Circular Plate
	Photon-Coupled Pair
	Polychloroprene
P C R	Photo-conductive Relay
P C S	Print Contrast Scale
P C S I R	Pakistan Council of Scientific and Industrial Research (Pakistan)
P C T	Photon-Coupled Transistor
P C T F E	Poly-monochloro-trifluoroethylene
P C U	Passenger Car Unit
	Power Conversion Unit
P C V	Positive Crankcase Ventilation
P D	Positive Displacement
	prefix to numbered series of amendments to Standards already issued by BSI
P D A	Post Deflection Acceleration
	Probability Discrete Automata
P D C E	Parametric Design and Cost Effectiveness
P D F	Probability Density Function
P D G	Precision Drop Glider
P D M	Physical Distribution Management
	Pulse Delta Modulation
	Pulse Duration Modulation
P D P	Positive Displacement Pump
	Programme Definition Phase
	Project Definition Phase
P D R	Periscope Depth Range
	Precision Depth Recorder
P D S	Power Density Spectra
P D S M S	Point-Defence Surface Missile System
P D T	Picture Description Test

P E	Permanent Echo
	Polyester
	Polyether
	Polyethylene
P E A C U	Plastic Energy Absorption in Compression Unit
P E C S	Portable Environmental Control System
P E E P	Pilot's Electronic Eyelevel Presentation
P E M	Production Engineering Measure
P E M A	Procurement Equipment and Missiles—Army
P E N A	Primary Emission Neutron Activation
P E O S	Propulsion and Electrical Operating System
P E P	Peak Envelop Power
	Planetary Ephemeris Programme
	Programme Evaluation Procedure
P E P P	Planetary Entry Parachute Programme
P E R A	Production Engineering Research Association
P E R M	Programme Evaluation for Repetitive Manufacture
P E R T	Performance Evaluation Review Technique
	Programme Evaluation Review Technique
P E S T F	Proton Event Start Forecast
P E T	Patterned Epitaxial Technology
	Polyethylene Terephthalate
	Production Environmental Testing
P F	Packing Factor
	Phenol-formaldehyde
	Protection Factor
P F A	Pulverized Fuel Ash
P F D	Primary Flash Distillate
P F M	Pulse-Frequency Modulation
P F P A	Pitch Fibre Pipe Association
P F R	Prototype Fast-breeder Reactor
P G R	Precision Graphic Recorder
P H I	Position and Homing Indicator
P H O E N I X	Plasma Heating Obtained by Energetic Neutral Injection Experiment
P H S	Public Health Service (USA)
P H W	Pressurised Heavy Water
P I	Performance Index
	Polyimides
	Productivity Index
	Programmed Instruction
	Proportional Integral

P I A	Pakistan International Airlines Corporation (Pakistan)
P I A C	Petroleum Industry Advisory Council
P I A N C	Permanent International Association of Navigation Congresses
P I A P A C S	Psycho-physiological Information Acquisition, Processing And Control System
P I A R C	Permanent International Association of Road Congresses
P I B	Petroleum Information Board
	Polyisobutylene
	Prices and Incomes Board
P I B A C	Permanent International Bureau of Analytical Chemistry of Human and Animal Food
P I B M R I	Polytechnic Institute of Brooklyn, Microwave Research Institute (USA)
P I C	Particle-In-Cell
P I C A	Power Industry Computer Applications
P I D	Proportional Integral and Differential
	Proportional Integral Derivation
P I G H	Pan-American Institute of Geography and History
P I I	Positive Immittance Inverter
P I L	Pest Infestation Laboratory (of Agricultural Research Council)
	Pitt Interpretive Language (University of Pittsburgh, USA)
P I L C	Paper Insulated Lead Covered
P I L O T	Permutation Indexed Literature Of Technology
	Piloted Low-speed Test
P I M	Precision Indicator of the Meridian
	Pulse Interval Modulation
P I N S	Portable Inertial Navigation System
P I N S A C	PINS Alignment Console
P I O S A	Pan Indian Ocean Science Association
P I P	Probabilistic Information Processing
P I R A	Paper and Board, Printing and Packaging Industries Research Association
P I T	Processing of Index Terms
	Programme Instruction Tape
P I T A C	Pakistan Industrial Technical Assistance Centre
P I T B	Petroleum Industry Training Board
P K N	Polski Kometet Normalizacyjny (Poland) (Standards Commission)

P L	Payload
	Production Language
	Programming Language
P L A	Moon, Planets, Comets and Interplanetary Medium Advisory Committee (of ESRO)
	Port of London Authority
	Proton Linear Accelerator
P L A C E	Programming Language for Automatic Checkout Equipment
P L A N I T	Programming Language for Interactive Teaching
P L A S T E C	Plastic Technical Evaluation Center (USDOD)
P L A T	Pilot Landing Aid Television
P L A T O	Programmed Logic for Automatic Teaching Operations
P L D	Phase-Lock Demodulator
	Pulse-Length Discriminator
P L L	Phased-Locked Loop
P L O D	Planetary Orbit Determination
P L P	Pattern Learning Parser
P L S S	Portable Life-Support System
P L U T O	Pipe Line Under The Ocean
	Plutonium Loop Testing Reactor
P M	Photo-Multiplier
P M A	Permanent Magnet Association
P M A F	Pharmaceutical Manufacturers Association Foundation (USA)
P M B X	Private Manual Branch Exchange
P M E	Photomagneto-electric Effect
	Protective Multiple Earthing
P M M A	Paper Machinery Makers Association
P M P	Project Master Plan
P M R	Pacific Missile Range (USAF)
P M S	Phanazinium Methosulphate
P M S R P	Physical and Mathematical Sciences Research Paper
P M T	Photomultiplier
P N	Performance Number
P Ndb	Perceived Noise decibels
P N E U R O P	European Committee of Manufacturers of Compressed Air Equipment
P N L	Pacific Naval Laboratory (of DRB, Canada) (now Defence Research Establishment Pacific)
P N T D	Personnel Neutron Threshold Detector

P N W	prefix to series issued by Pacific Northwest Forest and Range Experiment Station (Forest Service of USDA)
P O C S	Patent Office Classification System (US Patent Office)
P O D	Post Office Department (USA)
P O E	Port of Embarkation
P O G O	Polar Orbiting Geophysical Observatory
P O I	Programme of Instruction
P O L	Petroleum, Oil and Lubricants
P O M M	Preliminary Operating and Maintenance Manual
P O M S	Panel on Operational Meteorological Satellites
P O S E	Programme for Optimizing Sales Effort
P O S H	Permuted On Subject Headings
P O T C	PERT Orientation and Training Center (USDOD)
P O W S	Pyrotechnic Outside Warning System
P P A	Photo-Peak Analysis
P P A A R	Princeton University, Pennsylvania University, Army (US Army Electronics Command) Avionics Research
P P B S	Planning, Programming and Budgeting System
P P C	Procurement Policy Committee (of HM Treasury) Pulsed Power Circuit
P P D R	Pilot Performance Description Record
P P E	Polyphenylether
P P G	Programme Pulse Generator
P P I	Plan-Position Indicator
P P L	Private Pilot's Licence
P P M	Planned Preventive Maintenance Pulse Position Modulation
P P O	Promocion Professional Obrera (Spain) (Organisation for training semi-skilled workers)
P P S	Primary Propulsion System
P R	Preliminary Report Progress Report Project Report Pseudo Random
P R A I S	Pesticide Residue Analysis Information Service (of the Laboratory of the Government Chemist)
P R B	Public Roads Bureau (Dept of Commerce, USA)
P R B S	Pseudo Random Binary Sequence
P R C	Poultry Research Centre (of Agricultural Research Council)
P R E S S	Pacific Range Electromagnetic Signature Studies

PRESTO	Programme for Rapid Earth-to-Space Trajectory Optimization
PRF	Pulse Repetition Frequency
PRFCS	Pattern Recognition Feedback Control System
PRIDE	Programmed Reliability In Design
PRIME	Precision Integrator for Meteorological Echoes
	Precision Recovery Including Manoeuvrable Entry
	Priority Management Efforts
PRINCE	Parts Reliability Information Center (of NASA)
PRL	Personnel Research Laboratory (USAF)
PRM	Power Range Monitor
PROFILE	Programmed Functional Indices for Laboratory Evaluation
PROMPT	Programme Reporting, Organisation and Management Planning Technique
PROP	Profit Rating Of Profits
PROXI	Projection by Reflection Optics of Xerographic Images
PRTR	Plutonium Recycle Test Reactor
PS	Polystyrene
	prefix to Standards issued by PSI
PSAC	President's Science Advisory Committee (USA)
PSALI	Permanent Supplementary Artificial Lighting of Interiors
PSCC	Power System Computation Conference
PSI	Pakistan Standards Institution (Pakistan)
	Preprogrammed Self Instruction
	Present Serviceability Index
PSIEP	Project on Scientific Information Exchange in Psychology (of American Psychological Association)
PSK	Phase Shift Keying
PSMS	Permanent Section of Microbiological Standardization (of IAMS)
PSNS	Puget Sound Naval Shipyard (USN)
PSRP	Physical Sciences Research Paper
PST	Polished Surface Technique
PSTC	Pressure Sensitive Tape Council (USA)
PSW	Pacific Southwest Forest and Range Experiment Station (Forest Service of USDA)
PsyCHES	Psychiatric Case History Event System
PTA	Planar Turbulence Amplifier

P T C	Personnel Transfer Capsule
	Phenylthiocarbamide
P T C S	Propellant Tanking Computer System
P T F E	Polytetrafluorethylene
P T M	Pulse Time Modulation
P T P	Point-To-Point Programming
P T R	Pool Test Reactor
P T S	Permanent Threshold Shift
P T V	Predetermined Time Value
P U F F S	Passive Underwater Fire control sonar Feasibility Study
P U F F T	*Purdue University* Fast FORTRAN Translator
P V	Positive Volume
P V A	Polyvinyl Acetate
P V A L	Polyvinyl Alcohol
P V C	Polyvinyl Chloride
P V D	Paravisual Director
P V O R	Precision VHF Omnirange
P V T	Polyvinyl Toluene
P W F	Present Worth Factor
P W L	Piece-Wise Linear
P W M	Pulse Width Modulation
	Pulse Width Multiplier
P W R	Pressurised Water Reactor

Q

Q A	Quality Assurance
Q C	Quality Control
Q C & T	Quality Control and Test
Q C E	Quality Control Engineering
Q D R I	Qualitative Development Requirements Information (issued by US Army Material Command)
Q P L	Qualified Products List
Q R	Quality and Reliability
Q R A	Quick Reaction Alert
Q R B M	Quasi-Random Band Model
Q R C	Quick Reaction Capability
Q S G	Quasi-Stellar Galaxy
Q S O	Quasi-Stellar Object
Q S O P	Quadripartite Standing Operating Procedures
Q S R S	Quasi-Stellar Radio Sources
Q U A M	Quadrature Amplitude Modulation
Q U I C O	Quality Improvement through Cost Optimization
Q U I P	Questionnaire Interpreter Programme

R

R	Recommendation
	Report
	Research
R & D	Research and Development
R & M	Reports and Memoranda
R A B F M	Research Association of British Flour-Millers
R A B P C V M	Research Association of British Paint, Colour and Varnish Manufacturers
R A C	Royal Automobile Club
R A C E	Rapid Automatic Check-out Equipment
R A C E P	Random Access and Correlation for Extended Performance
R A C I C	Remote Area Conflict Information Center (of BMI)
R A C S	Remote Access Computing System
	Remote Automatic Calibration System
R A D	Radiation Absorbed Dose
	Random Access Disc
R A D A	Random Access Discrete Address
R A D A R	Radio Detection And Ranging
R A D A S	Random Access Discrete Address System
R A D C	Rome Air Development Center (USAF)
R A D I A C	Radioactivity Detection Indication And Computation
R A D V S	Radar Altimeter and Doppler Velocity Sensor
R A E	Radio Astronomy Explorer satellite
	Royal Aircraft Establishment
R A E N	Radio Amateur Emergency Network
R Ae S	Royal Aeronautical Society
R A F T	Radially Adjustable Facility Tube
R A I S	Rail Air International Service
R A M A C	Random Access Method of Accounting and Control
R A M P	*Raytheon* Airborne Microwave Platform
R A M P A R T	Radar Advanced Measurements Programme for Analysis of Re-entry Techniques
R A M P S	Resource Allocation and Multi-Project Scheduling
R A N	Request for Authority to Negotiate
R A P	Redundancy Adjustment of Probability
	Rocket Assisted Projectile
R A P C O N	Radar Approach Control

R A P I D	Research in Automatic Photocomposition and Information Dissemination
R A P R A	Rubber and Plastic Research Association
R A R	Rapid Access Recording
R A R D E	Royal Armament Research and Development Establishment (MOD)
R A S S	Rapid Area Supply Support
R A S T A	Radiation Special Test Apparatus
R A T A N	Radar And Television Aid to Navigation
R A T E R	Response Analysis Tester
R A T I O	Radio Telescope In Orbit
R A T O G	Rocket-Assisted Take-Off Gear
R A T S C A T	Radar Target Scatter
R B	Return to Bias
R B A	Road Bitumen Association
R B E	Relative Biological Effectiveness
R C	Research Centre
R C A	Reinforced Concrete Association
R C A F	Royal Canadian Air Force
R C A T	Radio Code Aptitude Test
R C J	Reaction Control Jet
R C N	Reactor Centrum Nederland (Netherlands) (Netherlands Reactor Centre)
R C S	Reaction Control System
R C U	Road Construction Unit
R D	Research and Development
R D A	Reliability Design Analysis
R D E	Radial Defect Examination
R D P S	Radar Data Processing System
R D T & E	Research Development Testing and Evaluation
R D T L	Resistor Diode Transistor Logic
R D T R	Research Division Technical Report
R E & R	Research, Engineering and Reliability
R E A C T	Register Enforced Automated Control Technique
R E A D	Real-time Electronic Access and Display Remote Electronic Alphanumeric Display
R E A D I	Rocket Engine Analyser and Decision Instrumentation
R E A R	Reliability Engineering Analysis Report
R E C M F	Radio and Electronic Component Manufacturers Association
R E D S O D	Repetitive Explosive Device for Soil Displacement

REEP	Regression Estimation of Event Probabilities
REHVA	Representatives of European Heating and Ventilating Associations
REI	Research-Engineering Interaction
REM	Rapid Eye Movement
	Roentgen Equivalent Man
RENFE	Red Nacional de los Ferrocarriles Espanoles (Spain) (Spanish National Railways)
REON	Rocket Engine Operations—Nuclear
REPLAB	Responsive Environment Programmed Laboratory
REPT	Report
RER	Reseau Express Regional (France)
RESA	Scientific Research Society of America (USA)
RESD	Research and Engineering Support Division (of Institute for Defense Analysis, USA)
REST	Radar Electronic Scan Test
RETMA	Radio, Electronics, Television Manufacturers Association (now EIA) (USA)
REVS	Rotor-Entry Vehicle System
RF	Radio Frequency
	Rating Factor
RFA	Redundant Force Analysis
RFI	Radio Frequency Interference
RFCWA	Regional Fisheries Commission for West Africa (Ghana)
RFP	Request for Proposal
RGT	Resonant Gate Transistor
RH	prefix to series on Radiological Health issued by Public Health Service (USA)
RHA	Road Haulage Association
RHEL	Rutherford High Energy Laboratory
RHI	Range-Height Indicator
RHOGI	Radar Homing Guidance
RHR	Rejectable Hazard Rate
RI	Report of Investigation
	Royal Institution
RIA	Rock Island Arsenal (US Army)
RIAS	Research Institute for Advanced Studies (USA)
RIBA	Royal Institute of British Architects
RIC	Royal Institute of Chemistry
RICA	Research Institute for Consumer Affairs
RICASIP	Research Information Center and Advisory Service on Information Processing (USA)

R I C S	Range Instrumentation Control System
R I F T	Reactor In Flight Test
R I G	Reaktor - Interessen - Gemeinschaft (Austria)
R I L E M	Reunion Internationale des Laboratoires d'Essais et de Recherches sur les Materiaux et les constructions (International Union of Testing and Research Laboratories for Materials and Structures)
R I N A	Registro Italiano Navale (Italy)
R I P P L E	Radioactive Isotope Powered Pulse Light Equipment
	Radioisotope Powered Prolonged Life Equipment
R I T	Rocket Interferometer Tracking
R K W	Rationalisierungs Kuratorium der Deutschen Wirtschafts (Germany) (German Productivity Organisation)
R L	Radiation Laboratory
	Research Laboratory
	Resistor Logic
R M	Radio Monitoring
	Research Memorandum
R M C	Rod Memory Computer
R M E A	Rubber Manufacturing Employers Association
R M C S	Royal Military College of Science (MOD)
R M I C	Research Materials Information Center (of ORNL, USAEC)
R M P	Re-entry Measurements Programme
R M S	Root-Mean-Square
	Royal Microscopical Society
R M U	Remote Manoeuvring Unit
R N	Research Note
	Road Note (series issued by the Road Research Laboratory, Ministry of Transport)
R N A	Ribonucleic Acid
R N D	Rijksnijverheidsdienst (Netherlands) (Government Industrial Advisory Service)
R N I B	Royal National Institute for the Blind
R N I D	Royal National Institute for the Deaf
R N P	Ribonucleoprotein
R N P L	Royal Naval Physiological Laboratory (MOD)
R N P R C	Royal Navy Personnel Research Committee (of Medical Research Council)
R N S S	Royal Naval Scientific Service (MOD)
R O A	Return on Assets

R O C	Receiver Operating Characteristics
R O F	Royal Ordnance Factory (MOD)
R O I	Return On Investment
R O L F	Remotely Operated Longwall Face
R O M	Read-Only Memory
R O O S T	Re-usable One Stage Orbital Space Truck
R O S E	Remotely Operated Special Equipment Retrieval by On-line Search
RO S P A	Royal Society for the Prevention of Accidents
R O T	Re-usable Orbital Transport
R O T I	Recording Optical Tracking Instrument
R P	Recovery Phase
	Research Paper
	Rocket Projectile
R P D	Retarding Potential Difference
R P E	Rocket Propulsion Establishment (MINTECH)
R P G	Report Programme Generator
R P L	Radiophysics Laboratory (of CSIRO, Australia)
R P S	Royal Photographic Society of Great Britain
R Q A	Recursive Queue Analyzer
R Q L	Reference Quality Level
R R	Research Report
	Return Rate
R R E	Royal Radar Establishment (MINTECH)
R R E A C	*Royal Radar Establishment* Automatic Computer
R R I S	Record Room Interrogation System
	Remote Radar Integration Station
R R L	Road Research Laboratory (Ministry of Transport)
R R N S	Redundant Residue Number System
R R S	Radiation Research Society (USA)
	Radio Research Station
R R U	Radiobiological Research Unit
R S A	Royal Society of Arts
R S A C	Reactor Safety Advisory Committee (Canada)
R S C	Royal Society of Canada
R S G B	Radio Society of Great Britain
R S H	Royal Society of Health
R S I C	Radiation Shielding Information Center (of ORNL)
	Redstone Scientific Information Center (Redstone Arsenal, US Army)
R S L	Radio Standards Laboratory (of NSB)

R S M	Royal School of Mines
	Royal Society of Medicine
R S N	Radiation Surveillance Network
R S R S	Radio and Space Research Station (of Science Research Council)
R S S I	Regional Science Research Institute (USA)
R T	Rated Time
R T C A	Radio Technical Commission for Aeronautics (USA)
R T D	Residence Time Distribution
R T G	Radioisotope Thermoelectric Generator
R T I T B	Road Transport Industry Training Board
R T L	Resistor Transistor Logic
R T M	Real-Time Monitor
	Research Technical Memoranda
R T P	Reinforced Thermoplastic
R T S	Royal Television Society
R T S D	Resources and Technical Services Division (of the American Library Association)
R T T D S	Real Time Telemetry Data System
R U M	Remote Underwater Manipulator
R U S I	Royal United Services Institution
R V	Re-entry Vehicle
R V C	Relativity Velocity Computer
R W	Resistance Welding
R W M	Rectangular Wave Modulation
R W M A	Resistance Welder Manufacturers Association (USA)
R Z	Return to Zero
R zh	Referativny Zhurnal (Abstract Journal)

S

S & T	Scientific and Technical
S & T I	Scientific and Technical Information
S A	Springfield Armory (US Army)
	Stability Augmentation
S A A	South African Airways
	Standards Association of Australia
	Surface Active Agent
S A A B	Svensk Aeroplan AB (Sweden)
S A A E B	South African Atomic Energy Board (South Africa)

S A B C A	Societe Anonyme Belge de Constructions Aeronautiques (Belgium)
S A B E	Society for Automation in Business Education (USA)
S A B E N A	Societe Anonyme Belge d'Exploitation de la Navigation Aerienne (Belgium)
S A B S	South African Bureau of Standards
S A C	Society for Analytical Chemistry
S A C M	Societe Alsacienne de Constructions Mecaniques (France)
S A C O M	Ships Advanced Communications Operational Model
S A D	Sentence Appraiser and Diagrammer
S A D A	Seismic Array Data Analyser
S A D A S	*Sperry* Airborne Data Acquisition System
S A D C	Sequential Analogue-Digital Computer
S A D I E	Sterling And Decimal Invoicing Electronically
S A D L	Sterilization Assembly Development Laboratory (of NASA at JPL)
S A D S A C	*Seiler* ALGOL Digitally Simulated Analogue Computer
S A D S C A T	Self Assigned Descriptors from Self And Cited Titles
S A E	Society of Automotive Engineers (USA)
S A F E	Safe Assessment and Facilities Establishment (of JAIF)
	Space and Flight Equipment Association (USA)
S A G	Standard Address Generator
S A G E	Semi-Automatic Ground Environment
S A G E M	Societe d'Applications Generales d'Electricite et de Mecanique (France)
S A H Y B	Simulation of Analogue and Hybrid Computers
S A I L S	Simplified Aircraft Instrument Landing System
S A I M S	Selected Acquisitions Information and Management System
S A I P	Societe d'Applications Industrielles de la Physique (France)
S A I S	South African Interplanetary Society (South Africa)
S A I S A C	Ship's Aircraft Inertial System Alignment Console
S A I T	Societe Anonyme Internationale de Telegraphie (Belgium)
S A K I	*Solatron* Automatic Keyboard Instructor
S A L M	Society of Air Line Meteorologists (USA)

S A M	School of Aerospace Medicine (USAF)
	Semantic Analysing Machine
	Semi-Automated Mathematics
	Simulation of Analogue Methods
	Society for Advancement of Management (USA)
	Surface-to-Air Missile
	Symbolic and Algebraic Manipulation
	Systems Analysis Module
S A M - D	Surface-to-Air Missile Development
S A M A	Scientific Apparatus Makers Association (USA)
S A M E	Society of Military Engineers (USA)
S A M E S	Societe Anonyme de Machines Electrostatiques (France)
S A M I	Socially Acceptable Monitoring Instrument
S A M M	Societe d'Applications des Machines Motrices (France)
S A M P E	Society of Aerospace Material and Process Engineers (USA)
S A M S O	Space And Missiles Organisation (of USAF Systems Command)
S A M S O M	Support-Availability Multi-System Operations Model
S A N C A R	South African National Council for Antarctic Research (South Africa)
S A N D	Shelter Analysis for New Designs
S A O	Smithsonian Astrophysical Observatory (USA)
S A P	Start of Active Profile
S A P A R	Societe d' Appareillage Electrique (France)
S A P I R	System of Automatic Processing and Indexing of Reports
S A P R O	Societe Anonyme de Pipeline a Produits (Switzerland)
S A Q	Schweizerische Arbeitsgmeneinschaft fur Qualitatsbeforderung (Switzerland) (Swiss Association for the Promotion of Quality)
S A R	Search and Rescue Radio
S A R B E	Search and Rescue Beacon Equipment
S A T A N A S	Semi-Automatic Analogue Setting
S A R P S	Standards And Recommended Practices (series issued by ICAO)
S A R S T	Societe Auxiliare de la Recherche Scientifique et Technique (France)
S A S	Stability Augmentation Safety System
	Surface Active Substances

S A S E	Statistical Analysis of a Series of Events
S A S M I R A	Silk and Art Silk Mills Research Association (India)
S A S S Y	Supported Activity Supply System
S A T	Societe Anonyme de Telecommunications (France)
	Society of Acoustic Technology (now British Acoustical Society)
	Stabilization Assurance Test
	Stepped Atomic Time
S A T C O	Signal Automatic Air Traffic Control
S A T C O M	Committee on Scientific and Technical Communication (of National Academy of Sciences *and* National Academy of Engineering) (USA)
	Satellite Communication Agency (USDOD)
S A T E R C O	Societe Anonyme de Terrassements et de Constructions (Belgium)
S A T I R E	Semi-Automatic Information Retrieval
S A T R A	Shoe and Allied Trades Research Association
S A T S	Short Airfield for Tactical Support
S A V E	Society of American Value Engineers (USA)
	System for Automatic Value Exchange
S A W C	Special Air Warfare Center (USAF)
S A W E	Society of Aeronautical Weight Engineers (USA)
S A W M A R C S	Standard Aircraft Weapons Management And Release Control System
S B A	Small Business Administration (USA)
	Standard Beam Approach
S B A C	Society of British Aerospace Companies
S B A S I	Single-Bridge *Apollo* Standard Initiator
S B B	Societe Belge des Betons (Belgium)
S B B N F	Ship and Boat Builders National Federation
S B C C	Southern Building Code Congress
S B N	Standard Book Number
S B P	Society of Biological Psychiatry (USA)
S B R	Styrene Butadiene Rubber
S B R (O E P)	Styrene Butadiene Rubber (Oil Extended)
S B T	Submarine Bathythermograph
S B T C	Sino-British Trade Council
S C	Special Committee
	Sudden Commencement
	Superimposed Coding
	Synchro-Cyclotron
S C A D S	Scanning Celestial Attitude Determination System

S C A N	Selected Current Aerospace Notices (issued by NASA)
	Stockmarket Computer Answering Network
	Switched Circuit Automatic Network
S C A N D O C	Scandinavian Documentation Center (USA)
S C A N S	Scheduling and Control by Automated Network System
S C A P	Silent Compact Auxiliary Power
S C A P E	Self Contained Atmospheric Personnel Ensemble
S C A R	Scandinavian Council for Applied Research
	Scientific Committee on Antarctic Research
	Submarine Celestial Altitude Recorder
S C A R F	Santa Cruz Acoustic Range Facility
S C A T	Speed Command of Attitude and Thrust
S C B	Stage Check-out Building
S C C A P E	Scottish Council for Commercial, Administrative and Professional Education
S C D C	Steel Castings Development Committee
S C E A	Signal Conditioning Electronic Assembly
S C E P T R E	Systems for Circuit Evaluation and Prediction of Transient Radiation Effects
S C E R T	Systems and Computer Evaluation and Review Technique
S C F	Self-Consistent Field
	Stress Concentration Factor
S C I	Society of Chemical Industry
	Societe de Chimie Industrielle (France)
S C I C	Semiconductor Integrated Circuit
S C I P	Scanning for Information Parameters
S C I R	Standing Committee for Installation Rebuilding (of MOD and MPBW)
S C M A	Southern Cypress Manufacturers Association (USA)
S C N	Sensitive Command Network
S C O L M A	Standing Conference on Library Materials for Africa
S C O M O	Satellite Collection of Meteorological Observations
S C O O P	Scientific Computation of Optimal Programmes
S C O P E	Schedule-Cost-Performance
	Specifiable Co-ordinating Positioning Equipment
S C O R	Scientific Committee on Oceanographic Research
S C O R E	Satellite Computer Operated Readiness Equipment

S C O R E	Service Corps of Retired Executives (USA)
	Signal Communications by Orbital Relay Equipment
S C O R P I O	Sub-critical Carbon-moderated Reactor assembly for Plutonium Investigations
S C P	Safety Control Programme
S C R	Silicon Controlled Rectifier
S C R A M J E T	Supersonic Combustion Ramjet
S C R A P	Super Calibre Rocket Assisted Projectile
S C R D E	Stores and Clothing Research and Development Establishment (MOD)
S C S	Soil Conservation Service (USDA)
	Space Cabin Simulator
	Stabilization Cabin Simulator
S C S A	Soil Conservation Society of America (USA)
S C S E	South Carolina Societies of Engineering (USA)
S C U B A	Self-Contained Underwater Breathing Apparatus
S C U M R A	Societe Centrale de l'Uranium et des Minerais et Metaux Radioactifs (France)
S D A D	Satellite Digital and Analogue Display
S D C	Society of Dyers and Colourists
	Submersible Diving Chamber
S D C A	Society of Dyers and Colourists of Australia
S D C E	Society of Die Casting Engineers (USA)
S D E C E	Service de Documentation Exterieure et de Contre-Espionnage (France)
S D F C	Space Disturbance Forecast Center (of ESSA)
S D I	Selective Dissemination of Information
S D L	System Descriptive Language
S D M	Statistical Delta Modulation
	Standardization Design Memoranda (series issued by MOD)
S D R	Small Development Requirement
S D S	Space Documentation Service (of EURODOC)
S E A	Societe d'Electronique et d'Automatisme (France)
	Systems Effectiveness Analyzer
S E A C	*Standard's* Eastern Automatic Computer (NBS)
S E A C O M	South East Asia Commonwealth Cable
S E A S	Committee for the Scientific Exploration of the Atlantic Shelf
S E A S C O	South East Asia Science Co-operation Office (India)
S E A T O	South-East Asia Treaty Organisation

S E A V O M	Societe d'Etudes et d'Applications Vide Optique Mecanique (France)
S E C	Sanitary Engineering Center (of US Public Health Service)
	Secondary Electron Conduction
	Secondary Emission Conductivity
	Simple Electronic Computer
S E C A M	Sequential Colour And Memory (Sequential couleur a memoire)
S E C A N	Societe d'Etudes et de Constructions Aero-Navales (France)
S E C A P	System Experience Correlation and Analysis Programme
S E C A R	Secondary Radar
S E C E M	Sociedad Espanola Construcciones Electro-Mecanicas (Spain)
S E C N A V	Secretary of the Navy (USN)
S E C O	Bureau de controle pour la securite de la construction en Belgique (Belgium) (Office for Research on Safety Precautions in Belgian Construction Work)
S E C O R	Sequential Collation Of Range
S E C U R E	Systems Evaluation Code Under Radiation Environment
S E D A	Societe d'Etudes pour le Developpement de l'Automatisme (France)
S E D A D	Societe d'Etude et Developpement des Applications Derivees electroniques et mechaniques (France)
S E D A M	Societe d'Etudes et de Developpement des Aeroglisseurs Marins (France)
S E D E I S	Societe d'Etudes et de Documentation Economiques, Industrielles et Sociales (France)
S E D I X	Selected Dissemination of Indexes
S E D S	Space Electronic Detection System
S E E	Society of Environmental Engineers
S E E N	Societe d'Etudes et d'Entreprises Nucleaires (France)
S E F O R	*South-west* Experimental Fast Oxide Reactor
S E G	Society of Exploration Geophysicists
	Systems Engineering Group
S E I N	Societe d'Electronique Industrielle et Nucleaire (France)

SEIT	Satellite Educational and Informational Television
SEL	Stanford Electronics Laboratories (of Stanford University, USA)
SELNI	Societa Elettronucleaire Italiana (Italy)
SEM	Scanning Electron Microscope
SEMA	Societe d'Economie et Mathematique Appliquees (France)
	Spray Equipment Manufacturers Association
SEMCOR	Semantic Correlation
SEMIRAD	Secondary-Electron Mixed-Radiation Dosimeter
SEMLAT	Semiconductor Laser Array Technique
SEMPE	Socio-Economic Model of the Planet Earth
SEMS	Severe Environmental Memory System
SEMT	Societe d'Etudes de Machines Thermiques (France)
SEN	prefix to Standards issued by SVS
SENA	Societe d'Energie Nucleaire Franco-Belge des Ardennes
SENTA	Societe d'Etudes Nucleaires et de Techniques Nouvelles (France)
SEPIA	Societe d'Etudes de Protection des Installations Atomiques (France)
SEPM	Society of Economic Paleontologists and Mineralogists (USA)
SEPOL	Soil Engineering Problem—Oriented Language
SEPR	Societe d'Etude de la Propulsion par Reaction (France)
SERCEL	Societe d'Etudes Recherches et Constructions Electroniques (France)
SEREB	Societe pour l'Etude et la Realisation d'Engins Ballistiques (France)
SEREL	Societe d'Exploitation et de Recherches Electroniques (France)
SERL	Services Electronics Research Laboratory
SERT	Society of Electronic and Radio Technicians
	Space Electrical Rocket Test
SES	Solar Energy Society (USA)
	Standards Engineers Society (USA)
	Suffield Experimental Station (Defence Research Board, Canada) (now Defence Research Establishment Suffield)
	Surface Effect Ship
SESA	Society for Environmental Stress Analysis (USA)

S E S C O	Societe Europeene des Semiconducteurs (France)
S E S O C	Surface Effect Ship for Ocean Commerce
S E T	Selective Employment Tax
	Solar Energy Thermionic conversion system
S E T E L	Societe Europeene de Teleguidage (France)
S E T I	Societe Europeene pour le Traitment de l'Information (France)
S E T P	Society of Experimental Test Pilots (USA)
S E T U	Societe d'Etudes et de Travaux pour l'Uranium (France)
S E U S S	South-East United States Survey
S E V	Schweizerischer Elektrotechnischer Verein (Switzerland) (Swiss Electrotechnical Institution)
	Soviet Ekonomickeskoi Vzaimopomoschchi (Council for Mutual Economic Assistance)
	prefix to Standards issued by SNV
S F A	Scientific Film Association (now part of BISFA)
	Societe Francaise d'Astronautique (France)
S F A R	System Failure Analysis Report
sf B	Samarbetskommitten for Byggnadsfragor (Sweden) (Cooperative Committee for the Building Industry)
S F B	Semiconductor Functional Block
S F C	Solar Forecast Center (of USAF)
	Specific Fuel Consumption
S F D	Sudden Frequency Deviation
	System Function Description
S F E	Societe Francaise des Electriciens (France) (French Society of Electricians)
S F E A	Space and Flight Equipment Association (USA)
S F E C	Societe de Fabrication d'Elements Catalytiques (France)
S F E R	Societe Francaise des Electroniciens et Radioelectriciens (French Society of Electronic and Radio Technicians)
S F F	Solar Forecast Facility (of USAF)
S F I M	Societe de Fabrication d'Instruments de Mesure (France)
S F I T	Swiss Federal Institute of Technology (Switzerland)
S F I T V	Societe Francaise des Ingenieurs et Techniciens Vide (France) (French Society of Vacuum Engineers and Technicians)

S F O F	Space Flight Operations Facility (of NASA)
S F P E	Society of Fire Protection Engineers (USA)
S F S	Suomen Standardisoimisliitto (Finland) (Standards Institute)
S F T S	Standard Frequency and Time Signals
S G	Spheroidal Graphite
S G A E	Studiengesellschaft fur Atomenergie (Austria)
S G H W R	Steam Generating Heavy Water Reactor
S G P	Society of General Physiologists (USA)
S G R C A	Sodium Graphite Reactor Critical Assembly
S G S	Societa Generale Semiconduttori (Italy)
sh	prefix to numbered series issued by the Ship Division of the National Physical Laboratory
S H A B	Soft and Hard Acids and Bases
S H A L	Subject Heading Authority List
S H A R E	Society to Help Avoid Repetitive Effort (USA)
S H A R P	SHIPS Analysis and Retrieval Project
S H F	Societe Hydrotechnique de France (Hydraulic Engineering Society)
	Super High Frequency
S H I E F	Shared Information Elicitation Facility
S H I P	prefix to numbered series issued by the Ship Division of the National Physical Laboratory
S H I P S	Bureau of Ships (USN)
S H I R T D I F	Storage, Handling and Retrieval of Technical Data in Image Formation
S H L M A	Southern Hardwood Lumber Manufacturers Association (USA)
S H N	Servicio de Hidrografia Naval (Argentina) (Naval Hydrographic Service)
S H O R A N	Short Range Navigation
S H O T	Society for the History Of Technology (USA)
S H O W	Scripps Institution—University of Hawaii—Oregon State University—University of Wisconsin (USA)
S I	Smithsonian Institute (USA)
	Society of Illustrators (USA)
	Statutory Instrument (issued by Parliament and published by HMSO)
	Systeme International d'unites (International System of Units)
	prefix to Standards issued by SII

S I A	Societe Suisse des Ingenieurs et des Architectes (Switzerland) (Swiss Society of Engineers and Architects)
	Subminiature Integrated Antennae
S I A M	Society for Industrial and Applied Mathematics (USA)
S I B	Shipbuilding Industry Board
	Snake In the Box
S I C	Semiconductor Integrated Circuit
	Societe Intercontinentale des Containers (France)
	Standard Industrial Classification
S I C N	Societe Industrielle de Combustible Nucleaire (France)
S I C S	Semiconductor Integrated Circuits
S I D	Society for Information Displays (USA)
	Sudden Ionosphere Disturbance
	Syntax Improving Device
S I D A S E	Significant Data Selection
S I D S	Stellar Inertial Doppler System
S I E	Science Information Exchange (of Smithsonian Institution, USA)
S I F	Selective Identification Feature
S I G M A	Societe Industriale Generale de Mecanique Appliquee (France)
S I I	Standards Institution of Israel
S I L	Speech Interference Level
S I M A	British Scientific Instrument Manufacturers Association
S I M I	Societa Italiana Macchine Idrauliche (Italy)
S I M I L E	Simulator of Immediate Memory In Learning Experiments
S I M M	Symbolic Integrated Maintenance Manual
S I M O	Societe Industrielle des Minerais de l'Ouest (France)
S I M S	Single-Item, Multi-Source
	Symbolic Integrated Maintenance System
S I M U L A	Simulation Language
S I N B	Southern Interstate Nuclear Board (USA)
S I N S	Ships Inertial Navigation System
S I N T E F	Selskapet for Industriell og Teknisk Forskning (Norway) (Engineering Research Institute)
S I N T O	Sheffield Interchange Organization

SINTRA	Societe Industrielle des Nouvelles Techniques Radioelectriques et de l'Electronique Francaise (France)
SIO	Scripps Institution of Oceanography (USA)
SIOUX	Sequential Iterative Operation Unit X
SIPRE	Snow Ice and Permafrost Research Establishment (US Army)
SIPROS	Simultaneous Processing Operating System
SIR	Semantic Information Retrieval
SIRA	British Scientific Instrument Research Association
	Safety Investigation Regulations (of Civil Aeronautics Board, USA)
SIRS	Satellite Infrared Spectrometer
SIS	Shorter-Interval Scheduling
	Svenska Interplanetariska Sallskapet (Sweden) (Swedish Interplanetary Society)
	prefix to Standards issued by SVS
SISS	Single-Item, Single-Source
SIT	Society of Instrument Technology
	Stevens Institute of Technology (USA)
SITA	Societe Internationale de Telecommunications Aeronautiques (International Society of Aeronautical Telecommunications)
SITC	Standard International Trades Classification (of United Nations)
SITE	Spacecraft Instrumentation Test Equipment
SIXPAC	System for Inertial Experiment Priority and Attitude Control
SJ	Statens Jarnvagar (Sweden) (Swedish State Railways)
SJCC	Spring Joint Computer Conference (USA)
SJCM	Standing Joint Committee on Metrication
SK-EOQC	Svenska Kommittee for EOQC (Sweden) (Swedish Committee for participation in EOQC)
SKOR	*Sperry Kalman* Optimum Reset
SL	Stor-Stockholms Lokalttrafiken (Sweden)
SLA	Special Libraries Association (USA)
SLA	Spacecraft LM Adapter
	Special Libraries Association (USA)
SLAC	Stanford Linear Accelerator Center (Stanford University, USA)
SLAET	Society of Licensed Aircraft Engineers and Technicians

S L A M	Supersonic Low-Altitude Missile
S L A P	Symbolic Language Assembler Programme
S L A R	Side-Looking Airborne Radar
S L A S H	*Seiler* Laboratory ALGOL Simulated Hybrid
S L A T E	Small Lightweight Altitude Transmission Equipment
S L B M	Ship *or* Submarine Launched Ballistic Missile
S L C	Simulated Liquistic Computer
S L C B	Single-Line Colour-Bar
S L C C	*Saturn* Launcher Computer Complex
S L E A T	Society of Laundry Engineers and Allied Trades
S L E D G E	Simulating Large Explosive Detonable Gas Experiment
S L E P	Second Large ESRO Project
S L I C	Selective Listing In Combination
S L M	Statistical Learning Model
S L O	Swept Local Oscillator
S L P	Skip-Lot Plan
S L R V	Surveyor Lunar Roving Vehicle
S L S	Segment Long Spacing
	Sidelobe Suppression
	Side Looking Sonar
S L T	Solid Logic Technology
S L T C	Society of Leather Trades Chemists
S M	Scientific Memorandum
	Special Memorandum
	Student Manual
S M A	Science Masters Association
	Staff Management Association
S M A R T	*Salton's* Magical Automatic Retriever of Texts
	Systems Management Analysis, Research and Test
S M A R T I E	Simple Minded Artificial Intelligence
S M B A	Scottish Marine Biological Association
S M C	Supply and Maintenance Command (US Army)
S M L M	Simple-Minded Learning Machine
S M M	Standard Method of Measurement
S M M P	Standard Methods of Measuring Performance
S M M T	Society of Motor Manufacturers and Traders
S M O G	Special Monitor Output Generator
S M O W	Standard Mean Ocean Water
S M P S	Simplified Message Processing Simulation
S M P T E	Society of Motion Picture and Television Engineers (USA)

S M R	Standard Malaysian Rubber
S M R A	Spring Manufacturers Research Association (now Spring Research Association)
S M R D	Spin Motor Rate Detector
S M R E	Safety in Mines Research Establishment (of Ministry of Fuel and Power)
S M S	Surface Missile System
	prefix to Standards issued by svs
S M S A	Silica and Moulding Sands Association
S M S G	School Mathematics Study Group
S M T I	Selective Moving Target Indicator
S N	Science *or* Scientific Note
S N A M E	Society of Naval Architects and Marine Engineers (USA)
S N A P	Simplified Numerical Automatic Programmer
	Space Nuclear Auxiliary Power
	Systems for Nuclear Auxiliary Power
S N C B	Societe Nationale des Chemins de Fer Belges (Belgium) (Belgian National Railways)
S N C F	Societe Nationale de Chemins de Fer Francaise (France) (French National Railways)
S N D T	Society of Non-Destructive Testing (USA)
S N E C M A	Societe Nationale d'Etude et de Construction de Moteurs d'Aviation (France)
S N E M S A	Southern New England Marine Sciences Association (USA)
S N M	Society of Nuclear Medicine (USA)
S N M M S	Standard Navy Maintenance and Material Management System (USN)
S N O P	Standardized Nomenclature of Pathology
S N O R T	Supersonic Naval Ordnance Research Track (USN)
S N P A	Societe Nationale des Petroles d'Aquitaine (France)
S N P M	Standard and Nuclear Propulsion Module
S N P O	Space Nuclear Propulsion Office (of NASA)
S N R	Signal to Noise Ratio
S N T	Society for Non-destructive Testing (USA)
S N V	Schweizerische Normenvereinigung (Switzerland) (Swiss Standards Association) (also known as Association Suisse de Normalisation)
S O C	Separated Orbit Cyclotron
	Specific Optimal Controller
	Superposition of Configurations

S O C C	Salvage Operational Control Centre
S O C I A	Societe pour l'Industrie Atomique (France)
S O C K O	Systems Operational Checkout
S O C M	Stand-Off Cluster Munitions
S O C O L	Societe de Construction d'Enterprises Generales (Belgium)
S O C R A T E S	System for Organizing Content to Review And Teach Educational Subjects
S O D A C	Society of Dyers and Colourists
S O E R O	Small Orbiting Earth Resources Observatory
S O F A R	Sound Fixing And Ranging
	Sound Fuzing and Ranging
S O F N E T	Solar Observing and Forecasting Network (of USAF)
S O F T	Simple Output Format Translator
S O G E P P A R	Societe de Gestion et de Participation (Belgium)
S O G E T R A	Societe Generale de Travaux (Belgium)
S O G E V	Societe Generale du Vide (France)
S O G R E A H	Societe Grenobloise d'Etudes et Applications Hydrauliques (France)
S O I	Standards Organisation of Iran (Iran)
S O L A R	Serialized On-Line Automatic Recording
S O L O G S	Standardization of Operations and Logistics
S O P H Y A	Supervisor of Physics Analysis
S O N A R	Sound Navigation And Ranging
S O P E L E M	Societe d'Optique, Precision, Electronique et Mecanique (France)
S O R	Specific Operating Requirement
S O R C A	Societe de Recherche Operationelle et d'Economie Appliquee (Belgium)
S O R E A S	Syndicat des Fabricants d'Organes et d'Equipment Aeronautiques et Spatiaux (France)
S O R E F A M E	Sociedades Reunidas Fabriacoes Metalicas (Portugal)
S O R I N	Societa Ricerche Impianti Nucleari (Italy)
S O T I M	Sonic Observation of the Trajectory and Impact of the Missiles
S P	Special Paper *or* Publication
	Specification
S P A	Society for Personnel Administration (USA)
	Systems and Procedures Association (USA)
S P A C	Spatial Computer
S P A C E	Sequential Position And Covariance Estimation
	Sidereal Polar Axis Celestial Equipment

S P A D	Satellite Position Predictor And Display
S P A D A T S	Space Detection and Tracking System
S P A D E	SPARTA Acquisition Digital Equipment
S P A M	Ship Position and Attitude Measurement
S P A N	Statistical Processing and Analysis
S P A R	Seagoing Platform for Acoustics Research
S P A R C	Space Air Relay Communications
S P A R S A	Sferics Pulse, Azimuth, Rate and Spectrum Analyzer
S P A R T A	Special Anti-missile Research Tests in Australia
S P A S U R	Space Surveillance
S P A Y Z	Spatial Property Analyzer
S P B	Special Boiling Point
S P E	Society of Plastics Engineers (USA)
S P E C O N	System Performance Effectiveness Conference
S P E E D	Subsistence Preparation by Electronic Energy Diffusion
S P E R T	Special Power Excursion Reactor Test
S P E T	Solid Propellant Electric Thruster
S P F A	Steel Plate Fabricators Association (USA)
S P G S	Secondary Power Generating Subsystem
S P I	Society of the Plastics Industry (USA)
	Specific Productivity Index
S P I C	Society of the Plastics Industry of Canada (Canada)
S P I D E R	Sonic Pulse-echo Instrument Designed for Extreme Resolution
S P I E	Scavenging—Precipitation—Ion—Exchange
	Self-Programmed Individualized Education
	Society of Photographic Instrumentation Engineers (USA)
S P I W	Special Purpose Individual Weapon
	Special Purpose Infantry Weapon
S P L	Software Programming Language
	Sound Pressure Level
S P M	Sequential Processing Machine
S P M S	System Programme Management Survey
S P O	System Programme Office
S P O C K	Simulated Procedure for Obtaining Common Knowledge
S P O T	Satellite Positioning and Tracking
S P R	Simplified Practice Recommendation (series issued by NBS)
S P R I	Scott Polar Research Institute

S P R C	Self-Propelled Robot Craft
S P R I T E	Solid Propellant Rocket Ignition and Evaluation
S P R T	Sequential Probability Ratio Test
S P S	Symbolic Programming System
S P S E	Society of Photographic Scientists and Engineers (USA)
S P U R	Space Power Unit Reactor
S Q A	Supplier Quality Assurance
S Q A P S	Supplier Quality Assurance Provisions
S Q C	Statistical Quality Control
S Q U I D	*Sperry* Quick Updating of Internal Documentation
	Superconducting Quantum Interference Device
S R	Scientific Report
	Special Regulation *or* Report
	Summary Report
S R A	Shop Replaceable Assembly
	Spring Research Association
S R A M	Short Range Attack Missile
S R B I I	Societe Royale des Ingenieurs et des Industriels (Belgium) (Royal Society of Engineers and Industrialists)
S R C	Science Research Council
	Systems Research Center (Case Institute of Technology) (USA)
S R C R A	Shipowners Refrigeration Cargo Research Association
S R C F E	Southern Regional Council for Further Education
S R D A S	Service Recording and Data Analysis System
S R D S	Standard Reference Data System
	Systems Research and Development Service (of FAA)
S R E	Sodium Reactor Experiment
S R G	Shift-Register Generator
S R I	*Spalling* Resistance Index
	Stanford Research Institute (USA)
S R M U	Space Research Management Unit (of Science Research Council)
S R R	Shift Register Recognizer
S R R B	Search and Rescue Radio Beacon
S R S	Statistical Reporting Service (of USDA)
S R S A	Scientific Research Society of America (USA)
S R T	Society of Radiologic Technologists (USA)

S R T I	Societe de Recherches Techniques et Industrielles (France)
S R U	Shop Replaceable Unit
	Societe du Raffinage d'Uranium (France)
S R V	Space Rescue Vehicle
S S A	Smoke Suppressant Additive
S S B	Single Sideband
S S B S C O M	SSB Suppressed-Carrier Optical Modulator
S S C	Ship Structure Committee (USA)
S S C N S	Ships Self-Contained Navigation System
S S D	Single Station Doppler
	Space Systems Division (USAF)
S S E	Special Support Equipment
S S E B	South of Scotland Electricity Board
S S E C	Secondary Schools Examination Council
	Selective Sequence Electronic Calculator
S S F F	Solid Smokeless Fuels Federation
S S G S	Standardized Space Guidance System
S S I D A	Steel Sheet Information and Development Association
S S M	Standard Stores Memoranda (numbered series issued by MOD)
S S M T	Stress Survival Matrix Test
S S P	Societe Suisse de Physique (Switzerland) (Physical Society of Switzerland)
S S R	Secondary Surveillance Radar
	Synchronous Stable Relaying
S S R C	Social Sciences Research Council (USA)
S S S A	Soil Science Society of America (USA)
S S T	Supersonic Transport
	prefix to numbered series issued by Office of Supersonic Transport Division, Federal Aviation Agency (USA)
S T	Select Time
St	prefix to series issued by Standards Division of the National Physical Laboratory
S T A A S	Surveillance and Target Acquisition Aircraft System
S T A D A N	Satellite Tracking and Data Acquisition Network (of NASA)
S T A F	Scientific and Technological Applications Forecast
S T A G	Strategy and Tactics Analysis Group (US Army)
S T A N	Standard or Standardisation

S T A R	Scientific and Technical Aerospace Report
	Speed Through Air Re-supply
	Star and Stellar Systems Advisory Committee (of ESRO)
S T A R T	Spacecraft Technology And Re-entry Tests
S T A T E	Simplified Tactical Approach and Terminal Equipment
S T C	Scientific and Technical Committee (of ESRO)
	System Test Complex
S T D	Salinity Temperature Depth
	Standard
	Subscriber Trunk Dialling
S T E M	Stored Tubular Extensible Member
S T E P	Simple Transition Electronic Processing
	Standard Terminal Programme
S T E T	Specialised Technique for Efficient Typesetting
S T I	Statens Teknologiske Institutt (Norway) (Government Technological Institute)
S T I B O K A	Stichting voor Bodemkartering (Netherlands) (Institute for Soil Survey)
S T I D	Scientific and Technical Information Division (of NASA)
S T I N F O	Scientific and Technical Information
S T I N G S	Stellar Inertial Guidance System
S T O L	Short Take-Off and Landing
S T O P S	Shipboard Toxicological Operational Protective System
S T O R E T	Storage and Retrieval
S T P	Standard Temperature and Pressure
S T P T C	Standardization of Tar Products Test Committee
S T R A D	Signal Transmission Reception and Distribution
S T R A P	Stellar Tracking Rocket Attitude Positioning
	Strategic Actions Planner
S T R A T C O M	Strategic Communications Command (US Army)
S T R E S S	Structural Engineering System Solver
S T R I P	Strategic Intermediate Planner
S T R O P	Strategic Optimizing Routine
S T T A	Service Technique des Telecommunications de l'Air (France)
S T U	Submersible Test Unit
S T U F F	System To Uncover Facts Fast
S T W P	Society of Technical Writers and Publishers (USA)

S U	Stanford University (USA)
S U B D I Z	Submarine Defence Identification Zone
S U D A A R	Stanford University, Division of Aeronautics and Astronautics (USA)
S U E D E	Surface Evaluation and Definition
S U G A R	*Sydney University* Giant Airshower Recorder
S U H L	*Sylvania* Ultrahigh Level Logic
S U I P R	Stanford University Institute for Plasma Research (USA)
S U M T	Sequential Unconstrained Minimization Technique
S U N	Solar Astronomy and General Astronomy Advisory Committee (of ESRO)
S U N Y	State University of New York (USA)
S U P A R C O	Space and Upper Atmosphere Research Committee (Pakistan)
S U P P S	Regional Supplementary Procedures (series issued by ICAO)
S U P R O X	Successive Approximation
S U R C A L	Surveillance Calibration
S U R F	Support of User Records and Files
S U R I	Syracuse University Research Institute (USA)
S U R R D	Southern Utilization Research and Development Division (USDA)
S U S I E	Stock Updating Sales Invoicing Electronically
S V I B	Strong Vocational Interest Blank
S V M I U	Associazione Italiana per lo Sviluppo della Ricerca nelle Macchine Utensili (Italy) (Association for the Development of Machine Tool Research)
S V S	Sveriges Standardisering-kommission (Sweden) (Standards Institute)
S V T L	Services Valve Test Laboratory
S V T P	Sound Velocity, Temperature and Pressure
S W A	Single Wire Armoured
S W E	Society of Women Engineers (USA)
S W E A T	Student Work Experience And Training
S W I E E E C O	Southwestern IEEE Conference and Exhibition (USA)
S W I F T	Selected Words In Full Title
	Software Implemented *Friden* Translator
S W O A	Scottish Woodland Owners Association
S W P A	Steel Works Plant Association

S Y B E L E C	Syndicat Belge d'Etudes et de Recherches Electroniques (Belgium) (Belgian Union for Electronics Study and Research)
S Y C O M	Synchronous Communications
S Y N T O L	Syntagmatic Organization of Language
S Y S T R A N	Systems Analysis Translator

T

T	Translation
T & E	Test and Evaluation
T A	Training Adviser
	Turbulence Amplifier
T A A	Trans-Australia Airlines (Australia)
	Transportation Association of America (USA)
T A A S	Three Axis Attitude Sensor
T A B	Technical Abstract Bulletin
	Technical Activities Board (of IEEE)
	Technical Analysis Branch
	Title Announcement Bulletin
T A C	Trapped Air Cushion
T A C A N	Tactical Air Navigation
T A C D E N	Tactical Data Entry Device
T A C E	Turbine Automatic Control Equipment
T A C F I R E	Tactical Fire direction system
T A C L A N	Tactical Landing system
T A C M A R	Tactical Multifunction Array Radar
T A C N A V	Tactical Navigation
T A C O D A	Target Coordinate Data
T A C O L	Thinned Aperture Computed Lens
T A C S	Tactical Air Control System
T A C S A T C O M	Tactical Satellite Communications
T A C T	Technological Aids to Creative Thought
T A E R S	Transportation Army Equipment Record System
T A G	Transient Analysis Generator
T A I C	Tokyo Atomic Industrial Consortium (Japan)
T A L	Trans-Alpine pipeline
T A L A R	Tactical Landing Approach Radar
T A L I C	Tyneside Association of Libraries for Industry and Commerce
T A M	Telephone Answering Machine
T A M I S	Telemetric Automated Microbial Identification System

T A P	Time-sharing Assembly Programme
	Transportes Aereos Portugueses (Portugal)
T A P P	Tarapur Atomic Power Project (India)
	Two Axis Pneumatic Pickup
T A P P I	Technical Association of the Pulp and Paper Industry (USA)
T A R A B S	Tactical Air Reconnaissance and Area Battlefield Surveillance
T A R C	The Army Research Council (US Army)
T A R E	Telemetry Automatic Reduction Equipment
T A R G E T	Thermal Advanced Reactor Gas-cooled Exploiting Thorium
T A R I F	Technical Apparatus for Rectification of Indifferent Films
T A R S	Terrain And Radar Simulator
T A R T	Twin Accelerator Ring Transfer
T A S C	Tactical Articulated Swimmable Carrier
T A S I	Time Assignment Speech Interpolation
T A S S	Tactical Avionics System Simulator
T A T	Transatlantic Telephone cable
T A W C	Tactical Air Warfare Center (USAF)
T B O	Time Between Overhaul
T C	Tariff Commission (USA)
	Technical Committee
	Thermo-Current
T C C	Temperature Coefficient of Capacitance
	Thermofor Catalytic Cracking
	Transfer Channel Control
T C D	Transistor Controlled Delay
T C I	Theoretical Chemistry Institute (of Wisconsin University, USA)
T C M F	Touch-Calling Multi-Frequency
T C R	Temperature Coefficient of Resistance
T C S T	Trichlorosilanated Tallow
T C X O	Temperature-Compensated Crystal Oscillator
T D	Thoria Dispersed
T D C	Top Dead Centre
T D D L	Time-Division Data Link
T D M	Time-Division Multiplex
T D M S	Telegraph Distortion Measurement Set
	Time-shared Data Management System
T D P	Technical Development Plan

T D R	Technical Data *or* Documentary Report
	Time-Delay Relay
	Time Domain Reflectometry
T E	Thermo-electric
T E A	Tyrethylaluminium
	Tunnel-Emission Amplifier
T E A M	Technique for Evaluation and Analysis of Maintainability
T E A M S	Test Evaluation And Monitoring System
T E C H M E M O	Technical Memorandum
T E C H R E P T	Technical Report
T E C O M	Test and Evaluation Command (us Army)
T E D	Translation Error Detector
T E E	Telecommunications Engineering Establishment
T E I C	Tissue Equivalent Ionization Chamber
T E L	Tetraethyl Lead
T E L I	Technisch-Literarische Gesellschaft (Germany) (Technical Literature Association)
T E L S I M	Teletypewriter Simulator
T E L T I P S	Technical Effort Locator and Technical Interest Profile System (us Army)
T E L U S	Telemetric Universal Sensor
T E M	Transmission Electron Microscope
	Transverse Electric and Magnetic field
T E M A	Telecommunication Engineering and Manufacturing Association
T E M P O	Technical Military Planning Operation
T E P G	Thermionic Electrical Power Generator
T E R	Transmission Equivalent Resistance
T E R P	Terrain Elevation Retrieval Programme
T E T R A	Terminal Tracking telescope
T E X T I R	Text Indexing and Retrieval
T F B	Towed Flexible Barge
T F E	Tetrafluoroethylene
T F R	Terrain-Following Radar
T F T	Thin-Film Transistor
T F X	Tactical Fighter Experiment
T G A	Thermo-Gravimetric Analysis
T G C A	Transportable Ground Control Approach
T H	prefix to numbered series issued by the Test House of the National Physical Laboratory
T H E	Technical Help to Exporters (section of British Standards Institute)

T H O M I S	Total Hospital Operating and Medical Information System
T H T R	Thorium High Temperature Reactor
T H T R A	Thorium High Temperature Reactor Association
T I	Teknologisk Institut (Denmark) (Technological Institute)
	Thermionic
T I A S	Target Identification and Acquisition System
T I C	Transducer Information Center (of Battelle Memorial Institute, USA)
T I C A	Technical Information Centre Administration
T I E	Technical Integration and Evaluation
T I F R	Tata Institute of Fundamental Research (India)
T I G	Tungsten Inert Gas
T I I F	Tactical Image Interpretation Facility
T I L	Technical Information and Library services (MINTECH)
T I M S	The Institute of Management Sciences
T I N R O	Tikhookeanskiy Nauchno Issledovatel'skiy Institut Rybnogo Khozyaystva i Okeanologii (USSR) (Pacific Scientific Research Institute of Fisheries and Oceanology)
T I O	Time Interval Optimization
T I P	Technical Information Project
T I P A	Tank and Industrial Plant Association
T I R	Technical Information or Intelligence Report
	Transports Internationale Routiers
T I R O S	Television Infrared Observation Satellite
T I R P	Total Internal Reflection Prism
T I R R	Texas Institute for Rehabilitation and Research (USA)
T I S	Technical Information Service
T L C	Thin-Layer Chromatography
T L D	Thermoluminescent Dosimeter
T L E	Theoretical Line of Escape
T L P	Threshold Learning Process
T L S	Terminal Landing System
T L V	Threshold Limit Value
T M	Technical Manual or Memorandum or Monograph
	Training Manual
T M A M A	Textile Machinery and Accessory Manufacturers Association
T M L	Tetra-Methyl-Lead

T M N	Technical and Management Note
T M S	Temperature Measurements Society (USA)
	The Metallurgical Society (of AIME) (USA)
T M T	Turbine Motor Train
T M V	Tobacco Mosaic Virus
T N	Technical Note
T N D C	Thai National Documentation Centre (Thailand)
T N O	Toegepast Natuurwetenschappelijk Onderzoek (Netherlands) (Central National Council for Applied Scientific Research)
T N T	Trinitroluene
T O E	Tables of Organisation and Equipment
T O M	Typical Ocean Model
T O P P	Terminal Operated Production Programme
T O P S	Total Operations Processing System
T O P System	Transducer Operated Pressure System
T O S	Tactile Operations System
	TIROS Operational Satellite
T O S S	TIROS Operational Satellite System
T O W	Tube-launched, Optically-tracked, Wire-guided
T P	Tandem Propeller
	Technical Pamphlet *or* Paper *or* Publication
	Transactions Paper
T P G	Transmission Project Group (of CEGB)
T P I	Tropical Products Institute (of ODM)
T P P C	Total Package Procurement Concept
T P R C	Thermophysical Properties Research Center (of Purdue University, USA)
T P S	Technical Problem Summary
T P T	Tramway de Pithiviers a Toury (France)
T P V	Thermophotovoltaic
T Q C A	Textile Quality Control Association (USA)
T R	Technical Report
T R A C	Text Reckoning And Compiling
	Transient Radiation Analysis by Computer
T R A C A L S	Traffic Control, Approach and Landing System
T R A C E	Tactical Readiness And Checkout Equipment
	Tape-controlled Reckoning And Checkout Equipment
	Tele-processing Recording for Analysis by the Customer Engineer
	Time-shared Routines for Analysis, Classification and Evaluation

T R A C E	Tolls Recording And Computing Equipment
	Transportable Automated Control Environment
T R A C O N	Terminal Radar Control
T R A D A	Timber Research and Development Association
T R A D E X	Target Resolution And Discrimination Experiment
T R A N S	Transaction *or* Translation
T R A N S I M	Transportation Simulator
TRANSNUCLEAIRE	Societe pour les Transports de l'Industries Nucleaire (France)
T R A P	Terminal Radiation Programme
T R E A T	Transient Reactor Test
T R E E	Transient Radiation Effects on Electronics
T R E N D	Tropical Environment Data
T R F	Tuned Radio Frequency
T R G	Technical Research Group
	Training
T R I	Tin Research Institute
T R I A L	Technique for Retrieving Information from Abstracts of Literature
T R I N D E L	Travaux Industriels pour l' Electricite (France)
T R I U M F	Tri-University Meson Facility (Canada)
T R L	Transistor-Resistor Logic
T R M	Thermal Remanent Magnetization
T R N	Technical Research Note
T R S	Time Reference System
	Torry Research Station (MINTECH)
	Tough Rubber Sheathed
T R T A	Traders Road Transport Association
T R U M P	Total Revision and Upgrading of Maintenance Procedures
T S A	Time Series Analysis
	Training Situation Analysis
T S C L T	Transportable Satellite Communications Link Terminal
T S D	Temperature-Salinity-Density-Depth
T S E	Twist Setting Efficiency
	Turk Standardlari Enstitusu (Turkey) (Turkish Standards Institute)
T S H	Thyroid-Stimulating Hormone
TS I A M	T'sentral'nyy Nauchno Issledovatel'skiy Institut Aviatsionnogo Motorostroyeniya (USSR) (Central Scientific Research Institute of Aero-Engine Construction)

TS N I D A	Tsentral'nyy Nauchno Issledovatel'skiy Dizel'nyy Institut (USSR) (Central Scientific Research Diesel Institute)
TS N I E L	Tsentral'naya Nauchno Issledovatel'skaya Elektrotekhnicheskaya Laboratoriya (USSR) (Central Scientific Research Electrical Engineering Laboratory)
TS N I I	Tsentral'nyy Nauchno Issledovatel'skiy Institut (USSR) (Central Scientific Research Institute)
TS N I I Ch M	Tsentral'nyy Nauchno Issledovatel'skiy Institut Chernoy Metallurgii (USSR) (Central Scientific Research Institute of Ferrous Metallurgy)
TS N I I M F	Tsentral'nyy Nauchno Issledovatel'skiy Institut Morskogo Flota (USSR) (Central Scientific Research Institute of the Maritime Fleet)
TS N I I P O	Tsentral'nyy Nauchno Issledovatel'skiy Institut Protivopozharnoy Oborony (USSR) (Central Scientific Research Institute for Fire Prevention)
TS N I I P S	Tsentral'nyy Nauchno Issledovatel'skiy Institut Promyshlennykh Sooruzhenii (USSR) (Central Scientific Research Institute of Industrial Structures)
TS N I I S	Tsentral'nyy Nauchno Issledovatel'skiy Institut Svyazi (USSR) (Central Scientific Research Institute of Communications)
TS N I I T M A Sh	Tsentral'nyy Nauchno Issledovatel'skiy Institut Tekhnologii i Mashinostroyeniya (USSR) (Central Scientific Research Institute of Technology and Machine Building)
TS NILELEKTROM	Tsentral'naya Nauchno Issledovatel'syaya Laboratoriya Elektricheskoy Obrabotki Materialov (USSR) (Central Scientific Research Laboratory for Electrical Treatment of Materials)
T S R	Technical Summary Report
T S S	Time Sharing System
T S U S	Tariff Schedules of the United States
T T	Technical Translation
T T A	Turbine-Alternator Assembly
T T B W R	Twisted Tape Boiling Water Reactor
T T C P	Tripartite Technical Cooperation Programme
T T F	Timber Trade Federation
T T G	Technical Translation Group
T T I	Time-Temperature Indicator
T T L	Transistor-Transistor Logic

T T S	Teletypesetting
	Temporary Threshold Shift
T U	Tulsa University (USA)
T U B - I R	Teschnische Universitat, Berlin—Institut fur Raumfahrttechnik (Germany) (Technical University, Berlin—Institute for Space Technology)
T U C	Trades Union Congress
T U C C	Triangle Universities Computation Center (USA)
T U D	Technology Utilization Division (of NASA)
T U R P S	Terrestrial Unattended Reactor Power System
T U V	Technische Uberwachungs-Vereine (Germany) (Technical Supervisory Societies)
T V A	Tennessee Valley Authority (USA)
T V C	Thrust Vector Control
T W	Travelling Wave
T W C R T	Travelling Wave Cathode Ray Tube
T W I	Training Within Industry
T W T	Travelling Wave Tube
T X E	Telephone Exchange Electronic

U

U A I	Union des Associations Internationales (Union of International Associations)
U A I D E	Users of Automatic Information Display Equipment
U A R A E E	United Arab Republic Atomic Energy Establishment
U B M	Unit Bill of Material
U C	University of Chicago (USA)
U C C A	Universities Central Council on Admissions
U C C R S	Underwater Coded Command Release System
U C E A	University Council for Educational Administration (USA)
U C I M U	Unione Contruttori Italiana Macchine Utensili (Italy) (Union of Italian Machine Tool Manufacturers)
U C L A	University of California, Los Angeles (USA)
U C P T E	Union pour la Coordination de la Production et du Transport de l'Electricite (Union for the Coordination of the Production and Transport of Electrical Power)
U C R L	University of California, Lawrence Radiation Laboratory (USA)

U D A R	Universal Digital Adaptive Recognizer
U D C	Universal Decimal Classification
U D O F F T	Universal Digital Operational Flight Trainer Tool
U D O P	UHF Doppler
U D P G	Uridine Diphosphate Glucose
U D P G A	Uridine Diphosphate Glucuronic Acid
U E R	Union Europeene de Radiodiffusion (European Broadcasting Union)
U F	Urea-formaldehyde
U F A W	Universities Federation for Animal Welfare
U F C	Uniform Freight Classification (USA)
U F O	Unidentified Flying Object
U G C	University Grants Committee
U H F	Ultra High Frequency
U H T	Ultra High Temperature
U I A	Union International des Architects (International Union of Architects)
	Union of International Associations
U I C	Union Internationale des Chemins de fer (International Union of Railways)
U I C C	Union Internationale Contre le Cancer (International Union Against Cancer)
U I E O	Union of International Engineering Organisations
U I M	Union of International Motor-boating
U I T	Union Internationale des Telecommunications (International Telecommunications Union (of UNO))
U I T P	Union Internationale des Transports Publics (International Union of Public Transport)
U K A C	United Kingdom Automation Council
U K A E A	United Kingdom Atomic Energy Authority
U K R A S	United Kingdom Railway Advisory Service
U K S M	United Kingdom Scientific Mission
U L	Underwriters Laboratories (USA)
U L B	Universal Logic Block
U L I C P	Universal Log Interpretation Computer Programme
U M F	Urea-Melamine Formaldehyde
U M I S T	University of Manchester Institute of Science and Technology
U M P	Upper Mantle Project (of ICSU)
U N	United Nations Organisation
U N A D S	*Univac* Automated Documentation System

U N A M A C E	Universal Automatic Map Compilation Equipment
U N C A S T	United Nations Conference on the Applications of Science and Technology
U N C T A D	United Nations Conference on Trade And Development
U N E S C O	United Nations Educational, Scientific and Cultural Organisation
U N E T A S	United Nations Emergency Technical Aid Service
U N E	prefix to Standards issued by IRATRA
U N I	Ente Nazionale Italiano de Unificazione (Italy) (Italian Standards Association)
U N I C O M	Universal Integrated Communications
U N I D O	United Nations Industrial Development Organization
U N I P E D E	Union Internationale des Producteurs et Distributeurs d'Energie (International Union of Producers and Distributors of Electrical Energy)
U N I T A R	United Nations Institute for Training and Research (of UNO)
U N O	United Nations Organisation
U N S C E A R	United Nations Scientific Committee on the Effects of Atomic Radiation
U P A D I	Union Panamericano de Associanciones de Ingenieros (Pan-American Federation of Engineering Societies)
U P L I F T S	*University of Pittsburgh* Linear File Tandem System
U P R	Ultrasonic Paramagnetic Resonance
U P U	Universal Postal Union (of UNO)
U R A	Universities Research Associates (USA)
U R I P S	Undersea Radioisotope Power Supply
U R P A	University of Rochester, Department of Physics and Astronomy (USA)
U R R I	Urban-Regional Research Institute (Michigan State University, USA)
U R S	Universal Regulating System
U R S I	Union Radio-Scientifique Internationale (International Scientific Radio Union)
U R V	Undersea Rescue Vehicle
U S A	United States of America
U S A A V L A B S	United States Army Aviation Materiel Laboratories

U S A A V N S	United States Army Aviation School
U S A A V N T A	United States Army Aviation Test Activity
U S A B A A R	United States Army Board for Aviation Accident Research
U S A B E S R L	United States Army Behavioral Science Research Laboratory
U S A B R L	United States Army Ballistics Research Laboratories
U S A C D C	United States Army Combat Developments Command
U S A C D C A V N A	United States Army Combat Developments Command Aviation Agency
U S A C D C C B R A	United States Army Combat Developments Command Chemical-Biological-Radiological Agency
U S A C D I A	United States Army Developments Command Infantry Agency
U S A E C	United States Atomic Energy Commission
U S A E C O M	United States Army Electronics Command
U S A E P G	United States Army Electronic Proving Ground
U S A E R D L	United States Army Engineer Research and Development Laboratories
U S A F	United States Air Force
U S A F I	United States Armed Forces Institute (USDOD)
U S A F S C	United States Air Force Systems Command
U S A I D	United States Agency for International Development (USA)
U S A L M C	United States Army Logistics Management Center
U S A M	Unified Space Applications Mission (of NASA)
U S A M C	United States Army Materiel Command
U S A M R D G	United States Army Medical Research and Development Command
U S A M R L	United States Army Medical Research Laboratory
U S A P H S	United States Army Primary Helicopter School
U S A P R O	United States Army Personnel Research Office (now USABESRL)
U S A R E U R	United States Army Europe
U S A R I E M	United States Army Research Institute of Environmental Medicine
U S A R J	United States Army Japan
U S A R P	United States Antarctic Research Programme
U S A R P A	United States Army Radio Propagation Agency
U S A R P A C	United States Army Pacific

USARV	United States Army Vietnam
USASCAF	United States Army Service Center for Army Forces
USASCC	United States Army Strategic Communications Command
USASI	United States of America Standards Institute
USATEA	United States Army Transportation Engineering Agency
USATECOM	United States Army Test and Evaluation Command
USBM	United States Bureau of Mines
USC	United States Congress
USC&GS	United States Coast and Geodetic Survey (USDC)
USCEE	University of Southern California, Department of Electrical Engineering (USA)
USCG	United States Coast Guard (USA)
USD	Ultimate Strength Design
USDA	United States Department of Agriculture
USDC	United States Department of Commerce
USDL	United States Department of Labor
US DOD	United States Department of Defense
USFS	United States Frequency Standard
USFWS	United States Fish and Wildlife Service (US Dept of the Interior)
USGPO	United States Government Printing Office
USGR	United States Government Report
USGRDR	United States Government Research and Development Report
USGS	United States Geological Survey (US Dept of the Interior)
USIA	United States Information Agency
USIAS	Union Syndicale des Industries Aeronautiques et Spatiales (France)
USL	Underwater Sound Laboratory (USN)
USN	United States Navy
USMA	United States Maritime Administration (US Dept of Commerce)
	United States Military Academy
USNEL	United States Navy Electronics Laboratory (now reorganised as Navy Undersea Warfare Center *and* Navy Command, Control and Communications Center)
USNRDL	United States Naval Radiological Defense Laboratory

U S N U S L	United States Navy Underwater Laboratory
U S O E	United States Office of Education
U S P H S	United States Public Health Service
U S R L	Underwater Sound Reference Laboratory (USN)
U S S R	Union of Soviet Socialists Republics
U S T S	United States Travel Service (US Dept of Commerce)
U S W	Undersea Warfare
U S W B	United States Weather Bureau
U T A	Union de Transports Aeriens (France)
U T A C	Union Technique de l'Automobile, du motorcycle et du Cycle (France) (Technical Association for the Motor, Motorcycle and Cycle Industries)
U T E C	Utah University College of Engineering (USA)
U T I A S	University of Toronto, Institute for Aerospace Studies (Canada)
U T M	Universal Transverse Mercator
U T S	Ultimate Tensile Strength
	Underwater Telephone System
U U T	Unit Under Test
U X B	Unexploded Bomb

V

V A	Value Analysis
V A B	Vertical Assembly Building
V A E P	Variable, Attributes, Error Propagation
V A L S A S	Variable Length word Symbolic Assembly System
V A M	Vector Airborne Magnetometer
	Vogel's Approximation Method
V A M I	Vsesoyuznyy Alyuminiyeo Magniyevyy Institut (USSR) (All-Union Aluminium Magnesium Institute)
V A M P	Vector Arithmetic Multi-processor
	Visual-Acoustic-Magnetic Pressure
V A P S	VSTOL Approach System
V A R A D	Varying Radiation
V A R R	Variable Range Reflector
V A S C A	Electronic Valve and Semi-Conductor Manufacturers Association
V A S I	Visual Approach Slope Indicator
V A S T	Versatile Avionic Shop Test system
V A T E	Versatile Automatic Test Equipment

V A T L S	Visual Airborne Target Location System
V B B	Vattenbyggnadsbyran (Sweden)
V B L	*Voyager* Biological Laboratory
V C I	Volatile Corrosion Inhibitor
V C O	Voltage Controlled Oscillator
V D	Verbal Discrimination
V D E	Verband Deutscher Elektrotechniker (Germany) (German Association of Electrical Engineers)
V De H	Verein Deutscher Eisenhuttenleute (Germany) (German Iron and Steel Research Association)
V D E W	Vereinigung Deutscher Elektrizitatswerke (Germany) (Association of German Electricity Supply Undertakings)
V D G	Verein Deutscher Giessereifachleute (Germany) (German Association for Foundry and Casting Operations)
V D I	Verein Deutscher Ingenieure (Germany) (German Association of Engineers)
V D M A	Verein Deutscher Maschinenbau-Anstalten (Germany) (German Association of Machinery Manufacturers)
V D R I	Verein Deutscher Revisions-Ingenieure (Germany) (German Association of Engineering Inspection)
V D S	Variable Depth Sonar
V D S I	Verein Deutscher Sicherheits-Ingenieure (Germany) (German Association of Safety Engineers)
V E	Value Enginering
V E A	Value Engineering Association
V E B	Variable Elevation Beam
V E M	Vaso-Excitor Material
V E R A	Versatile Experimental Reactor Assembly
V E V	Voice Excited Vocoder
V F O	Variable Frequency Oscillator
V F R	Visual Flight Rules
V F W	Vereinigte Flugtechnische Werke (Germany)
V G P I	Visual Glide Path Indicator
V H F	Very High Frequency
V I	Veiligheidsinstituut (Netherlands) (Safety Institute)
V I A M	Vsesoyuznyy Nauchno Issledovatel'skiy Institut Aviatsionnykh Materialov (USSR) (All-Union Scientific Research Institute of Aviation Materials)

V I C	Variable Instruction Computer
V I N I T I	Vsesoyuznyy Institut Nauchnoy i Teknicheskoy Informatsii (USSR) (All-Union Institute of Scientific and Technical Information)
V I P	Variable Information Processing
V I P S	Voice Interruption Priority System
V I S T A	Volunteers In Service To America
V I T	Vertical Interval Test
V I T A L	Variably Initialized Translator for Algorithmic Languages
V L A	Very Large Array
V L F	Very Low Frequency
V M C	Visual Meteorological Conditions
V M D	Vertical Magnetic Dipole
V N I I	Vsesoyuznyy Nauchno Issledovatel'skiy Instrumental'nyi Institut (USSR) (All-Union Scientific Research Institute of Instruments)
V N I I E M	Vsesoyuznyy Nauchno Issledovatel'skiy Institut Elektromekhaniki (USSR) (All-Union Scientific Research Institute of Electromechanics)
V N I I F T R I	Vsesoyuznyy Nauchno Issledovatel'skiy Institut Fiziko-Technicheskikh i Radiotekhnicheskikh Izmereniy (USSR) (All-Union Scientific Research Institute of Physical-technical and Radiotechnical Measurements)
V N I I G I M	Vsesoyuznyy Nauchno Issledovatel'skiy Institut Gidrotekhniki i Melioratsii (USSR) (All-Union Scientific Research Institute of Hydraulic Engineering and Land Reclamation)
V N I I M	Vsesoyuznyy Nauchno Isslesdovatel'skiy Institut Metrologii (USSR) (All-Union Scientific Research Institute of Metrology)
V N I I N P	Vsesoyuznyy Nauchno Issledovatel'skiy Institut Neftyanoy Promyshlennosti (USSR) (All-Union Scientific Research Institute of the Petroleum Industry)
V N I I S	Vsesoyuznyy Gosudarstvennyy Nauchno Issledovatel'skiy Institut Stekla (USSR) (All-Union State Scientific Research Institute of Glass)
V N I I T S	Vsesoyuznyy Nauchno Issledovatel'skiy Institut Tsementnoy promyshlennosti (USSR) (All-Union Scientific Research Institute of the Cement Industry)

V N I I T S	Vsesoyuznyy Nauchno Issledovatel'skiy Institut Tverdykh Splavov (USSR) (All-Union Scientific Research Institute of Hard Alloys)
V N I R O	Vsesoyuznyy Nauchno Issledovatel'skiy Institut Rybnogo khozyaystva i Okeanografii (USSR) (All-Union Scientific Research Institute of Fishing and Oceanography)
V O A	Vereniging Ontwikkeling Arbeidstechniek (Netherlands) (Work Study Association)
V O D	Velocity Of Detonation
V O R	VHF Omni-Range
V O R D A C	VOR Distance Measuring Equipment for Average Coverage
V R I C	Variable Resistive Components Institute (USA)
V S	Variable Sweep
V S B	Vestigial Sideband
V S C F	Variable-Speed Constant-Frequency
V S E G I N G E O	Vsesoyuznyy Nauchno Issledovatel'skiy Institut Gidrogeologii i Inzhenernoy Geologii (USSR) (All-Union Scientific Research Institute of Hydro-geology and Engineering Geology)
V S I	Vertical Speed Indicator
V S M	Verein Schweizerischer Maschinen-Industrielle (Switzerland)
V S M F	Visual Search Microfilm File
V S S	Variable Stability System
V S T O L	Vertical and Short Take-Off and Landing
V S W R	Voltage Standing Wave Ratio
V T	Variable Time
V T L	Variable Threshold Logic
V T M	Voltage-Tunable Magnetism
V T O H L	Vertical Take-Off and Horizontal Landing
V T O L	Vertical Take-Off and Landing
V T O V L	Vertical Take-Off Vertical Landing
V TS	Vychislitel'nyy Tsentre (USSR) (Computer Centre)
V T T	Valtion Teknillinen Tutkimuslaitos (Finland) (State Institute for Technical Research)
V T V M	Vacuum Tube Voltmeter
V U M S	Vyzkumny Ustav pro Matematickych Stroju (Czechoslovakia) (Research Institute for Mathematical Machines)

V U O S O	Vyzkumny Ustav Obrasecich Stroju a Obrabeni (Czechoslovakia) (Machine Tool and Metal Cutting Research Institute)
V V I A	Voyenno Vozdushnaya Inzhenernaya Akademiya (USSR) (Air Force Engineering Academy)
V V S	Vereniging Voor Statistick (Netherlands) (Statistical Society)
V W P I	Vacuum Wood Preservers Institute (USA)

W

W A D C	Wright Air Development Center (USAF)
W A D E X	Word and Author Index
W A G R	Western Australian Government Railways (Australia)
	Windscale Advanced Gas-cooled Reactor
W A L	Watertown Arsenal (US Army)
W A M	Worth Analysis Model
W A P	Work Assignment Procedure
W A S P	Workshop Analysis and Scheduling Procedure
W A T S	Wide Area Telephone Service
W A V F H	World Association of Veterinary Food Hygienists
W B A N	Weather Bureau, Air Force and Navy (USA)
W B C O	Waveguide Below Cut-Off
W B G T	Wet Bulb Globe Thermometer
W B P	Weather and Boil Proof
W D C	World Data Centre
W E C O M	Weapons Command (US Army)
W E M A	Winding Engine Manufacturers Association
W E R	Worth Estimating Relationship
W E S	Waterways Experiment Station (US Army)
	Women's Engineering Society
W E S C O N	Western Electronics Show and Convention (USA)
W E S R A C	Western Research Application Center (of University of Southern California, USA)
W E U	Western European Union
W F A	White Fish Authority
W F M H	World Federation for Mental Health
W G B C	Wave Guide operating Below Cut-Off
W H O	World Health Organisation (of UNO)
W H O I	Woods Hole Oceanographic Institution (USA)
W H P C	Wage and Hour and Public Contracts division (US Dept of Labor)
W H R A	Welwyn Hall Research Association

W H R C	World Health Research Centre
W I B	Werkgroep Instrument Beoordeling (Netherlands) (Working Group on Instrument Behaviour)
W I R A	Wool Industries Research Association
W I S	Wisconsin University (USA)
W I S - T I C	Wisconsin University, Theoretical Chemistry Institute (USA)
W J C C	Western Joint Computer Conference (USA)
W K S	Bundesversuchs-und forschungsanstalt fur Warme-, Kalte- und Stromungstechnik (Austria) (Government Testing and Research Station for Heat, Cold and Flow Technology)
W L A	Wingfoot Lighter-than-Air Society (USA)
W M A	World Medical Association
W M O	World Meteorological Organisation (of UNO)
W M S	World Magnetic Survey
W M S I	Western Management Science Institute (of University of California (USA))
W M S O	Wichita Mountains Seismological Observatory (USA)
W O G	Water, Oil or Gas
W P A F B	Wright Patterson Air Force Base (USAF)
W P C	Wood Plastic Combination *or* Composite
	World Petroleum Congress
	World Power Conference
W P C F	Water Pollution Control Federation (USA)
W P R L	Water Pollution Research Laboratory (MINTECH)
W P S A	World's Poultry Science Association
W R	Wissenschaftsrat (Germany) (Science Council)
W R A	Water Research Association
	Weapon Replaceable Assembly
W R A I N	Walter Reed Army Institute of Nursing (US Army)
W R A I R	Walter Reed Army Institute of Research (US Army)
W R A P	Weighted Regression Analysis Programme
W R E	Weapons Research Establishment (Dept of Supply, Australia)
W S D	Working Stress Design
W S E	Washington Society of Engineers (USA)
	Western Society of Engineers (USA)
W S E D	Weapon Systems Evaluation Division (of IDA)
W S E I A I C	Weapon System Effectiveness Industry Advisory Committee (USDOD)

W S L	Warren Spring Laboratory (MINTECH)
W S M R	White Sands Missile Range (US Army)
W T R	Western Test Range (of NASA)
W U	Washington University (USA)
W V A	World Veterinary Association
W W P A	Western Wood Products Association (USA)

X

X - sonad	Experimental Sonic Azimuth Detector
X B T	Expendable Bathythermograph
X H M O	Extended Huckel Molecular Orbit
X O	Crystal Oscillator
X R M	X-Ray Microanalyser
X R P M	X-Ray Projection Microscope

Y

Y A G	Yttrium Aluminium Garnet
Y E A	Yale Engineering Association (USA)
Y I G	Yttrium Iron Garnet
Y M B A	Yacht and Motor Boat Association

Z

Z A D C A	Zinc Alloy Die Casters Association
Z A E D	Zentralstelle fur Atomkernenergie Dokumentation (Germany) (Atomic Energy Documentation Centre)
Z A V	Zentralstelle fur Arbeitsvermittlung (Germany) (Central Placement Office)
Z D	Zero Defects
Z D A	Zinc Development Association
Z D T	Zero-Ductility Transition
Z E B R A	Zero Energy Breeder Reactor Assembly
Z E E P	Zero Energy Experimental Pile
Z E N I T H	Zero Energy Nitrogen Heated Thermal reactor
Z E R L I N A	Zero Energy Reactor for Lattice Investigations and study of New Assemblies
Z E T A	Zero Energy Thermonuclear Apparatus
Z H S	Zero Hoop Stress
Z I F	Zentralinstitut fur Fertigungstechnik (Germany) (Central Institute for Production Engineering)

Z I S	Zentralinstitut fur Schweisstechnik (Germany) (Central Institute for Welding Technique)
Z P R	Zero Power Reactor
Z V E I	Zentralverband der Elektrotechnischen Industrie (Germany)

VAB, VAPS, VASI, VBL, VFR, VFW, VGPI, VIAM, VIPS, VMD, VOR, VORDAC, VSCF, VSI, VSTOL, VTOHL, VTOL, VTOVL, VVIA, WADC, WTR

Agriculture
ABLE, ABMAC, ABRO, ADSA, AEA, AEC, AECB, AIC, AMS, AOAC, ARC, ARS, ASAE, ASCS, CAB, CACA, CAES, CEA, CICA, CIDA, CNEEMA, CNRA, CSAE, DEA, DSI, EAC, ECA, EHF, EHS, ELMIA, FAO, FAS, FCIM, FEF, FIPA, FMD, IAAC, IAIAS, ICAI, IDF, IFAP, IICA, IRSIA, ITT, IWC, MAFF, NAAS, NACA, NIAE, PIL, PRC, USDA

Air conditioning
ARI, ASHRAE, CEDRIC, COSTIC, HEVAC

Air pollution
AP, APCA, CMVPCB, IUAPPA

Aluminium
AA, ADA, AIAG, CIDA, OEAS, VAMI

Animals
ABRO, AVMA, BVA, CVMA, EAAP, IAP, ICLA, IGZN, ILAR, IRAD, PIL, PRC, UFAW, WAVFH, WPSA, WVA

Apparatus
ACEEA, BEAB, BLWA, CECED, CEE, EWF, SAMA

Architecture
AIA, BSA, CIAM, DAI, FAS, IUA, RIBA, SIA, UIA

Arctic and Antarctic areas
AAL, AINA, ANARE, ANCAR, ARLIS, CPR, CRREL, IAA, INACH, SANCAR, SCAR, TAAF, USARP

Associations for science and technology
AA, AAAS, ACLS, ACSP, ACT, AFOSR, AFSAB, AMSOC, ANAAS, ANVAR, ANRT, ARDC, ARO, ARO-D, ARPA, ASRCT, BA, BASRA, CAAS, CCRST, CDRA, CENATRA, CIAI, CIMRST, CISIR, CNR, CNRS, COSPUP, COSRIMS, CRSIM, CSIR, CSIRO, CSP, DFG, DRB, DRME, DSB, DVTWV, FCST, FGAF, ICAITI, ICSU, IIRS, INAT, INSA, IRI, IRSIA, ISCT, IVA, IVIC, JSC, JTI, JUSE, KTH, LFTI, MPG, NAS, NAS/NRC, NRAC, NRC, NRDC, NRE, NSB, NSF, NTNF, NZDSIR, PSAC, PCSIR, RI, RIAS, RSC, SCAR, SFIT, SRC, SRSA, TARC, TIFR, TNO, TsNII, UNCAST, UNESCO, URA, VTT, WR

Astronautics see Aeronautics and astronautics

Astronomy and astrophysics
AAO, CIPASH, CLARC, COS, FAGS, GARP, HARP, HMNAO, IAU, IFA, ITA, JILA, LAS, NAO, NRAO, QSG, QSO, QSRS, SAO, VLA

Atomic energy
AAEC, ACRS, AE, AEA, AECB, AECL, AEE, AEET, AERE, AFC, AFINE, AGR, AHSB, AIEA, AIENDF, ANL, ANP, ANS, APF, ART, ARTE, ATEN, AWRE, BCD, BCMM, BEN, BEPO, BGRR, BHW, BMR, BNL, BNX, BWPR, BWR, CANDU, CEA, CEN, CEN-Ca, CEN-FAR, CEN-G, CEN-S, CERCA, CERN, CHF, CINS, CIR, CNA, CNEN, CRNL, CSE, DAPHNE, DF, DFR, DIMPLE, DMTR, EAES, EANDC, EBR, EBWR, ECFA, ENEA, ETP, ETR, EURATOM, EUREX, FAPIG, FARET, FBR, FERD, FFTF, FIEN, FORATOM, FPA, FRAMTOME, FRCTF, GAAA, GCFR, GIAT, GIIN, GKIAE, GLEEP, GSN, HANE, HASL, HASP, HDMR, HECTOR, HERALD, HERMES, HERO, HFBR, HFIR, HIFAR, HORACE, HTGCR, HTGR, HWCTR, HWOCR, IAEA, IANEC, IBR, ICPP, IEA, IFA, IKO, ILW, ING, INIS, INSJ, INSTN, IRS, ITL, JAEC, JAERI, JAFC, JAIF, JAPCO, JCAE, JCAR, JEN, JPDR, JRIA, LACBWR, LCRE, LENA, LITR, LLW, LMFBR, LOFT, LRL, LSBR, LWBR,

LWR, MAIG, MCR, MITR, MPBE, MPRE, MSRE, MTR, NAIG, NBSR, NDL, NERO, NERVA, NESTOR, NINA, NIRNS, NMCS, NPD, NPFO, NRDS, NRTS, NRU, NRX, NSPP, NUCLEX, NUDAC, NUDETS, OGRDP, OIYaI, ORNL, ORR, PENA, PF, PFR, PHW, PLUTO, PRTR, PTR, PWR, RCN, REON, RHEL, RIFT, RIG, RIPPLE, RSAC, RTG, SAAEB, SAFE, SCORPIO, SCUMRA, SEEN, SEFOR, SEIN, SELNI, SENA, SENTA, SEPIA, SG, SGAE, SGRCA, SINB, SLAC, SNAP, SNPO, SOC, SOCIA, SORIN, SPERT, SPIE, SPUR, SRE, TAIC, TAPP, TARGET, TART, THTR, THTRA, TRANSNUCLEAIRE, TREAT, TRIUMF, TTBWR, TURPS, UAREE, UKAEA, URIPS, USAEC, VERA, WAGR, ZAED, ZEBRA, ZEEP, ZENITH, ZERLINA, ZETA, ZPR

Automobile engineering
AA, AAMVA, ASAE, BINA, BPICA, DAF, DERV, FISITA, FVRDE, IOMTR, JAMTS, MAA, MIRA, NIITAvtoprom, PCV, RAC, SMMT, UTAC

Automation
IFAC, INTERKAMA, SABE, SEDA, UKAC

Bakeries and baking
BBIRA, BEMS

Bearings
BRBMA, ENIPP

Behavioural sciences
AIR, APRC, APRE, BESRL, FPRC, HumRRO, ICAP, RNPL, RNPRC, USABESRL, USAPRO

Biochemistry
BS, CBS, FEBS, IUB

Biology
ABL, ABLE, AIBS, BES, BIBRA, BIOS, BIOSIS, BPA, BW, CBE, CFBS, EMBO, FASEB, IBP, IUBS, MAMBO, NBL, VBL

Boilers
ABMA, ASB

Brewing
BBEA

Brushes
BBMRA

Building
ABC, ACDB, AEPB, APROBA, ASBC, ASBI, BCSA, BILG, BOAC, BRI, BRS, CEBTP, CECM, CEDOC, CEFB, CIB, CIDB, CIDE, CIRIA, CITB, CITC, CSTB, CSTC, DBA, DBR, DSTV, EIB, FGW, FHA, FIBTP, FIDOR, FMCE, HLG, IABSE, IBCC, IBM, IBSAC, ICBO, IFHP, IH, IOMB, ISMCM, ITB, ITBTP, MPBW, NBA, NBO, NBRI, NHBRC, SBCC, SCIR, SECO, sfB, SMM

Business equipment
BEMA, BETA, OMEF

Cartography see Mapping

Cement
CCA, CEMBUREAU, GPC, VNIITS

Ceramics
ACS, BCRA, CRIC, EVKI, GIKI, IPSC, NICE

Chemical engineering
ABCM, ABMAC, AIChEe, BCPMA, CIA, IChemE, SCI

Chemistry
ACS, ATR, CDEE, CI, CIC, DECHEMA, EDC, GDC, IFKh, IKh, ILMAC, IONKh, IRCHA, IUPC, LGC, RIC, SAC, WIS-TIC

Chromatography
GCMS, GLC, GSC, TLC

Civil engineering
ASCE, CER, CERA, CIRIA, ICE, ICES

Clocks and watches
BCWMA, CETEHOR, LSRH

Coal and coke
BCR, BCRA, BCURA, CECA, CERCHAR, COED, CPPA, CTRA, DGMK, ECSC, INICHAR

Colour
AATCC, BCC, CIC, DCASA, ISCC, OCCA, SDC, SDCA, SODAC

Combustion engineering
BICEMA, BICERI, CEA, CIMAC

Commerce see Trade

Compressed air see Pneumatics

Computers see Data processing

Concrete
ACI, BCCF, BPCF, CCA, CMMA, DBV, IRABA, NRCMA, RCA, SBB

Consumers organisations
BEUC, C&MS, CA, IOCU, ILC, RICA

Contamination
AACC

Copper
CDA

Corrosion
CEBELCOR, EFC, NACE, VCI

Cranes (see also Materials handling)
ACM, LMCA

Crystallography
IK, IUCr

Cutlery
CATRA

Data processing
ABAC, ABACUS, ACE, ACM, ACU, ADAC, ADAPSO, ADC, ADIS, ADP, ADPS, ADRS, ADSAF, ADX, AGILE, AICA, AIMS, AIRS, ALDP, ALGOL, ALMS, ALP, ALPHA, ALS, AMBIT, AMIS, AMNIP, AMOS, AMTCL, AMTRAN, ANI, APACHE, APS, ARAL, ASTRAC, ATS, AUTODIN, AUTOMAST, AUTOSATE, AUTO-STATIS, AUTOSTRAD, BAIT, BCS, BEACON, BEST, BILA, BLODIB, BOLD, BORAM, BPKT, CADC, CADFISS, CAIS, CAL, CALM, CAM, CAP, CAPS, CAPERTSIM, CAPRI, CARD, CASPAR, CCST, CECE, CHILD, CLARA, CLEO, CMC, COBLOC, COBOL, CODASYL, COGENT, COINS, COMPARE, COMPASS, COMSOAL, CORC, COSA NOSTRA, COSINE, COSMIC, COSMOS, CPU, CRAFT, CRAM, CRESTS, CS, CSL, CUDOS, DAC, DACOR, DAD, DADEE, DAM, DAPS, DARES, DAS, DATAN, DDA, DDAS, DDS, DDT, DEACON, DECUS, DEUCE, DISAC, DITRAN, DOCUS, DPMA, DYSTAC, EAM, EANDRO, EASARS, EASL, ECMA, EDP, EDPE, EDPS, EDSAC, EDUCOM, EDVAC, EJCC, EMA, ENIAC, ERCR, EROP, ESB, FACE, FACSI, FADAC, FAHQMT, FASE, FIDAC, FIND, FJCC, FLAP, FLIP, FORBLOC, FORMAC, FORMAC, FORTRAN, FOSDIC, FSL, GAMLOGS, GAP, GASP, GAT, GATAC, GEESE, GEMS, GENDA, GEPAC, GOCI, GPCP, GPSS, GRA, GRACE, GRAF, GRASP, GRED, GUIDE, HAM, HARTRAN, HAYSTAQ, HIVOS, HODRAL, HSDA, HSM, HTSS, HYBLOC, HYFES, HYTRESS, IAA, IAG, IAS, ICC, ICES, ICRH, ICS, IITRAN, IMPS, INAC, IROD, JCC, JOSS, JOVIAL, KALDAS, LADAPT, LEANS, LITE, LOGEL, LOPAD, LPD, LPRINT, LSFFAR, LUCID, LYRIC, MAC, MACS, MAD, MADAM, MAGIS, MAGPIE, MALT, MAP, MASIS, MASS, MASTER, MCDP, MCDS, MESS, METRIC, MIAC, MICR, MICS, MINDAC, MIRF, MIS, MISSIL, MMPT, MOBIDIC, MOBULA, MOC, MOLDS, MOP, MOST, MSTS, MT, MTDS, MULTICS, MUMMS, NAMES, NAPSS, NAVDAC, NC, NCC, NICOL, NODAC, NSRDS, NTDS, OCR, OCR-A, OCR-B, OLRT, OPPOSIT, OPR, OPS, PAC, PACED, PACT, PADRE, PAL, PAPA, PASS, PAT, PCAM, PCE, PIAPACS, PICA,

Education and training

ACE, AISEC, AIISUP, ASEE, ASME, ASTD, ATI, BACIE, BITO, CAT, CATIB, CEI, CELC, CGLI, CITB, CITC, CNAA, COSINE, COSIP, CRAC, CTC, CTEB, DES, EDC, EDUCOM, EEMJEB, EFLC, EIP, EITB, EMRIC, FACTMA, FE, EPA, GAS, GTC, HCITB, HEW, IAESTE, ITB, ITS, IUC, JCTFI, MMFPITB, NABE, NACEIC, NAEC, NCET, NCPEA, NEA, NEBSS, NFER, NVGA, OTJ, PITB, PPO, RTITB, SABE, SCCAPE, TA, TSA, TWI, UCCA, USOE

Electrical engineering

ACEC, AEG, AKEW, ASEA, BEAIRA, BEAMA, BECTO, BEPC, CEB, CEGB, CEI, CERL, CIGB, CIGRE, CTS, DFB, ECA, ECMC, EDA, EDF, EFI, EID, ENEL, ERA, FACEJ, FPA, HEPC, IEC, IEE, IEEE, IEETE, IES, IPCEA, KEMA, LCIE, MESG, MHD, MIC, MICS, MKS, MKSA, NEC, NECTA, NEMA, NFEA, NICEIC, NIIEP, NIIKP, NSHEB, PAM, PICA, PILC, PME, RMS, SAPAR, SFE, SSEB, SWA, TEPG, TPG, TRINDEL, TRS, TsNIEL, UNIPEDE, VDE, VDEW, ZVEI

Electro-chemistry

ICETK, LNBEE

Electro-magnetism

EMC, EMETF, EMI, EMM, EMP

Electro-mechanics

IEM, VNIIEM

Electronics (see also Radar, Tele-communications)

AAS, ACCEL, ACR, ACTO, ADGE, ADMSC, AEW&C, AERDL, AFC, AFCEA, AFICCS, AGED, AGET, APC, ATL, AUDREY, AUTOVON, BADGE, BED, BFO, BWO, CCO, CFA, CFAR, CIRCAL, CMCLT, CODED, COMPARE, CORAPRAN, CRO, CSL, DAFC, DAIS, DARE, DCTL, DL, DLT, DM, DOFIC, DOM, DPCM, DTL, DTPL, DVM, EAEC, ECAP, ECC, ECCM, ECOM, ECRC, EDD, EDE, EEA, EECL, EEM, EFS, EIA, EIMO, ELSIE, EMEC, EPIC, ERC, ERDA, ESS, EUROCAE, FET, FNIE, FTFET, HCE, IC, ICE, IEETE, IERE, IFME, IGFET, IMEA, INEL, IP, IRE, JEDEC, JEIDA, JERC, LAEDP, LSA, LVDT, MADS, MALE, MANDRO, MBT, MERA, MIB, MIS, MISFET, MNS, MOPA, MOSAIC, MOSFET, MOST, MR ATOMIC, MTOS, MTS, NADGE, NAECON, NAVELEX, NBT, NDRO, NEC, NEEP, NERC, NIC, NRZ, OMTS, OPA, OSIC, PACED, PAM, PCC, PCM, PCP, PCT, PDA, PDM, PFM, PII, PLD, PLL, PM, PME, PMT, PPM, PRF, PWM, RDTL, RECMF, RGT, RL, ROC, RTL, RZ, SCEPTRE, SCIC, SCR, SEC, SEMLAT, SERL, SERT, SESCO, SFB, SFER, SGS, SIC, SICS, SID, SLO, SLT, SRG, SWIEECO, SYBELEC, TC, TCC, TCD, TCR, TCXO, TE, TEA, TFT, TI, TPV, TREE, TRL, TRM, TTL, TWCRT, TWT, ULB, USAECOM, USAEPG, USNEL, VARR, VASCA, VCO, VFO, VRCI, VSCF, VSWR, VTL, VTVM, WBCO, WESCOM, WGBC, XO

Electroplating

AES, DGG, TsNILELEKTROM

Engineering (general)

EEUA, EIA, EIC, EITB, EJC, ESC, ESNE, EUSEC, FEANI, FIDIC, ICES, IVA, KIVI, LACES, LES, MES, MEXE, NAE, NCSE, NSPE, SAE, SCSE, SIA, SINTEF, SNAME, SRBII, SWE, UIEO, UPADI, VDI, WES, WSE, YEA

Environmental science

IER, IES, SEE

Excavators

EMA

Explosives

BRL, CARDE, CRIPE, EED, ERDE, HDL, HEAT, HEP, LEED, LOX, LRBA, MDF, NG, RARDE, REDSOD, SOCM, TNT, USABRL, VOD

7

Management

ACADI, ACMS, ADS, AFAP, AIF, AIM, AIMA, AMA, AMETA, AMIS, AMS, APICS, APO, APROBA, ASAE, ASTRA, AWV, BIB, BIM, BPC, CAPERTSIM, CAS, CBA, CBI, CCM, CCPMO, CECIOS, CER, CIOS, CIPM, CNBOS, CNOF, CNOS, CNP, COM-SOAL, COP, CPA, CPFF, CPM, DCCA, DCF, DIF, DOC, ECONOMAN, ELD, EOQ, FEI, FICS, FIFO, FIRM, GERT, GPA, GSPI, IBAM, IILS, IMAS, IMI, IMPACT, IOC, ISOC, IUC, IWM, JIMA, LCES, LESS, LIFO, MAGPIE, META, METRIC, MIM, MIMS, MINDD, MINSD, MINSOP, MINT, MISS, MODI, MTM, NAPA, NCIP, NCMA, NLRB, NOMA, NPA, NPACI, NPT, O&M, OBAP, ODLRO, OKW, OMTC, OPPOSIT, OPZ, OSR, PA, PAEM, PASS, PDP, PEM, PEP, PERA, PERM, PERT, PI, PMTS, POSE, PPBS, PRIME, PROMPT, PROP, RAMPS, RKW, ROA, ROI, SAIMS, SAM, SCERT, SCOPE, SET, SIMS, SISS, SLP, SMA, SPA, SPI, SUSIE, TIMS, TOE, TPPC, TUC, TUV, WAM, WAP, WASP, WER, WMSI, ZIF

Mapping

ACSM, GIMRADA, ICA, IMW, UNA-MACE, UTM

Marine engineering (see also Ships and shipping)

BMEC, BPU, ßSRA, HSD, HYSTAD, IESS, IMarE, ISSC, NCRE, NECIES, SBBNF, SNAME, SSC, SIB

Marketing see Trade

Materials—research and testing

AMIC, AML, AMRA, AMS, BAM, BNCM, DVM, IMMS, IMR, ISMCM, NAMC, NMC, RMIC, SAMPE, SCRDE, USAAVLABS, VIAM

Materials handling (see also Cranes)

AHSE, CEMA, FEM, ICHCA, IMH, LEMA, LIFT, MHEA, MHEDA, PASE

Mathematics (see also Statistics)

AMS, AMSC, AMTRAN, COSRIMS, GAMM, IMAG, IMU, LMS, LP, MAA, MC, MRC, SAM, SEMA, SIAM, SMSG, VAMP, VUMS

Measurement (see also Weights and measures)

BIMCAN, CPEM, ECC, IMEKO, IN-TERKAMA, MKS, MKSA, NRLM, SI, TMS, VNIIFTRI, VNIIM

Mechanical engineering

ADETIM, ASME, CCAM, CMERI, IMechE, IOPM, ITM, JSME, NMERI

Mechanical handling see Materials handling

Mechanics

IMEKh, IUTAM

Medical science (see also Dentistry)

AAIN, AAL, AAN, AAPS, ACGIH, ACPM, ADH, AFD, AFIP, AHF, AIHA, AIHC, AMA, AMD, AMEDS, AMRL, APHA, APHI, APRC, APRE, ARIEM, ARNMD, ASCP, ASME, ATP, BAIT, BMA, BUIC, CAMI, CERBOM, CIOMS, CMA, DIA, DNA, DRML, ECG, ECS, EEG, EOG, FACTMA, FDA, FPRC, GSA, GSC, HPA, IAM, IAMC, ICMMP, ICNV, ICS, IDF, IED, IFGO, IFME, IHF, IMA, IMO, INSERM, INTAPUC, IPA, ISA, ISN, ISU, IUNS, LATS, LDH, LH, LSD, MAC, MEDAC, MERDL, MIRD, MRC, MRI, MRL, MUST, NAMI, NAMRU, NAVMED, NCHS, NIH, NINDB, NMFRL, NMRI, NSAM, NSMC, NTA, PADRE, PAHO, PHS, PIAPACS, PSYCHES, REB, RH, RNA, RNIB, RNID, RSH, RSM, SAM, SAMI, SBP, SNM, SNOP, THOMIS, TIRR, TLV, TSH, UDPG, UDPGA, UICC, USAMRDG, USAMRL, USPHS, VEM, WFMH, WHO, WHRC, WMA, WRAIN, WRAIR

Metallurgy

AIME, ASM, ASVILMET, BNFMRA, CELME, CIMM, CNRM, CRIF, DGM,

MPL, MTD, NRCP, NEWRADS, NRDL, PF, RAD, RADIAC, RBE, REM, RH, RRS, RRU, RSIC, RSN, SCEPTRE, SEMIRAD, TLD, TRAP, TREE, UCRL, UNSCEAR, USNRDL, VARAD

Radio
ARD, ARMS, ARRL, BBC, BREMA, BRVMA, CIRM, CISPR, EARC, EBU, FIAR, IARU, IERE, IRE, IRPA, NAB, NHK, ORTF, RAEN, RECMF, RSGB, SERT, SFER, UER, URSI, USARPA

Radiobiology
AFRRI, ARCRL

Railways
AAR, ACI, AICMR, AREA, ATC, BR, BRB, CFF, CIT, CNR, CSD, DB, DLW, DR, ELSIE, FACS, FRS, FS, IUR, LAMA, LIFT, LRTL, NRGS, NRAB, NS, NSB, RENFE, SJ, SNCB, SNCF, TMT, TPT, UIC, UKRAS, WAGR

Refrigeration
ARI, ASHRAE, ASRE, BRA, IIR, NCHVRFE, NFCIT, SRCRA

Reliability see Quality and reliability

Roads and road transport
AASHO, ATTI, BPR, CBR, CGRA, CRCP, CSF, CTA, HRB, IHC, IHE, IRF, IRRD, IRTE, ITE, NCHRP, NMFC, NRB, PFA, PIARC, PRB, PSI, RCU, RHA, RRL, RTITB, TRTA

Rockets (see also Missile technology)
AFRPL, AIR, ARA, ARIP, ARS, ASROC, DGRR, EXAMETNET, HVAR, LRPL, LSFFAR, LSMR, NRDS, REON, RIT, RP, RPE, SCRAP, SERT

Rubbers and plastics
ABS, BPF, CAB, CEP, EPR, EPT, ERF, EV, EVATMI, FEP, FRP, GFRP, GRP, HAF, INTERPLAS, IOP, IRAD, IRHD, IRI, NIIPM, NIIRP, NIPPM, NRPRA, NWO, OPP, PBTF, PCP, PCTFE, PE, PEACU, PET, PIB, PLASTEC, PS, PTFE, PVA, PVAL, PVC, PVT, RAPRA, RMEA, RTP, SBR, SBR(OEP), SMR, SPE, SPI, SPIC, TFE, UF, UMF, WPC

Safety (see also Fire protection)
ACEAA, AHSB, ATL, BASEEFA, BCISC, BEAB, CIS, IASA, IISO, ISPEMA, NOSA, NSC, NSCA, ROSPA, SECO, USABAAR, VDSI, VI

Satellites see Aeronautics and astronautics

Sedimentology
IAS

Seismology
IAEE, IASPEI, LASA, WMSO

Sericulture
ISC

Sewerage
ATV, BSPMA, EST

Ships and shipping
ICS, IMCO, MA, MDHB, NCSORG, PLA, SES, SESCO, SINS, TsNIIMF, USMA

Shoes
SATRA

Soil
CSSS, ISSS, LGM, REDSOD, SCS, SCSA, SEPOL, SSSA, STIBOKA

Solar energy
AFASE, SES, SET

Spectrometers
IRIS, SIRS

Spectroscopy
ESCA, GCMS

Spray equipment
SEMA

Springs
SMRA, SRA

Standards and specifications
AAR, AASHO, AATCC, ABCA, ABNT, ACI, ADA, AFNOR, AGMA, AIA, AMS, API, AS, ASA, ASBC, ASCE, ASHRAE, ASME, ASTM, AU, AWS, AWWA, BINA, BOM, BS, BSI, CAMESA, CCIR, CCITT, CEE, CEMA, CEN, CFC, CGA, CGSB, CI, CIGRE, CISPR, CP, CS, CSA, DCDMA, DEF, DGN, DIN, DNA, DS, DTD, EIA, ENO, ESB, FES, FSPT, GOST, IBN, IBS, ICC, IEC, IEE, IEEE, IES, IIRS, IN-ANTIC, INDITECNOR, INORCOL, IP, IRAM, IRATRA, IS, ISA, ISI, ISO, ITE, JANS, JEDEC, JIS, JISC, JZS, MAS, MIL, MIL-STD, MIN-TECH, MOD, MPBW, MS, MSS, NBN, NBS, NCSL, NEMA, NEN, NF, NFPA, NNI, NOM, NORVEN, NPL, NSF, NZSI, NZSR, NZSS, OCS, ONA, ONORM, PD, PKN, PS, PSI, RSL, SAA, SABS, SAE, SARPS, SBAC, SDM, SEN, SES, SEV, SFS, SI, SII, SIS, SMS, SNV, SOI, SPR, SSM, St, STPTC, SVS, TAPPI, TSE, UFC, UL, UNE, UNI, USASI

Statistics
ASA, CBS, FSUC, IASI, ISI, ISPO, NCHS, SASE, SPAN, SPRT, SRS, TSA, VVS

Steam
ICPS, IFC

Steel see Iron and steel

Structural engineering (see also Building)
AIPC, AISC, ISE, ISMES, STRESS, TSNIIPS

Sugar
BSMMA, ISC, ISSCT

Sun
ICARVS, OSO, SFC, SFF, SOFNET, SUN

Surveying
ACMS, DMTS, DVW, FIG, GEISHA, IFS

Tanks—fighting vehicles
AFV, ATAC, AVBL, FVRDE, IFVME, MAW, MBT

Tar
STPTC

Telecommunications (see also Electronics)
AF, AFLCON, AFTN, AGED, AM, AMA, BPO, CANTA, CANTAV, CANTRAN, CCIR, CCITT, CCT, CEPT, CIT, CNET, CNR, COMPAC, COMSAT, CRPL, CSSB, CTFM, CTL, DDD, DRTE, DSA, EHF, EUM-AFTN, FBFM, FCC, FDM, FM, FMFB, FMIC, FSK, FTS, IDA, IDAST, IDCSP, IDOC, IFRB, IMPATT, IMPI, IPFM, IPOEE, ISD, ITSA, ITU, IWCS, LAMCS, LID, LINCOMPEX, LMT, LOF, LUF, MARS, MF, MIB, MODEMS, MOF, MOTNE, MUF, PABX, PAX, PMBX, PCR, PSK, RADA, RSL, SATCOM, SCAN, SCORE, SEACOM, SFTS, SHF, SITA, SN, SNR, SSB, SSBSCOM, SSD, SSR, STD, STRAD, STTA, TACSATCOM, TAM, TASI, TAT, TCC, TCMF, TDDL, TDM, TDMS, TDR, TEE, TEMA, TER, TRF, TSCLT, TXE, UDOP, UHF, UIT, USASCC, UTS, VHF, VIPS, VLF, VOR, VORDAC, VSB, WATS

Telemetry
ACTS, CTDH, DRIFT, TARE, TELUS

Telephony see Telecommunications

Television
BATC, BBC, CATV, CFT, DTDS, EBU, FDS, IFTC, LLLTV, LSCC, NCTA, NEFTS, NTSC, ORTF, PAL, PAL-D, PLAT, RATAN, RTS, SECAM, SEIT, SLCB, SMPTE, TIROS, VIT

Testing (see also Materials—research and testing)
ABEM, AFFTC, AFMTC, APG, APGC, ASTM, ATE, AVR, BAM, BSNDT, CERES, DIMATE, EID, GPATS, HYT-

A / D	Altitude/Depth
A A A	American Airship Association (USA)
A A A A	Army Aviation Association of America (USA)
A A E	American Association of Engineers (USA)
A A W	Anti-Air Warfare
A B	Automated Bibliography
A B C	Already Been Converted
A C C A P	Autocoder to COBOL Conversion-Aid Programme
A C C E S S	Automatic Computer-Controlled Electronic Scanning System
A C E L	Aerospace Crew Equipment Laboratory (of Naval Air Engineering Center, USN)
A C T	Analogical Circuit Technique
A C T P	Advanced Computer Techniques Project
A D M	Atomic Demolition Munitions
A D T A	Augmented Target Docking Adaptor
A E A	Advanced Engine, Aerospike
A E B	Advanced Engine, Bell
A E D S	Association for Educational Data Systems (USA)
A E S	Aerospace Electrical Society (USA)
	Airways Engineering Society (USA)
A E S E	Association of Earth Science Editors (USA)
A F	Air Foundation (USA)
A F A F C	Air Force Accounting and Finance Center (USAF)
A F T O	Air Force Technical Order (USAF)
A I D	Aeronautical Inspection Directorate (MINTECH)
A I I E	American Institute of Industrial Engineers (USA)
A I O P	Association Internationale d'Oceanographie Physique (International Association of Physical Oceanography)
A I P E	American Institute of Plant Engineers (USA)
A I R	Air Injection Reactor
A L C A T E L	Societe Alsacienne de Constructions Atomiques, de Telecommuncations et d'Electronique (France)
A L C O R	*ARPA-Lincoln* Coherent Observable Radar
A L P A C	Automatic Language Processing Advisory Committee (of NAS)
A L P S	Assembly Line Planning System
A L R C	Anti-Locust Research Centre (of ODM)
A M H S	American Material Handling Society (USA)
A M S	Army Map Service (US Army)
A N M C C	Alternate Military Command Center (USDOD)
A O Q	Average Outgoing Quality

A P	Association of Professions (USA)
A P B	Air Portable Bridge
A P D S	Armour Piercing Discarding Sabot
A P L	Associative Programming Language
A P R O	Aerial Phenomena Research Organisation (USA)
A R A	American Rheumatism Association (USA)
A R M A N	Artificial Methods Analyst
A S	prefix to Aerospace Standards issued by SAE (USA)
A S A	Acoustical Society of America (USA)
A S C E N D	Advanced System for Communications and Education in National Development
A S D I R S	Army Study Documentation and Information Retrieval System (US Army)
A S G L S	Advanced Space-Ground Link Sub-system
A S N E	American Society of Naval Engineers (USA)
A S S R	Airborne Sea and Swell Recorder
A S T A	Association of Short-Circuit Testing Authorities
A S T R A	Applied Space Technology—Regional Advancement
A T C	Armoured Troop Carrier (a vessel)
A T C A	Air Traffic Control Association (USA)
A T E A	Army Transportation Engineering Agency (US Army)
A T G M	Anti-Tank Guided Missile
A T L A S	Anti-Tank Laser Assisted System
A T L I S	Army Technical Libraries and Information Systems (US Army)
A T O L	Assisted Take-Off and Landing
A T S	Automatic Trim System
A U T O - T R I P	Automatic Transportation Research Investigation Programme
A V C O M	Aviation Materiel Command (US Army)
A W R A	American Water Resources Association (USA)
A W T R	Advanced Waste Treatment Processes
B A C	Background Analysis Center (University of Michigan, USA)
B A K	Barrier Arresting Kit
B A L L O T S	Bibliographic Automation of Large Library Operations using Time Sharing
B A S I C	Beginner's All-purpose Symbolic Instruction Code
B A T	Battalion Anti-Tank

B C L	Biological Computer Laboratory (Illinois University, USA)
B D C	Book Development Council
B G R V	Boost Glide Re-entry Vehicle
B H S L	Basic Hytran Simulation Language
B I A A	British Industrial Advertising Association
B I G A	Bundesamt fur Industrie, Gewerbe und Arbeit (Switzerland)
B I P E	Bureau d'Informations et de Previsions Economiques (France)
B I S P A	British Independent Steel Producers Association
B I T	Built-In-Test
B L A C	British Light Aviation Centre
B M E	Bio-Medical Engineering
B O F	Basic Oxygen Furnace
B R I C S	Bureau of Research Information Control System (of USOE)
B R L E S C	*Ballistic Research Laboratories* Electronic Scientific Computer
B S	Biological Society (USA)
B T O	British Trust for Ornithology
C A A D R P	Civil Aircraft Airworthiness Data Recording Programme
C A C M	Central American Common Market
C A D I C	Computer Aided Design of Integrated Circuits
C A E P E	Centre d'Assemblage et d'Essais des Propulseurs et des Engins (France)
C A I N T	Computer Assisted Interrogation
C A R A	Combat Air Rescue Aircraft
C A S E	Coordinated Aerospace Supplier Evaluation (an organisation of aerospace industrial concerns in USA)
C A S S	Commanded Active Sonobuoy System
C A S S I S	Communications And Social Science Information Service
C A V E	Consolidated Acquanauts Vital Equipment
C B	Certification Body (of CEE)
C C B	Command Communications Boat
C C H M S	Central Committee for Hospital Medical Services (of British Medical Association)
C C S	Controlled Combustion System
C C S L	Compatible *or* Comparative Current Sinking Logic

C D C E	Central Data Conversion Equipment
C D P S	Computing and Data Processing Society (Canada)
C E X	Civil Effects
C F E	Compagnie Belge de Chemins de Fer et d'Entreprises (Belgium)
C F F	Critical Fusion Frequency
C F P	prefix to numbered series of Canadian Forces Publications issued by Dept. of National Defence, Canada
C G	Centre of Gravity
C G E	Compagnie Generale d'Electricite (France)
C G I	Commissione Geodetica Italiana (Italy) (Italian Geodetic Commission)
C G I	Ground Control Interceptor
C I C S	Committee for Index Cards for Standards
C I M T C	Construction and Industrial Machinery Technical Committee (of SAE)
C I N F A C	Counterinsurgency Information Analysis Center (American University, USA)
C L S	Comparative Systems Laboratory (Western Reserve University, USA)
C N E A	Comision Nacional de Energia Atomica (Argentina) (National Atomic Energy Commission)
C N I	Communication, Navigation and Identification
C O L I D A R	Coherent Light Detecting And Ranging
C O M A N S E C	Computation and Analysis Section (of Defence Research Board, Canada)
C O M S A T S	Control Organisation Methods And Techniques Study
C O N B A T	Converted Battalion Anti-Tank
C O N T R E Q S	Contingency Transportation Requirements System
C O P A N T	Pan-American Standards Commission
C O P E P	Committee on Public Engineering Policy (of National Academy of Engineering, USA)
C O R O D I M	Correlation of the Recognition of Degradation with Intelligibility Measurements
C O S E M	Compagnie Generale des Semi-Conducteurs (France)
C O S M O S	Computer Orientated System for Manufacturing Order Synthesis
	Courtauld's Own System for Matrix Operations
C O W A R	Committee on Water Resources (of ICSU)
C P E	Contractor Performance Evaluation

C R G	Classification Research Group
C R O F	Controllerate Royal Ordnance Factories (MOD)
C T F	Chlorine Trifluoride
C U E	Computer Updating Equipment
C V R	Continuous Video Recorder
D A P C A	Development And Production Costs for Aircraft
D A R T	Digital Automatic Readout Tracker
D A T	Designation-Acquisition-Track
D A T S	Despun Antenna Test Satellite
D C	Dimensional Co-ordination
D C B R E	Defence Chemical, Biological and Radiation Establishment (of DRB, Canada)
D E V C O	Committee for Standardization in the Developing Countries (of ISO)
D G I	Direction Generale des Impots (France)
D I A	Defense Intelligence Agency (USDOD)
D I C O R S	Diver Communication Research System
D I L S	Doppler Inertial LORAN System
D M U	Diesel-Multiple-Unit
D N N	Det Norske Nitridaktieselskap (Norway)
D O P I C	Documentation of Programme In Core
D O R E	Defence Operational Research Establishment (of DRB, Canada)
D R A D S	Degradation of Radar Defence System
D R E A	Defence Research Establishment Atlantic (of DRB, Canada)
D R E A C	Drum Experimental Automatic Computer
D R E P	Defence Research Establishment Pacific (of DRB, Canada)
D R E S	Defence Research Establishment Suffield (of DRB, Canada)
D R E T	Defence Research Establishment Toronto (of DRB, Canada)
D T I E	Division of Technical Information Extension (of USAEC)
D V G W	Deutscher Verein vor Gas-und Wasserfachmannern (Germany)
D X	Destroyer Experimental
E A B	Engineering Activity Board (of SAE)
E C H M	Earth Coverage Horizon Measurement
E C H O	Evolution of Competing Hierarchical Organisation

E C R C	Electricity Council Research Centre
E C S	Etched Circuits Society (USA)
E D C	Error Detection and Correction
E D S	Environmental Data Service (of ESSA)
E E R J	External Expansion Ramjet
E F P	European Federation of Purchasing
E I E D	Electrically Initiated Explosive Device
E L S	Economic Lot Size
E M I C	Electronic Materials Information Centre (of RRE)
E M Q	Economic Manufacturing Quantity
E M R L	Engineering Mechanics Research Laboratory (Texas University, USA)
E M S C	Electrical Manufacturers Standards Council (of NEMA, USA)
E M U	Electrical-Multiple-Unit
E N I	Electro-Naval et Industriel (Belgium)
E O L	Expression-Oriented Language
E R D	Equivalent Residual Dose
E R I C	Educational Resources Information Center (USOE) (' Resources ' was formerly ' Research ')
E R O S	Eliminate Range Zero System
E R P	Economic Review Period
E R S	Earth Resources Satellite
	Experiment Research Society (USA)
E S	Electrochemical Society (USA)
E S C O M	Electricity Supply Commission (South Africa)
E S G	Electrostatic Gyro
E S P	Electro-Sonic Profiler
E S R T	Electroslag Refining Technology (division of BISRA)
E T R	Eastern Test Range (USAF)
E U V	Extreme Ultra-Violet
E V R	Electronic Video Recording and Reproduction
E W R	Entwicklungsring Sud (Germany)
F A T I M A	Fatique Indicating Meter Attachment
F A U	Florida Atlantic University
F F A	Flygetniska Forsoksanstalten (Sweden) (Aeronautical Research Institute)
F F V	Foersvarets Fabriksverk (Sweden)
F I D	Forecasts-In-Depth
F I N C O	Finance Committee (of ISO)
F O B S	Fractional Orbiting Bombardment System
F P S	Fluid Power Society (USA)

F R C	Fast Reaction Concept
	Fibre Reinforced Composite
F R T P	Fibreglass Reinforced Thermoplastic
F T L	Forsvarets Teletekniska Laboratorium (Sweden) (Military Electronics Laboratory)
G - E W S	Group on Engineering Writing and Speech (of IEEE)
G D I F S	Gray and Ductile Ironfounders Society (USA)
G E O P S	Geodetic Estimates from Orbital Perturbations of Satellites
G E R D	Gross National Expenditure on Research and Development
G I G O	Garbage In, Garbage Out
G R E M E X	*Goddard* Research Engineering Management Exercise (Goddard Space Flight Center, NASA)
H A T S	Helicopter Advanced Tactical System
H F	Hydrogen Fluoride
H F E	Human Factors in Electronics
H F S	Human Factors Society (USA)
H H H M U	Hydrazine Hand-Held Manoeuvring Unit
H I C	Hybrid Integrated Circuit
H N I L	High Noise Immunity Logic
H R S	High Speed Rail
H T V	High Temperature and Velocity
H V L	Half-Value Layer
H Y D R O L A N T	Hydrographic Warning—Atlantic (originated by NOO)
H Y D R O P A C	Hydrographic Warning—Pacific (originated by NOO (Honolulu Branch))
I B C	International Broadcasting Convention
I C A D	Integrated Control And Display
I C A S	International Congress of the Aeronautical Sciences
I C B P	International Committee for Bird Preservation
I C E T T	Industrial Council for Educational and Training Technology
I C M R T	International Center for Medical Research and Training (of NIH)
I C S I	International Commission of Snow and Ice (of IASH)
I D E A L S	Ideal Design of Effective And Logical Systems
I D S	Integrated Data Store

I G A A S	Integrated Ground/Airborne Avionics System
I I F	Institut International du Froid (International Institute of Refrigeration)
I I H R	Iowa University Institute of Hydraulic Research (USA)
I M A S	International Marine and Shipping Conference
I M I	Improved Manned Interceptor
I M L	Intermediary Musical Language
I M S	Industrial Mathematics Society (USA)
I N I I	Institutu Nacional de Investigacao Industrial (Portugal)
I O N	Institute of Navigation (USA)
I P S	Institute of Purchasing and Supply
I P S S B	Information Processing Systems Standards Board (of USASI)
I P T S	International Practical Temperature Scale
I R	Informal Report
I R F N A	Inhibited Red Fuming Nitric Acid
I R I A	Infrared Information and Analysis Center (University of Michigan, USA)
I R I S	Infrared Information Symposia (USA)
I S T	International Skelton Tables
I S T C	International Steam Tables Conference (later ICPS)
I T P P	Institute of Technical Publicity and Publications
I W F N A	Inhibited White Fuming Nitric Acid
J A C T R U	Joint Air Traffic Control Radar Unit
J A T O	Jet-Assisted Take-Off
J E C C	Japan Electronic Computer Company (Japan)
J E C M B	Joint Committee on Medicine and Biology (of IEEE and ISA)
J E O L	Japan Electron Optics Laboratory (Japan)
J I F D A T S	Joint Services In-Flight Data Transmission System (USDOD)
J N R	Japanese National Railways (Japan)
J N S D A	Japan Nuclear Ship Development Agency (Japan)
J P	Jet Propellant *or* Propelled *or* Propulsion
J R D C	Japan Research and Development Corporation (Japan)
J S E M	Japan Society for Electron Microscopy (Japan)
K E A S	Knots Equivalent Air Speed
K I S A	Korean International Steel Associates (Korea)

L A N S	Load Alleviation and Stabilization
L A S V	Low-Altitude Supersonic Vehicle
L E T I S	Leicestershire Technical Information Service
L F S W	Landing Force Support Weapon
L I A	Laser Industry Association (USA)
L I M I T	Lot-size Inventory Management Interpolation Technique
L I M P	Language-Independent Macro Processor
L I N S	LORAN Inertial System
L I T A S T O R	Light Tapping Storage
L O G A C S	Low Gravity Accelerometer Calibration System
L O R V	Low Observable Re-entry Vehicle
L O T	Large Orbital Telescope
L P I A	Liquid Propellant Information Agency (JHU)
L R C	Linguistics Research Center (University of Texas, USA)
L R T F	Long Range Technological Forecast
L U C R E	Lower Unit Costs and Related Earnings
L V T	Landing Vehicle Tracked
M & Q Form	prefix to numbered series 'Mines and Quarries' issued by Ministry of Power
M A M M A X	Machine Made and Machine Aided Index
M A R I D A S	Maritime Data System
M A R V	Manoeuvrable Anti-Radar Vehicle
M A S H	Manned Anti-Submarine Helicopter
M B R V	Manoeuvring Ballistic Re-entry Vehicle
M C M	Machines for Co-ordinating Multiprocessing
M D C	Missile Development Center (USAF)
M E S A	Miniaturized Electrostatic Accelerometer
M E S T I N D	Measurement Standards Instrumentation Division (of Instrument Society of America)
M I I G A i K	Moskovskiy Institut Inzhenerov Geodezii, Aerofotos'yemki i Kartografii (USSR) (Moscow Institute of Geodetic, Aerial Mapping and Cartographic Engineers)
M I R	Musical Information Retrieval
M M H	Monomethylhydrazine
M O B A T	Modified Battalion Anti-Tank
M R & D F	Malleable Research and Development Foundation (USA)
M R N L	Medical Research and Nutrition Laboratory (US Army)

M T M A - U K	Methods-Time Measurement Association of the United Kingdom
N A O S	North Atlantic Ocean Station
N A S	National Airspace System (USA)
N A T E C	Naval Air Technical Evaluation Centre (MOD)
N A V E A M S	Navigational Warning East Atlantic and Mediterranean (originated by MOD (Navy Dept))
N A V S E C	Naval Ship Engineering Center (USN)
N A V S E C - P H I L A D I V	Naval Ship Engineering Center—Philadelphia Division (USN)
Nav S H I P S	Naval Ship Systems Command (USN)
Nav S U P	Naval Supply Systems Command (USN)
N C E S	National Center for Education Statistics (USOE)
N E	Nuclear Explosive
N E D S A	Non-Erasing Deterministic Stack Automation
N E M E D R I	North European and Mediterranean Route Instructions (issued by MOD (Navy Dept))
N H R L	National Hurricane Research Laboratory (USA)
N I A I D	National Institute of Allergy and Infectious Diseases (USA)
N I I Sh P	Nauchno Issledovatel'skiy Institut Shinnoy Promyshlennosti (USSR) (Scientific Research Institute of the Tyre Industry)
N I W	Naval Inshore Warfare
N M S	Naval Medical School (USN)
N O I B N	Not Otherwise Indexed By Name
N O S	Not Otherwised Specified
N P N	Normal Propyl Nitrate
N Q R	Nuclear Quadrupole Resonance
N S R D C	Naval Ship Research and Development Center (USN)
N S R T	Near Surface Reference Temperature
O C S	Onboard Check-out System
O L D	Open Loop Damping
O M R V	Operational Manoeuvring Re-entry Vehicle
O P A D E C	Optical Particle Decoy
O P D A C	Optical Data Converter
O P D A R	Optical Direction And Ranging
O P M A C	Operations for Military Assistance to the Community
O R C	Operations Research Center (University of California, USA)

ORCO	Organisation Committee (of ISO)
OTH	Over The Horizon
PACT	Production Analysis Control Technique
PACV	Patrol Air Cushion Vehicle
PADE	Pad Automatic Data Equipment
PAIR	Performance And Integration Retrofit
PAR	Perimeter Acquisition Radar
PARSAC	Particle Size Analogue Computer
PCB	Plenum Chamber Burning
PCGN	Permanent Committee on Geographical Names
PDM	Polynomial Discriminant Method
PEHLA	Prufung Elektrischer Hochleistungs Apparate (Germany)
PERGO	Project Evaluation and Review with Graphic Output
PEST	Parameter Estimation by Sequential Testing
PF	Perchloryl-fluoride
PGH	Patrol Gunboat, Hydrofoil
PIC	Pesticides Information Center (of National Agriculture Library, USA)
PILE	Product Inventory Level Estimator
PLANET	Planned Logistics Analysis and Evaluation Technique
PMP	Parts-Material-Packaging
PMVI	Periodic Motor Vehicle Inspection
PRAW	Personnel Research Activity Washington (USN)
PRODAC	Production Advisers Consortium (of BCIRA, BWRA and PERA)
PROMPT	Production Reviewing, Organizing and Monitoring of Performance Techniques
PTI	Presentation of Technical Information Group
QF	Quality Factor
RAK	Rikets Almanna Kartverk (Sweden) (Geographical Survey Office)
RAX	Remote Access Computing System
RDE	Research and Development Effectiveness
REG	Rheoencephalography
RENE	Rocket Engine Nozzle Ejector
RETSPL	Reference Equivalent Threshold Sound Pressure
RFNA	Red Fuming Nitric Acid
RJ	Ramjet
RON	Research Octane Number

R P	Rocket Propellant *or* Propulsion
R R E G	Regional Rheoencephalography
R T D S	Real Time Data System
R T S R S	Real Time Simulation Research System
S & S C S	Scintillation and Semiconductor Counter Symposium
S A B M I S	Seaborne Anti-Ballistic-Missile Intercept System
S A B R E	Self-Aligning Boost and Re-entry System
S A L S	Solid-state Acousto-electric Light Scanner
S C N R	Scientific Committee of National Representatives (of SHAPE)
S D A	Source Data Automation
S D D	Selected Dissemination of Documents
S E P	Search Effectiveness Probability
S E P B O P	South-Eastern Pacific Biological Oceanographic Programme
S E T E	Secretariat for Electronic Test Equipment (of USDOD and NASA)
S F E N A	Societe Francaise d'Equipements pour la Navigation Aerienne (France)
S G L S	Space-Ground Link Sub-system
S H A P E	Supreme Headquarters, Allied Powers Europe
S I A O	Smithsonian Institute Astrophysical Observatory (USA)
S I D S	Speech Identification System
S M O D O S	Self Modulating Derivative Optical Spectrometer
S P I A - L P I A	Solid and Liquid Propellant Information Agency (JHU)
S P S	Space Summary Programme
S R F B	Space Research Facilities Branch (National Research Council, Canada)
S T A	Science and Technology Agency (Japan)
S T A C O	Standing Committee for the Scientific Principles of Standardization (of ISO)
S T C	SHAPE Technical Centre
S U S I E	Sequential Unmanned Scanning and Indicating Equipment
S W A C	*Standards* Western Automatic Computer (NBS)
S W A T	Stress Wave Analysis Technique
T A B S A C	Targets and Backgrounds Signature Analysis Center (University of Michigan, USA)

T A C V	Tracked Air Cushion Vehicle
T I D E	Transponder Interrogation and Decoding Equipment
T I F S	Total In-Flight Simulator
T P A	Technical Publications Association
T R I P	Transformation Induced Plasticity
T S	Technical Specification
T S C	Transportation Safety Committee (of SAE)
T T B	Troop Transport Boat
T V L	Tenth-Value Layer

U A G	Alaska University College Geophysical Institute (USA)
U D E	Unsymmetrical Diethylenetriamine
U D M H	Unsymmetrical Dimethylhydrazine
U J T	Unijunction Transistor
U L T	Unique Last Term
U M E S	*University of Michigan* Executive System
U S A M R N L	United States Army Medical Research and Nutrition Laboratory
U S A N D L	United States Army Nuclear Defense Laboratory
U S E	*Univac* Scientific Exchange (USA)
U S E S	United States Employment Service (USA)
U U A	*Univac* Users Association (USA)

V A L O R	Variable Locale and Resolution
Vd T U V	Vereinigung der Technischen Uberwachungs-Vereine (Germany)
V H O	Very High Output
V I F C S	VTOL Integrated Flight Control System
V I P	Visual Image Processor
V I P R E	Visual Precision
V P I	Virginia Polytechnic Institute (USA)
V R	Variety Reduction
V T I	Vsesoyuznyy Nauchno Issledovatel'skiy Teplotekhnicheskiy Institut (USSR) (All-Union Scientific Technical Thermotechnology Institute)

W A T	Weight, Altitude and Temperature
W F N A	White Fuming Nitric Acid
W I N C O N	Aerospace & Electronics Systems Winter Convention (USA)
W I R D S	Weather Information Remoting and Display System

W O M B A T	Weapons Of Magnesium Battalion Anti-Tank
W O R C	Washington Operations Research Council (USA)
W R E S A T	*Weapons Research Establishment* Satellite (WRE)
W W W	World Weather Watch (of WMO)
X	Experiment
X A C T	x (ie any computer) Automatic Code Translation